Sky Pilots

The American Military Experience Series
John C. McManus, Series Editor

The books in this series portray and analyze the experience of Americans in military service during war and peacetime from the onset of the twentieth century to the present. The series emphasizes the profound impact wars have had on nearly every aspect of recent American history and considers the significant effects of modern conflict on combatants and noncombatants alike. Titles in the series include accounts of battles, campaigns, and wars; unit histories; biographical and autobiographical narratives; investigations of technology and warfare; studies of the social and economic consequences of war; and in general, the best recent scholarship on Americans in the modern armed forces. The books in the series are written and designed for a diverse audience that encompasses nonspecialists as well as expert readers.

SKY PILOTS

The Yankee Division Chaplains
in World War I

MICHAEL E. SHAY

UNIVERSITY OF MISSOURI PRESS
Columbia

Copyright © 2014 by
The Curators of the University of Missouri
University of Missouri Press, Columbia, Missouri 65201
Printed and bound in the United States of America
All rights reserved
5 4 3 2 1   18 17 16 15 14

Cataloging-in-Publication data available from the Library of Congress
ISBN 978-0-8262-2031-8

∞ This paper meets the requirements of the
American National Standard for Permanence of Paper
for Printed Library Materials, Z39.48, 1984.

Jacket design: Susan Ferber
Interior design and composition: Richard Farkas
Typefaces: Minion Pro

Dedication

Rev. John H. ("Fr. Chevy") Chevalier, SSE (1919–1987)

He followed in his Master's footsteps to rural Alabama to minister to the "least of His brethren."

Angel of the Resurrection (St. Michael the Archangel) by sculptor Walker K. Hancock. Photo courtesy of Paul Shay.

St. Michael the Archangel, defend us in battle.
Protect us against the wickedness and snares of the devil.
—Traditional Christian Prayer

Contents

List of Illustrations   xi
Preface   xiii
Acknowledgments   xvii
Abbreviations   xxi
1. "Sky Pilots"   1
2. Early Days   31
3. Toul Sector   51
4. Aisne-Marne   67
5. St. Mihiel and Troyon   87
6. Verdun   97
7. Going Home   111
8. "Recalled to Life"   129
Afterword   167
Appendix   171
Notes   179
References   203
Index   213

Illustrations

Photographs

Angel of the Resurrection
1. Bishop Charles H. Brent, Senior AEF Chaplain   3
2. U.S. Army Chaplain School, Camp Zachary Taylor   7
3. Camp Bartlett, Westfield, MA, group of chaplains   11
4. Chaplain Markham W. Stackpole circa 1916   12
5. Chaplain Michael J. O'Connor   14
6. Chaplain Murray W. Dewart circa 1916   16
7. Chaplain George S. L. Connor   17
8. Chaplain Israel Bettan   21
9. Chaplain Malcolm E. Peabody   24
10. "Off to the Front," Chaplain Rollins delivers a sermon   36
11. Chaplain Rollins conducts a service in a dugout   37
12. Chaplain Anselm J. Mayotte   45
13. First YD funeral, near Vailly   48
14. Chaplain de Valles awarded the Croix de Guerre   56
15. Chaplain William J. Farrell   59
16. Chaplain Orville A. Petty receives the Silver Star   61
17. "Home on Leave," Chaplain Rollins   63
18. Chaplain Walton S. Danker   65
19. Chaplain O'Connor offers Mass from back of an ambulance   68
20. Chaplain Harrison Ray Anderson   69
21. Chaplain Albert G. Butzer, Sr.   82
22. Chaplain Michael Nivard   83
23. Chaplain Charles K. Imbrie   84
24. Chaplain Thomas Guthrie Speers, Sr.   94
25. Chaplain Arthur J. LeVeer   96
26. Chaplain John Francis Tucker   100
27. Chaplain John H. Creighton conducts a service near Verdun   103
28. Chaplain Robert Campbell, Jr., conducts a burial service near Verdun   119

xii   Illustrations

29. "Homeward Bound," Chaplains Edwards, de Valles, O'Connor, Evans, and Imbrie   126
30. Rev. Murray W. Dewart   133
31. Chauncey Allen Adams, DD   139
32. Rev. George F. Jonaitis   143
33. Dr. Moody and Robert Frost at Middlebury College   150
34. Archbishop John J. Mitty   156
35. Chaplain Aldred A. Pruden   168

Map

Partial map of France with highlights of YD service   xxiii

Preface

Living in the Boston suburb of Framingham, Massachusetts, my family was no stranger to priests. They were guests at our dinner table. We saw them in formal and informal settings, and they engendered our respect. Rev. Michael J. O'Connor ("Father Mike") was my parents' pastor at St. Bridget's, and he was counted among my maternal grandfather's many close friends. In fact, he celebrated the marriage of my parents. My mother regularly corresponded with a high school chum, Rev. Francis McGauley, S.J., who, as a missionary, remained in India for decades, knowing that if he left, even briefly, it was unlikely he would be allowed to return. Years later, when he was back in the States, I met Frank for the first time when he was a guest of my parents, but it was like I had always known him. Monsignor Edward F. Sweeney, Director of the Propagation of the Faith, and, for a short time, Pastor at St. Bridget's, frequently dined with us. Then there was Rev. John H. Chevalier, S.S.E., diminutive and slightly walleyed, who had known my Uncle Paul at St. Michael's College in Winooski, Vermont. He labored at St. Martin de Porres Parish, a small mission church in Gadsden, Alabama, that served the African-American community. My family had recently moved there from suburban Chicago when we first met. "Just call me Father Chevy," he would say, "I'm not a Cadillac." This humble man, comfortable in his own skin, did God's work under difficult circumstances in Gadsden, and later in Selma, at Our Lady Queen of Peace Parish. He died there on November 11, 1987.

Like Fr. Chevy, Army chaplains worked under difficult circumstances. During the First World War, more than 2,300 men served as chaplains in the United States Army, although initially, only a fraction of them served overseas in the AEF. As there was no organized chaplain corps, the job was largely what they and their commanding officers made of it. They were often referred to as "handymen" and at times assigned to other minor duties. For some, their primary duty was to see that the soldiers' conduct was pure and exemplary. As one soldier put it: "The chaplains . . . dwelt considerably upon maintaining the moral standard of the army. . . ." However, that was just one aspect of their duties. The war was a very difficult time for the young soldiers, many of them overseas and away from home for the first time. Army chaplains were affectionately dubbed "Sky Pilots" and "Holy Joes," and sometimes simply "Padre," by the men they served.[1] Most chaplains were there to lend an ear.

The chaplains in the First World War did not officially bear arms of any kind, at least those serving in the British and American forces.[2] The faith and courage of these men of the cloth under the most trying and terrible circumstances carried them through. They were incredibly brave men who risked life and limb to minister to the dead and dying as the shells flew overhead, unafraid to rush ammunition toward the front or to drive an ambulance hell-bent away from the front, carrying the wounded to safety. When the need arose, some pulled the lanyard on an artillery piece, while others tossed grenades. They suffered the same terrors and privations as the doughboys that they served; they dug the graves; they wrote the letters of condolence home.

Just how a chaplain acted in the front lines was more important to the troops than a church service conducted in the rear. "A chaplain's conduct at the front counts heavily with them; there, the chaplain proves his faith that there is an after world by his behavior under fire and in the face of war's strain . . . [and he can] . . . win all the influence [he] may desire by an exhibition of calm and unflinching courage. . . ." This sentiment was echoed by long-time Chaplain Leslie Groves, who said that the ideal chaplain "is the one who lives with the men, enduring the same hardships and encountering the same dangers, who is ruled not by selfishness but by love for all men . . . who can speak when the time comes the words that will be listened to."[3]

In his excellent memoir, *Good-bye to All That*, Robert Graves compares the Anglican chaplains to the Catholic ones in the British Army. According to Graves, who served as an officer in the Royal Welsh Fusiliers during the First World War, the former were not well thought of by the troops, while the latter were universally revered for their willingness to share the dangers of battle with their men. Perhaps apocryphally, he relates the story of the colonel of one battalion who had gone through four Anglican chaplains in four months. Exasperated, he finally asked that a Catholic chaplain be sent, claiming a mass change of faith in the men he commanded! In fairness to all chaplains, regardless of denomination, the esteem accorded each was in direct proportion to the degree of shared experience, and not his belief system. Who can ever forget the image of the four Army chaplains who gave up their life jackets so that others might live, praying together as the U.S. Army Transport *Dorchester* sank into the icy Atlantic in February 1943?[4]

If one were asked who was the most famous chaplain of World War I, he or she would answer, "Father Francis Duffy of the 165th Infantry Regiment ('Fighting 69th') of the 42nd ('Rainbow') Division." It is doubtful that one would be able to name another. Yet, if you were able to ask any doughboy today who his chaplain was, he would likely answer with alacrity. Hundreds of men filled that role during the war, virtually all now unsung. One of those was Rev. Michael J. O'Connor of the Yankee Division, who went on to become the Division Chaplain, and later a Brigadier General, in the Massachusetts National Guard. The Twenty-sixth Division was particularly fortunate to have a group of chaplains—Protestant, Catholic, and Jewish—who were second to none. In addition to Fr. O'Connor, Reverend Lyman Rollins of the 101st Infantry, an Episcopal clergyman from Marblehead, often went on raids with the men, including the fateful Hickey's Raid. He worked well with Fr. O'Connor, the division chaplain and a Catholic. Frequently, O'Connor would say Mass, and Rollins would preach the sermon. He talked straight to his men, and in one notable sermon, he used a string of the doughboy's "favorite oaths and epithets" just to make a point![5] It is very clear that in the Yankee Division, the doughboy's soul was as well looked after as was his body.

Acknowledgments

For some time now, as I researched my other books on the Yankee Division, I frequently came across references to the exploits of certain regimental chaplains. Since then, I have wanted to write about these brave men. Each time, however, I have had to put it off for one reason or another. Throughout the process of researching and writing this book, I have been aided by many others, like Brig. Gen. Leonid Kondratiuk, Director of the Massachusetts National Guard Museum and Archives in Concord, Massachusetts. Len is both knowledgeable and generous with his insights. Thanks also go to all the archivists and reference librarians, who remain a mainstay in my research. I am particularly grateful to the families of these brave men who took the time to share a part of their own family history, particularly to Harrison Ray Anderson, Jr. Lad was very enthusiastic about the project and generous with his help in locating letters and other family materials detailing his father's service. Sadly, he died in August 2012, well before I could share with him a copy of this volume. I would be remiss if I did not single out Terry Finnegan, historian and fellow devotee of all things YD. Terry is a great source and has been most generous with his insights. The following list is long, and, hopefully, I have not left anyone out:

Archives

Rev. Robert Altmann, Archivist, Diocese of La Crosse, La Crosse, WI
Deacon Jeffrey Burns, Archivist, Archdiocese of San Francisco, San Francisco, CA
Richard L. Baker, U.S. Army Military History Institute, Carlisle, PA
Bill Conley, Archivist, Oblates of St. Francis de Sales, Newark, DE
Eleanor Dornon, Archives Committee, Pilgrim Place, Claremont, CA
Lin Fredericksen, State Archives Division, Kansas Historical Society, Topeka, KS
Eva Garcelon-Hart, Archivist, Stewart-Smith Research Center, Middlebury, VT

Diane Guyer, Office of the Chancellor, Diocese of Springfield, Springfield, MA
Robert Johnson-Lally, Archivist, Archdiocese of Boston, Braintree, MA
Brig. Gen. Leonid Kondratiuk, National Guard Museum & Archives, Concord, MA
Msgr. John J. McDermott, Chancellor, Diocese of Burlington, Burlington, VT
Marcia G. McManus, Director, U.S. Army Chaplain Corps Museum, Ft. Jackson, SC
Deacon Timothy F. McNeil, Chancellor, Archdiocese of Omaha, Omaha, NE
Maria Medina, Archivist, Archdiocese of Hartford, Hartford, CT
Rev. Michael P. Morris, Archivist, and Kate Feighery, Archival Manager, Archdiocese of New York, Yonkers, NY
Karen Nelson, Brown Memorial Park Avenue Presbyterian Church, Baltimore, MD
Kevin Proffitt, Senior Archivist, American Jewish Archives, Cincinnati, OH
Sr. Lea Stephancova, Archivist, Diocese of Peoria, Peoria, IL
Msgr. Barry W. Wall, Archivist, Diocese of Fall River, MA

Public and University Libraries

Robbin Bailey, Reference Librarian, Concord Public Library, Concord, NH
Janet Cheung, Maryland Department, Enoch Pratt Free Library, Baltimore, MD
Suzanne Christoff, Special Collections and Archives, United States Military Academy
Susan Connor, Reference Department, Swampscott Public Library, Swampscott, MA
Jane Daugherty, Local History & Genealogy Div., Mobile Public Library, Mobile, AL
Kenneth R. Despertt, Reference Librarian, D.C. Public Library, Washington, D.C.
Dan Haacker, Assistant Director, Milton Public Library, Milton, MA
Elvernoy Johnson and Silvia Mejia, State Library of Massachusetts, Boston, MA
Susan Kasten, Reference Department, Newton Free Library, Newton, MA
Jim Massery, Archivist, Holyoke Public Library, Holyoke, MA

Cynthia Muszala, Library Assistant, Morristown & Morris Twp. Library, Morristown, NJ
Diane Pierce-Williams, Archivist, Milton Academy, Milton, MA
Paige Roberts, Archivist, Holmes Library, Phillips Academy, Andover, MA
Danielle M. Rougeau, Assistant Curator, Special Collections, Middlebury College, Middlebury, VT
Margaret Schaus, Lead Research Librarian, Haverford College, Haverford, PA
Roberta Schmidlen, Librarian, St. Albans Free Library, St. Albans, VT
Barbara Shatara, Librarian, Fletcher Free Library, Burlington, VT
Ellen M. Shea, Head of Research, and Lynda Leahy, Reference Librarian, Schlesinger Library, Radcliffe Institute, Cambridge, MA
Lynn Sullivan, Library Specialist, Omaha Public Library, Omaha, NE
L. Thurber, Reference Librarian, Nantucket Atheneum, Nantucket, MA
Ann Upton, Special Collections, Haverford College, Haverford, PA

Pastors, Sextons, Church Historians

Jim Allein, Archivist, Lancaster Presbyterian Church, Lancaster, NY
Don Allerton and Louise Howe, Fourth Presbyterian Church, Chicago, IL
Fred Benson, Sexton, and Sarah Twiss, Parish of the Epiphany, Winchester, MA
Fr. Michael Cronogue, S.S.E., Superior General, Society of St. Edmund, Colchester, VT
Dana Denault, Historian, St. Michael's Church, Marblehead, MA
Cathy Kobialka, Senior Clerk, Marblehead Cemetery Dept., Marblehead, MA
Rev. Peter Plagge, Pastor, Waterbury United Church of Christ, Waterbury, VT
Janice S. Randall, Emmanuel Church, 15 Newbury Street, Boston, MA
Susan Raymond, Montauk Community Church, Montauk, NY
Jack Wasko, Archivist, Church of the Ascension, Pittsburgh, PA

Historical Societies

Fabiola Cutler, Archivist, Aspinock Historical Society of Putnam, Inc., Putnam, CT
Iroquois County Genealogy Society, Watseka, IL
Richard C. Malley, Connecticut Historical Society, Hartford, CT

Individuals

Harrison Ray ("Lad") Anderson, Jr., Bellingham, WA
Kenneth J. Buck and Sylvia Buck, Warren, MA
Rev. Albert G. Butzer, III, First Presbyterian Church, Virginia Beach, VA
Murray Dewart, Brookline, MA
Marjorie Lindley, Independent Researcher, Laurium, MI
Gail Petty Riepe, Cockeysville, MD
Rev. Thomas G. Speers III, Simsbury, CT

State Records

Ronald Haynes, Office of the Adjutant General, Charleston, WV
Russell Horton, Archivist, Wisconsin Veterans Museum, Madison, WI
Paul Perrault, Vermont Office of Veteran's Affairs, Montpelier, VT

My brother Pat read portions of the manuscript and offered valuable suggestions to improve it, and my brother Paul took the stunning photograph of the St. Michael sculpture in Philadelphia. And, as always, to Marilyn, who plans the trips, helps with the research, and is a great listener and sounding board, as well as an all around good sport.

Abbreviations

ABMC	American Battle Monuments Commission
ADB	Archdiocese of Boston Archives, Braintree, MA
ADNY	Archdiocese of New York, Archives, Yonkers, NY
AGB	Albert G. Butzer, Sr., Papers
AWW	*United States Army in the World War*, 1917–19
CHS	Connecticut Historical Society, Hartford, CT
CRE	Clarence R. Edwards Papers, Massachusetts Historical Society, Boston, MA
CSL	Connecticut State Library and Archives, Hartford, CT
CTAG	Adjutant General, State of Connecticut, Hartford, CT
FPCA	Fourth Presbyterian Church, Archives, Chicago, IL
GCML	George C. Marshall Library, Lexington, VA
HRA	Harrison Ray Anderson, Sr., Personal Papers
IBP	Israel Bettan Papers, Jacob Rader Marcus Center, Hebrew Union College, Cincinnati, OH
KJB	Kenneth J. Buck, Tucker Family Papers, Warren, MA
MANG	Massachusetts National Guard Museum and Archives, Concord, MA
MHI	Military History Institute, Carlisle, PA
MPP	Mary Parkman Peabody Papers, Schlesinger Library, Radcliffe College, Boston, MA.
MWD	Murray Wilder Dewart, *Letters to Mitty*, Dewart Family Papers
NLM	National Library of Medicine, Bethesda, MD
TGS	Thomas Guthrie Speers, Sr., Papers

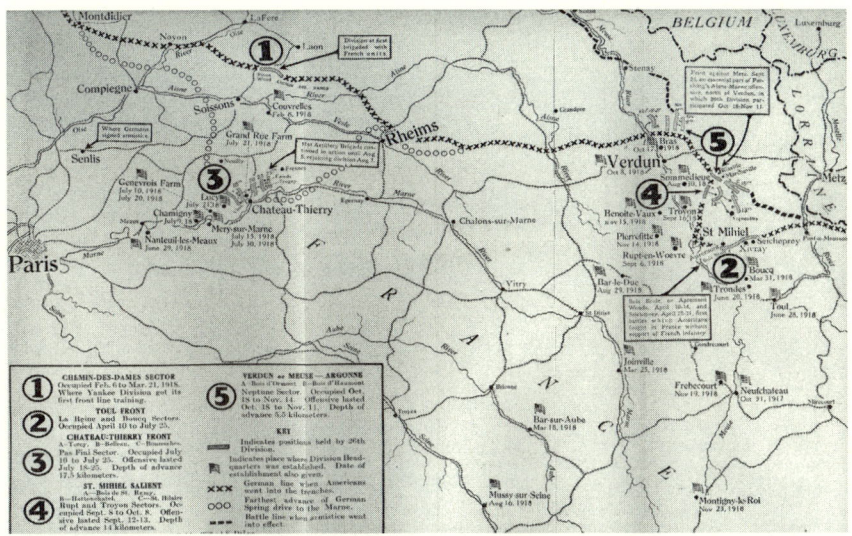

Map of France with Yankee Division highlights. Reprinted from Sibley, *With the Yankee Division in France*.

CHAPTER ONE

"Sky Pilots"

THE CHAPLAINCY EVOLVES

Ever since 1775, when General Artemas Ward took command of the aggregation of militias surrounding Boston, chaplains have been a part of what would become the United States Army. In fact, the Provincial Congress "was practically flooded with offers from patriotic preachers who wanted to serve," including Dr. Samuel Langdon, president of Harvard College, though the overall spiritual effect may very well have been minimal. In spite of twice-daily church services and an abundance of clergy, profanity persisted throughout the army.[1] The Continental Congress weighed in a year later, when it authorized the recruitment of chaplains, and George Washington himself followed up with General Orders dated July 9, 1776, in which he directed that a chaplain be assigned to each regiment. Commanding officers were ordered to seek out, "persons of good characters and exemplary lives."[2] Nevertheless, nearly 150 years would pass before a Chaplain's Corps would be formed and integrated into the Army after the close of the First World War.

ELIHU ROOT

Beginning in 1903, the truly transformational effects of the fundamental changes to the Army cannot be overstated, and they were primarily attributable to the vision and executive ability of Elihu Root. A successful New York attorney, Root was tapped by President William McKinley to be his Secretary of War, following the departure of Secretary Russell Alger from the Cabinet. The process begun by Root was continued by Maj. Gen. Leonard Wood, as Chief of Staff, and later Secretary of War, Henry L. Stimson, both of whom also vigorously seized upon the opportunity to reform the Army, from its inefficient and highly politicized bureau system to glacially slow promotions based strictly on seniority. In spite of resistance from die-hard senior officers, the most significant reform was the establishment of a General Staff and the appointment of a Chief of Staff to replace the rank of Commanding General. Promotions would gradually start to be made on merit and fitness, although the inevitable politics still played a role regarding promotions to the higher ranks. John J. Pershing was a prime example. There was also an emphasis on the training and education of officers in service schools, in an effort to make these leaders more professional. Also important was the effort to create a more modern army on a European model, with larger units like "maneuver" divisions, composed of infantry, artillery, and cavalry. Regiments would now have three battalions. In short, it was a complete makeover.[3]

Traditionally, a chaplain's duties were loosely defined, more often than not by the individual regimental commander.

> Aside from conducting religious services . . . chaplains were the morale officers of their day. Not all posts had chapels, so they had to hold services in whatever room was available. . . . They usually supervised the post school and library and gave lectures on assorted topics, and used stereopticon and lantern slides as well as movies to entertain the troops.[4]

As part of the reform effort, changes were made regarding the selection of chaplains. Instead of appointments by the Secretary of War, an examination was added, along with a background check, and more significantly, the various denominations were given increased input into the recommendation and selection of candidates. Once appointed, chaplains were accorded actual rank as officers, and the Army assigned assistants from the enlisted ranks and allocated transportation by the Quartermaster. More importantly, there was an increase in the overall number of chaplains to one per regiment. As early as 1908, Chaplain Aldred Adino Pruden proposed a board or commission be appointed to recommend chaplains to the General Staff. Gradually that idea took hold, and each of the major religious denominations established such entities, and they became the primary source of chaplain candidates. Later, the Protestant denominations would coalesce into the General Committee on Army and Navy Chaplains, while the Catholic Church would act through the National Catholic War Council.[5]

The Need

One thing is for certain—there were never enough chaplains in the AEF. As of April 1917, at the beginning of America's entry into the war, there was

Bishop Charles H. Brent, Senior AEF Chaplain, *third from left*. Courtesy of the Library of Congress.

still only a single chaplain assigned to each regiment, roughly composed of 1,200 men. The next month, Congress passed a defense bill without increasing the number of chaplains per regiment, while at the same time it increased the size of an infantry regiment to 3,600 men. At that time, in the Regular Army itself, there were a total of seventy-four chaplains, along with an additional seventy-two in the National Guard. General John J. Pershing, Commander in Chief of the AEF, recognized the need for chaplains and strongly recommended that one be assigned for every twelve hundred men (roughly the size of a new infantry battalion). Congress was slow to comply with this request, and when the law doing so was ultimately signed by President Wilson in May 1918, it was already late in the war. As a result, the Army played "catch-up" throughout the war, turning out about 150 new chaplains a month.[6]

Gradually, however, over the course of the conflict, the training and assignment of chaplains began to coalesce around the efforts of two men. The first, Bishop Charles H. Brent, a well-known Protestant missionary, was appointed as the Senior Chaplain for the AEF with his headquarters at Chaumont. His job was to coordinate the activities of all chaplains regardless of religion. The second, Chaplain Aldred A. Pruden, who had also lobbied hard for a chaplain school, designed the initial curriculum and served as the head of the school throughout the war.

Charles Henry Brent was born in Newcastle, Ontario, Canada, on April 9, 1862. He was ordained an Episcopal priest in 1887, three years following his graduation from Trinity College at the University of Toronto. Brent was assigned to St. Stephen's Church, an inner-city parish in Boston in 1891, and he became a United States citizen about the same time. In 1901, he was elected Bishop of the Philippines and consecrated the following year. He traveled there with William Howard Taft, who had been appointed to head the Second Philippine Commission and later as the governor of the islands. During his time there, Brent worked hard to convert the non-Catholic population, including the indigenous Moros and Igorots, as well as those in the Chinese enclave in Manila. He was the author of several works on religion and a fierce and vocal opponent of the opium trade, serving on various boards and commissions. While serving as Missionary Bishop of the Philippines, he returned periodically to the United States to lecture, first at the General Theological Seminary in New York in 1904, and again in 1907 at Harvard University.

In May 1908, he was elected Bishop of the Diocese of Washington, D.C., but he declined the appointment, preferring instead to remain a missionary bishop. He would serve the Philippines until 1918, at which time he was elected Bishop of the Diocese of Western New York, a position he accepted but did not assume until sometime in 1919 after he had returned from France. In the interim, he was selected as the Senior Chaplain for the AEF. While he stood high in Pershing's regard, some in the AEF thought that perhaps he tended to go on "interminably" about his ambitious plans for the placement of chaplains throughout the army.[7]

Bishop Brent arrived in France in December 1917 as a special representative of the YMCA when General Pershing tapped him to organize the AEF chaplains. He set about utilizing the limited resources available at that time. The bishop first turned to private organizations, like the Knights of Columbus, Red Cross, Salvation Army, Jewish Welfare Board, and the YMCA, all of which picked up the slack. Brent's decision to utilize these civilian agencies represented a departure from the entrenched attitude of many Army chaplains, dating back to the Civil War, when the YMCA-sponsored U.S. Christian Commission was viewed by many chaplains as an interloper and a direct competitor in what was their exclusive domain. Perhaps because Brent himself was not a regular military man, his decision was a logical one. Due to the acute shortage of Army chaplains, he referred to these agencies as the "saving element." Staffed by brave and dedicated men and women, the outside agencies served the doughboy at home and overseas, delivering creature comforts, writing materials, and spiritual aid and comfort. The Knights of Columbus sponsored dozens of priests, volunteers assigned to individual units, many of whom would eventually receive commissions in the Army. They, along with lay YMCA Secretaries, could be found throughout the AEF in France, including the front lines. At the same time Brent was unequivocal in his position regarding the role these organizations should play—they were "to aid the chaplain in his work."[8]

A Preliminary Board was established on January 10, 1918, for "the organization of chaplains and the coordination of all moral and spiritual agencies at work in the AEF." The board recommended the formation of a Chaplains' Office at Chaumont near General Headquarters, and after two revisions to its report, on May 1, 1918, General Order No. 66 established the GHQ Chaplains' Office and the Board of Chaplains to "develop an *esprit de corps* among the chaplains; to provide such literature on chaplains' opportunities and duties as will tend to develop the highest degree of efficiency; to prevent and forestall duplication of effort and to coordinate the activities of the various religious and welfare organizations operating" with the Army.

In addition to Bishop Brent, who was named Senior GHQ Chaplain, the other Board members were Rev. Francis B. Doherty, a Catholic priest and another old hand, having served in the Philippine War, and Rev. Paul D. Moody, both of whom were appointed as GHQ Chaplains. Paul Dwight Moody was born in Baltimore, Maryland, on April 11, 1879. He was the son of famed evangelist Dwight L. Moody, who was also the founder of the Northfield School (later Northfield Mount Hermon School). Upon graduation from Yale University in 1901, he embarked on ministerial studies in Scotland and at the Hartford Theological Seminary, from which he graduated in 1906. Moody taught school for a time and worked for two publishers. In April 1912, he was ordained as a Congregational minister at the South Church in St. Johnsbury, Vermont, and served there as minister until 1917. When the United States entered the war in Europe, he enlisted in the Vermont National Guard and was commissioned as a Chaplain (1st Lt.) in the 1st Vermont Infantry Regiment (later designated as the 103rd Infantry). Moody went to France with his regiment and served with it in the Chemin des Dames and Toul Sectors, until June 1918, at which time he became a permanent member of the Board of Chaplains headquartered at Chaumont.[9] He would be directly involved in the assignment of chaplains.

Like Bishop Brent, Paul Moody was imbued with the zeal of a missionary. As Chaplain of the 1st Vermont Infantry Regiment, he recognized the temptations testing the young soldiers in the camps, even before they went to France. He wrote:

> Unfortunately there are temptations which come upon men with greater force when cut off from the refining influences of home, and the government is coming to recognize more and more that these are dangerous, not merely because they affect the morals of the men, but also because they reduce their efficiency. If in any way the Church can help to stem the force of the appeals to the lower nature, it will be doing a service not alone for God but for country.[10]

Moody's views comported with those of Bishop Brent, and more importantly, with those of General Pershing, and could well have led to his appointment to the Board of Chaplains.

Virtually every aspect of the initial American war effort, including the chaplaincy, had to be learned on the job. So, while Bishop Brent was organizing the chaplains in France, the home front was not neglected. Recognizing the need for some uniformity, a plan to establish a school for chaplains was developed by Chaplain (Major) Aldred Adino Pruden, sometimes referred to as the "Father of Army Chaplaincy." Pruden was born in Virginia in 1866. Upon graduation from the Theological Seminary of Virginia in 1894, he was ordained an Episcopal minister. Pruden saw service in the Spanish-American War as a chaplain in the 1st North Carolina Volunteer Infantry and later in the Philippine War. He remained on active duty with the Army as a chaplain, and he was promoted to the rank of major in 1911.[11]

The War Department approved Pruden's school plan in February 1918, and the first Chaplain School class commenced at Fort Monroe, Virginia, on March 3, 1918, with Pruden as commandant, using a curriculum designed by him. Shortly thereafter, the U.S. Army Chaplain School moved to Camp Zachary Taylor in Kentucky. The course or training cycle lasted five weeks, and it included physical conditioning as well as subjects such as Military Law, First Aid, and Army Regulations. Each cycle consisted of approximately 140 students, and it was initially intended to train both chaplain candidates and commissioned chaplains in equal numbers. However, as the war progressed the Army found that those already commissioned could not be readily spared from their duties given the existing shortages. More than a thousand chaplains would graduate from the school prior to its closure in January 1919.[12]

Bishop Brent established a second school in France at Neuilly-sur-Suize, just south of Chaumont and AEF Headquarters. The purpose of this school was to supplement the initial training, with practical lessons geared specifically toward working in the front lines. At first, the course was one week long, but it was later expanded to ten days.[13]

For decades, a disproportionate number of Episcopal priests served as Army chaplains. Recognizing the fact that many other denominations were represented by the troops that served, steps were gradually taken to include a greater variety of clergymen, particularly Catholic priests, within the ranks of the chaplaincy. As early as 1906, President Theodore Roosevelt estimated that Catholics comprised more than 20 percent of the Army rank and file, but they were served by fewer Catholic chaplains. Later, in 1914, Secretary of War Lindley M. Garrison concluded that the actual number was 23.75 percent, and thereafter, the Army set the ratio at 25 percent. At

Army Chaplain School, Camp Zachary Taylor (Chaplain Pruden *seated, front row, ninth from right*). Courtesy of the Library of Congress.

the start of the First World War there were sixteen Catholic priests in the Regular Army, and another ten in the National Guard. In addition, there were 8 Navy chaplains who were Catholic priests. As of the Armistice, 1,026 Catholic priests were serving in the armed forces, 762 of whom had received commissions, with the balance serving under the auspices of organizations like the Knights of Columbus. This represented approximately thirty percent of the total number of chaplains.[14]

Despite the increase in the number of Army chaplains as a result of the Root reforms in 1903, even as late as 1916, efforts to appoint a Jewish chaplain from among them failed. It was not until October 6, 1917, that Congress authorized an additional twenty chaplains at large, six of whom were specifically allocated to Jewish chaplains. Those slots were immediately filled by rabbis already serving in the ranks. Later, with passage of the Defense Act of May 25, 1918, still more were authorized. Up to that point, Jewish troops were served primarily by chaplains of other faiths or lay troops within the ranks. "Acting Rabbi" to the Jewish soldiers in the Yankee Division was Benjamin Riseman, a real estate broker from Boston, who would serve under the auspices of the Jewish Welfare Board. These so-called "Star of David men," like the fifty-year-old Riseman, who had emigrated from Russia with his wife in 1890, would learn to perform Jewish services and to otherwise provide comfort and counseling where no Jewish chaplain was assigned to a unit.[15] Riseman would continue to serve, at least until the arrival of Rabbi Israel Bettan, a commissioned officer, late in the war.

There were also controversies regarding the awarding of rank and promotions, as well as the wearing of insignia. In March 1918, Pershing recommended that chaplains not wear insignia of rank, but only the Latin cross, as it could prove a barrier between the chaplain and the rank and file. This resulted in a special regulation two months later, although it was sometimes ignored, especially in the United States where the regulation did not apparently have widespread circulation. The controversy generated by this action would ultimately result in the relief of Major Pruden and others. It was not until 1926 when the insignia of rank were officially restored. The Latin cross, long the symbol of the chaplains, became the subject of controversy when, quite understandably, newly authorized Jewish chaplains protested the mandate. At one point, an insignia in the shape of a shepherd's crook was proposed for use by all as a compromise; however, Secretary Baker directed that the Latin cross remain the official insignia. Finally, in October 1918, an insignia in the shape of the two law tablets surmounted by a Star of David was authorized for Jewish chaplains.[16]

Birth of a Division

Prior to August 1917, the 26th Division simply did not exist. In April 1917, however, Maj. Gen. Clarence Ransom Edwards was given command of the Northeastern Department, which encompassed the six New England states. Just prior to that, he had been in command of the garrison at the Panama Canal, an important assignment. His primary task now was to form up a division out of the existing New England National Guard and, wherever necessary, supplement it with men from the National Army (draftees). In some respects, his task was easy, given that the six New England states were relatively small and, more importantly, contiguous, and each had a long military tradition, some dating back to Colonial militias, and most to the Civil War. Many Guardsmen had just recently returned from service on the border with Mexico, thus giving them, in essence, a "dry run."

If any man personified the spirit and drive of the division, it was General Edwards. His genuine affection for his troops, his "stout-hearted lads," was universally reciprocated by them, even long after the war. He was affectionately called "Daddy." Clarence Ransom Edwards was born into a very successful and politically connected family in Cleveland, Ohio, on New Year's Day 1859. He attended West Point, where he graduated dead last in his class. Despite his poor showing, his personal drive and his connections were rewarded with important assignments and regular promotions. Edwards would serve in the Southwest, the Philippines (where he was cited three times for bravery under fire), and the Panama Canal Zone, where he commanded the garrison and developed the plan for its defense. However, it was his twelve-year assignment as chief of the Bureau of Insular Affairs in Washington for which he was best known. There he hob-nobbed with the movers and shakers. He worked directly for Secretary of War Elihu Root, and he became a personal friend, advisor, and regular golfing partner of President William Howard Taft. It was this assignment that left him with the reputation of being a "political general." He also developed a reputation for getting things done, but also as one who was too openly critical of some fellow officers, including his superiors.[17]

The men who came to compose the Yankee Division assembled first at their local armories, and then at State Militia camps like Ethan Allen in Burlington; Keyes in Augusta, Maine; and Quonset Point in Rhode Island. Just before sailing, the division was further concentrated at Framingham and Westfield, Massachusetts, as well as some scattered camps like Niantic and New Haven, Connecticut. The weeding and sorting process was not without glitches. On the downside, that self-same Militia tradition, unit pride, and the politics associated with the National Guard and Militias created some hard feelings as units merged and changed designations, and sometimes, their functions. In addition, some officers were told that they would be assigned, if at all, to other divisions also then forming. As a result, unit pride sometimes trumped good sense. In one glaring example, a small mutiny took place on August 21, 1917, the day when the 5th and 9th Massachusetts Infantry Regiments were scheduled to be consolidated into the 101st Infantry Regiment. Hundreds of enlisted men from the 5th Massachusetts left their camp and seized an eastbound train in Framingham to take their protest to the Statehouse in Boston. Several officers and noncoms from the 5th Massachusetts, including Chaplain Lyman Rollins, a division stalwart, caught up with the men and convinced them to stop, thus averting a sure catastrophe.[18]

For Edwards, the problem was compounded at the higher level, as he was also tasked with selecting the location for a cantonment, or large military complex, for the processing and training of New England draftees. Most state governors and congressmen got into the act, vying for the honor (and the economic benefit) of being the state chosen. Ultimately, General Edwards recommended a site near Ayer, Massachusetts, which would be named Camp Devens, after Charles Devens, a Civil War–era general.

An American division in the First World War was, by today's standards, enormous, consisting of twenty-eight thousand men. Pershing wanted it that way. It was a "square division," comprised of four infantry regiments, with about thirty-six hundred men each, divided two each to a brigade.

Next came an artillery brigade comprised of three artillery regiments—two light and one heavy. The balance of the division consisted mainly of three machine gun battalions, a regiment of engineers, a field signal battalion, together with separate ammunition and sanitary trains, the latter composed of four field hospital companies and an equal number of ambulance companies. Rounding out the mix were various headquarters troops like military police. In short, an American division was a self-sustained fighting unit, two or three times larger than their Allied counterparts, as well as the Germans. What it lacked in experience would be generally offset by sheer firepower and numbers.

Like a giant "cut and paste" project, General Edwards built the Yankee Division with the disparate elements from virtually all of the New England National Guard units. First, he assembled his staff, with a headquarters in Boston. Curiously, he did not include a chaplain on his initial staff. That's not to say that there were no chaplains, since many of the existing infantry regiments had already made provision for them. The Yankee Division became the first fully formed division in France, due in no small credit to General Edwards and his staff. It was one of the first four divisions, two Regular (1st and 2nd) and two National Guard (26th and 42nd), which came to be known as the "Old Reliables." Of nearly thirty divisions to serve in France during the war, these four would suffer 30 percent of the casualties.[19]

Throughout the spring and early summer months the disparate units trained throughout New England. In late summer, they began to coalesce at larger encampments like Boxford (Camp Curtis Guild), Westfield (Camp Bartlett), and Framingham (Camp McGuinness) in Massachusetts, as well as Niantic and New Haven (Camp Yale) in Connecticut. Visitors were welcome, especially on weekends. As September drew near, going away events were planned. Camp Bartlett was the setting for just such an event on Sunday, September 9. The beautiful late summer day drew thirty thousand visitors. In addition to the usual inspections, the day began with a 7:00 a.m. Mass at the newly dedicated St. Paul's Chapel, celebrated by Rev. George S. L. Connor of Springfield, then attached to the 52nd Brigade Headquarters and acting as the Catholic chaplain at Camp Bartlett. The service was attended by nearly fifteen hundred officers and enlisted men. This was followed by an open-air Episcopal service conducted by the Right Reverend William Lawrence, Bishop of Massachusetts. Of special interest, ballots were received by the 103rd Infantry to be used by the soldiers from Maine, which was holding a referendum on a proposed amendment to the Constitution that would give women the right to vote. It was expected to pass handily, at least among that soldierly contingent.[20]

Camp Bartlett, Westfield, MA, Sunday, September 9, 1917. *Left to right:* Chaplain Walton S. Danker, Chaplain James E. Cochrane, Bishop William Lawrence, and Chaplain Paul D. Moody. Reprinted from Benwell, *History of the Yankee Division.*

Winnowing

All the while, the sorting process was going on, separating the fit from the unfit. The chaplaincy was no exception. Undoubtedly disappointed was longtime chaplain to the 2nd Maine Infantry, Rev. James E. Cochrane. It was felt that the sixty-four-year-old Monmouth native's place was at home and not in France. Cochrane had served as Chaplain of the 2nd Maine Infantry since November 1893 and held the rank of Captain. Throughout the war, he would continue to serve in the National Guard, and later the 57th Pioneer Infantry, followed by the 48th Infantry Regiment, until his discharge on October 30, 1919.[21] The story was the same with Herman Page, who served as a chaplain, without commission, to the 1st Massachusetts Field Signal Battalion while it remained encamped at Framingham. However, he, too, would not join the unit in France. Page eventually received his commission and served in various units within the United States.[22]

The same could have been said for forty-three-year-old Harris Elwood Starr, another clergyman from New Haven. However, for Starr, the need to work with the men of the Connecticut regiment was strong, as was his will. He had served as Chaplain of the 2nd Connecticut Infantry Regiment, but he had not been selected during the culling process, when the two state

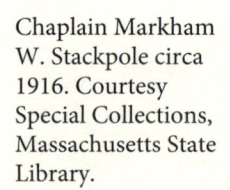

Chaplain Markham W. Stackpole circa 1916. Courtesy Special Collections, Massachusetts State Library.

National Guard regiments were merged to form the 102nd Infantry. Chaplain Orville Anderson Petty was selected in his stead. Although undoubtedly disappointed, Starr volunteered as a YMCA Secretary and served the 102nd Infantry Regiment in that capacity in France from September 1917 to May 1918. Starr returned home at that time and later attended the Army Chaplain School at Camp Zachary Taylor in Kentucky, where he was commissioned as a Chaplain (1st Lt.) on November 7. He would serve briefly in the 154th Depot Brigade at Fort Meade, Maryland, until his discharge on December 19, 1918.[23]

Age was not always a determinate factor. An original member of the division was Markham Winslow Stackpole, who had joined the 2nd Massachusetts Field Artillery, which later became the 102nd Field Artillery. Stackpole was born in Westborough, Massachusetts, on June 5, 1873. His parents, Stephen Henry Stackpole and Julia Langley Faunce, were both old New England stock. Stackpole attended both Colgate University and Harvard, graduating from the latter in 1896. He later attended Harvard Divinity School and Andover Theological Seminary, and following his ordination, he became associate minister of the Central Congregational Church in Boston. In 1908, he joined the faculty at Phillips Academy at Andover, where he was an instructor in Biblical Literature and the school minister. When the United States entered the war, he took leave to join the Army. Stackpole sailed for France with the 102nd Field Artillery in September 1917. With the exception of temporary assignments at Base Sections No. 1 and No. 6, he would serve with the regiment throughout the war.[24]

"The Bravest Thing"

Virtually all of the Yankee Division sailed to France in convoys, escorted by warships. Although the tactic would seem counterintuitive, naval strategists reasoned, correctly, that there was indeed safety in numbers. The bulk of the Division sailed for France from Hoboken, New Jersey, and Montreal, Canada, mostly on British ships and seized German liners, refitted and renamed, between September and October 1917. The doughboys did not just have to contend with seasickness and German U-boats. A small remnant, mostly the detail assigned to transport the artillery horses and mules, sailed a little later. One such ship, the intrepid *Montpelier*, laden with ice, thus slowing its passage, missed its assigned convoy and was forced to sail the North Atlantic alone, arriving at Brest in December.[25]

Perhaps the best-known chaplain in the division was Father Michael J. O'Connor from St. Francis de Sales Parish in Roxbury, Massachusetts. Like Fr. Duffy of the 42nd ("Rainbow") Division, O'Connor was also born in Ireland, and at the age of 19, he immigrated to Massachusetts in 1888. In 1897 he graduated from Holy Cross College in Worcester, Massachusetts, where he also played football. O'Connor was ordained to the priesthood in December 1901, and like Fr. Duffy, he also came to exemplify the spirit of the division that he served. Called "Father Mike" by all ranks, he began his service as a young man when he enlisted in Company E, 9th Regiment of Massachusetts Infantry in May of 1891. He saw service during the strikes in Lawrence, Massachusetts, and on the Mexican border, where he was regimental chaplain. In France, he began his tour as senior chaplain in the 101st Infantry Regiment, rising to the post of division chaplain.[26]

O'Connor was described as "a big, forcible, good-natured padre, an athlete and football player in college" and a person whom "the soldiers looked up to." He, too, seemed to be everywhere there was action, and he was slightly wounded and gassed, but he recovered from both. While in France, one soldier told of how Chaplain O'Connor came out to the trenches and heard confessions and gave out Holy Communion. "So you see he is with us every chance he gets," he told his mother, adding, "You ought to hear him give it to the Huns."[27]

Chaplain Michael J. O'Connor. Courtesy of Archives and Special Collections, College of the Holy Cross.

The *Henry R. Mallory*, a converted fruit transport, pulled away from the dock at Hoboken, New Jersey, during the late afternoon of September 7, 1917, carrying members of the 3rd Battalion, 101st Infantry to France. On Sunday, September 16, Fr. O'Connor celebrated Mass on a crowded aft deck, making use of his portable aluminum altar, while Chaplain Rollins held a Protestant service on the fore deck. Aside from the usual seasickness and the beautiful nightly displays of phosphorescence in the ship's wake, up to that point, the trip was generally uneventful. However, later that day, Private George T. Ahearn from East Boston, a member of Company M, developed acute appendicitis. It became imperative that he be transferred by lifeboat for treatment to one of the escorting warships. Fr. O'Connor volunteered to accompany the man. Late that same afternoon, a small lifeboat was lowered over the side. Four sailors manned the oars, with an officer at the tiller. Fr. Mike held tightly to the stricken man, who was seated in a chair, so that he would not fall over or be tossed out of the boat. Through the gigantic swells of the North Atlantic they rowed toward the waiting vessel. O'Connor described the trip: "As we rode the waves I could hear the cheers of those aboard, then silence as we disappeared from their view in the trough of the seas. As we rode on the crest of the oncoming waves the lusty cheers of our comrades came to our ears." Upon reaching the other ship, a net was lowered that contained a cot, and they gently placed the sick man in it. O'Connor takes up the story of the return to the troopship:

As we turned to leave for our own ship we were taken by a wave and almost stood on end. In the oncoming darkness we pulled toward the transport and arriving alongside we got a terrible battering against the side of the vessel's starboard. The ropes from the davits were lowered and as we were hauled upward the rolling of the vessel bumped us unmercifully.

The lifeboat banged again and again against the side, and no doubt as much from relief as anything else, the soldiers above began to laugh. Safe on deck, the doughty priest, his bruised pride still intact, wryly quipped, "I am the only one of you that can say that I was in a rowboat in mid-ocean!" A soldier who witnessed the event said, "It was as brave an act as I saw in the war."[28]

Flocking to the Colors

Who were these brave men who gave up their mostly comfortable lives to join those fighting with the Yankee Division in France? Many were already serving in that capacity in the various National Guard or Militia companies so prevalent throughout New England. One such was Walton Stoutenburgh Danker. A native of Little Falls, New York, Danker graduated from Trinity College in 1897, and three years later from the General Theological Seminary in New York. Danker enlisted in the 6th Massachusetts Infantry in 1904 and served as its chaplain for more than two years, after which he resigned. He reenlisted in 1909, serving on the Mexican border as Chaplain in the 2nd Massachusetts Infantry. In March of 1917, shortly before the declaration of war with Germany, he was drafted into federal service. Interspersed throughout this period, Danker served in parishes throughout the Northeast, including Bayonne, New Jersey; Milford, Massachusetts; and Brooklyn, New York. In the spring of 1917, he was serving as the Rector of St. John's Episcopal Church in Worcester, from which he took a leave of absence. In France, he would serve as the Regimental Chaplain of the 104th Infantry.[29]

Another veteran, Murray Wilder Dewart, was born in Chardon, Ohio, on February 14, 1874. He was the son of the Rev. James Hartley Dewart and his wife, Mary. Both of his parents had emigrated from Canada. The Dewart family moved to Minneapolis, Minnesota, when Murray was a boy, and he obtained his degree from the University of Minnesota in 1897, followed by postgraduate work at Harvard and General Theological Seminary in New York. He taught briefly at the Pomfret School in Connecticut and received a Divinity Degree from the Episcopal Theological School in Cam-

Chaplain Murray W. Dewart circa 1916. Courtesy Special Collections, Massachusetts State Library.

bridge, Massachusetts. Dewart was ordained a deacon in 1901, and the following year, he was ordained a priest by Bishop William Lawrence. His first assignment was at St. James Episcopal Church in Roxbury, Massachusetts. At the time of the Punitive Expedition to Mexico in 1916, he was in his fourth year as the Rector of the Parish of the Epiphany in Winchester, Massachusetts.[30]

That year, Dewart was granted a leave of absence by his parishioners, and the married father of three young boys joined his National Guard unit on the Mexican border as a chaplain. There, it was said that he "made himself beloved by all because of his natural qualities of leadership and friendship." He was hardly back and settled into his pastoral duties when war was declared against Germany in April 1917. Once again, he was granted a leave of absence, and with his commission as a Chaplain (1st Lt.) in hand, he joined the 101st Field Artillery on July 25, and on September 9, Dewart sailed with it to France aboard the *Adriatic*. Later that day, Colonel John H. Sherburne called the regimental officers together for a meeting. He asked Chaplain Dewart to conduct a brief service to mark the occasion and to ask the Lord's blessings on their endeavors. The trip was relatively uneventful, except for a "spy" scare, when a hapless soldier broke the blackout policy by turning on a light at night in mid-Atlantic. The offender was confined to the brig until he was able convince the authorities that he was not a spy. His confinement was likely a blessing, since some crew members wanted to summarily toss him overboard.[31]

Chaplain George S. L. Connor. Courtesy of Archives and Special Collections, College of the Holy Cross.

With the exception of a temporary assignment to a base hospital at Langres starting in August 1918, Dewart would serve throughout the war with the 101st Field Artillery. Murray's reason for becoming a chaplain was simple. In spite of his abhorrence for war, to him, his regiment "was a body of men, who, when under the stress of active service, would require moral and spiritual guidance and help." He felt that he had the power to do so, and so he freely accepted the responsibility.[32]

George S. L. Connor was no stranger to the men of western Massachusetts who eventually coalesced into the 104th Infantry. He had been a chaplain in the 2nd Massachusetts Infantry in the Massachusetts National Guard, and he had accompanied them to the border with Mexico and only recently returned. The son of Jeremiah J. and Ellen Connor, he was born in Holyoke, Massachusetts, on September 2, 1885, and he attended high school there. He was a 1907 graduate of Holy Cross College, where he played football all four years, having been elected Captain twice. For the rest of his life, he would be known as "Mr. Holy Cross" or simply "Cross" to his friends. Following his graduation, he studied for the priesthood at St. Bernard's Seminary in Rochester, New York, where he was ordained on June 10, 1911. His first assignment was as curate at St. Bernard's Church in Fitchburg, Massachusetts. Naturally, it was assumed that he would accompany the regiment to France. That was not to be, as he was assigned to the 101st Headquarters Train and Military Police. Connor received his commission as a Chaplain (1st Lt.) on October 11, 1917, and he sailed with his unit right after that.[33]

Other clergymen volunteered to serve with the Knights of Columbus, Salvation Army, Jewish Welfare Board, or the YMCA. Father John Baptist (Joao Baptista) de Valles made the transition from the Knights of Columbus to the Army. De Valles was born in Ponta Delgada on the island of San Miguel in the Azores. His parents, John and Maria, brought him to New Bedford, Massachusetts, as a youngster, joining the already large Portuguese population long settled in the region. At first it was the whaling industry that drew these people to America, but in the late nineteenth century they were drawn to the many area textile mills. Following his ordination on June 22, 1906, Father de Valles served parishes in Fall River and New Bedford. Just prior to his military service, he was the Administrator of St. Joseph's Church in North Dighton, Massachusetts.[34]

Nearly forty years old, de Valles volunteered as a chaplain with the Knights of Columbus and was assigned to the 104th Infantry Regiment, where he remained throughout the war. For him, it was more than simple patriotism. Just prior to going to the front, he wrote to Bishop Feehan to ask his forgiveness for any past "pain or offense" he may have given. He told him, in essence, his service would be his penance: "I am prepared to give up my life in doing my duty for the wounded and dying. I hope and pray the Almighty will accept all I have suffered since leaving America in expiation of my sins and errors."[35]

Frank Sibley, a reporter for the *Boston Globe* who was attached to the Yankee Division, described de Valles as "one of the most brilliant-looking, most fiery, high-spirited, tender-hearted men" that he knew in the Army. "His billet was always open," he wrote. Whether the priest was there or not, men freely came and went, and they helped themselves to cigarettes, candy, and other things provided by the Knights of Columbus and friends back home. However, de Valles himself thought that one stealthy doughboy went a little too far when he took the priest's "only other suit of underwear." An officer in the 104th Infantry described him as a "fine man." According to his orderly, Connell Albertine, the chaplain was known to carry cognac in his canteen, and as he made the rounds, he would share it with those on outpost duty. He was also a soft touch for a loan, just as long as the soldier promised not to spend it on prostitutes, or as he called it, "cohabitation." Each payday, he would tell Albertine to tear up the markers. The priest, who wore a distinctive cross on his chest, was always there with a kind word or a joke, and the men, whatever their faith, felt safe when he was around. On July 17, 1918, while in France, he was commissioned as a Chaplain (1st Lt.).[36]

At the time America entered the war, Rev. Charles Everett ("Doc") Hesselgrave, Ph.D., a graduate of Middlebury College and New York University, had been the Pastor of the Centre Congregational Church in South

Manchester, Connecticut, since December 1914. He had served as Pastor of the Stanley Congregational Church in Chatham, New Jersey, for the previous sixteen years. The forty-nine-year-old clergyman took a leave of absence from his ministerial duties to work under the auspices of the YMCA in France. Arriving in Soissons in February 1918, and at the time unassigned, he attached himself, first somewhat by chance, and later by choice, to the 101st Machine Gun Battalion, then conducting training exercises in the Chemin des Dames Sector. This unit was predominantly comprised of men from the Hartford, Connecticut, area, many of whom he already knew. Drawing supplies for his YMCA canteen and loading them on an empty ambulance, Hesselgrave began a non-stop journey with that unit all the way through St. Mihiel. In addition to his canteen duties, at times he also acted as the unofficial chaplain, since none had been assigned to the battalion, nor would one be until the division reached Verdun late in the war.[37]

Hesselgrave was not alone. In fact, many other clergymen, including three prominent Congregational ministers from New Haven, would serve the Yankee Division under similar circumstances. In addition to Harris Elwood Starr, they were Ernest L. Wismer, Oscar E. Maurer (known for his stirring sermons), and Roy M. Houghton.[38]

Robert C. Campbell, Jr., followed a similar path to the Yankee Division. One of ten children of Robert, Sr., a baker, and Elizabeth Campbell, both Irish immigrants, he and four of his brothers would eventually all serve in France at the same time. Campbell graduated from Bowdoin College and the Harvard Theological Seminary. Bowdoin would later confer a Doctor of Divinity upon him. Following his ordination, Robert served a parish in rural New Hampshire before coming to settle in Warren, Massachusetts, where he became Pastor of the Congregational Church, beginning in April 1917, just as war was declared with Germany. Campbell felt compelled to answer the call of duty, and he obtained a leave of absence to serve with the YMCA. By January 1918, he was in France, assigned to the Yankee Division area.[39]

Likewise, John Harvey Creighton would serve as a chaplain assigned to the Yankee Division, but without commission. Creighton was born in Alexandria, Virginia, on August 23, 1869. He was the son of W. F. and Harriet Creighton. The elder Creighton was a druggist. Creighton studied for the ministry, but he found his true calling in YMCA work. Prior to the war, he served as a YMCA Secretary in Philadelphia.[40]

WILL THEY FIGHT?

In the several decades leading up to the First World War, Americans were coming to grips with changes in the political and demographic landscape, as well as terms like anarchism, unionism, populism, and progressivism. It was a time of suspicion of things foreign; a time of the hyphenated American. The question on some people's minds was would these first and second generation immigrants fight; were they "American" enough? Many Yankee Division chaplains were first generation immigrants—ten, in fact, were born outside of the United States, one of them in Japan to American missionaries. Would Irish Catholics take up arms to support the British? Would they see this as America's fight? Shortly after the declaration of war, James Cardinal Gibbons gave the answer to President Wilson, and to the nation: "Our people, now as ever, will rise as one man to serve the nation. Our priests and consecrated women will once again, as in every former trial of our country, win by their bravery, their heroism and their service new admiration and approval." Wilson responded to Cardinal Gibbons in a letter in which he said that the resolutions of the Catholic archbishops "warm my heart and make me very proud indeed that men of such influence should act in so large a sense of patriotism and so admirable a spirit of devotion to our common country."[41]

The fact is that the war years were marked by a rise in so-called Americanism—a mixed-bag of genuine patriotic sentiment and an ugly xenophobia. Persons of foreign birth, particularly Germans, were looked upon with suspicion, and in some places, like Colorado and Collinsville, Illinois, it was worth your life. The federal government, through various boards and agencies, applied strict standards of censorship, and certain civil liberties like free speech were seriously curtailed. The Wilson Administration was, in fact, the most repressive since the Civil War. Criticism of the war effort, or the fact that the country was at war, often resulted in swift and draconian punishment—loss of mailing privileges for publications and imprisonment for persons like Eugene V. Debs. Union activity slowed, in part because of patriotism, and in part, because many looked upon it as radicalism, something that also drew swift punishment.[42] At some point it became downright silly, as in the case of renaming sauerkraut as "Liberty cabbage."

One of these new Americans was George Fediles Jonaitis. A native of Lithuania, he immigrated to the United States in 1898 at the age of fifteen and later became a naturalized citizen. After study at various places, including Boston College, St. Bonaventure College, and St. Paul Seminary in Minnesota, he studied at Louvain in Belgium. Jonaitis was ordained a priest at St. Cecilia's Cathedral in Omaha on May 2, 1910. By the time the United States entered the war, Father Jonaitis was serving as Pastor of St. Anthony's Lithuanian Catholic Church, also in Omaha. In April 1918, he and a number of his parishioners enlisted in the Army. Shortly thereafter, when it was discovered that he was a priest, he was commissioned as a Chaplain (1st Lt.)

and sent to Camp Taylor, Kentucky, for further training. Jonaitis was sent to France and went on to serve as chaplain of the 3rd Battalion, 102nd Infantry Regiment. Jonaitis sailed for France as a casual, and he is said to have erected a temporary altar on deck from which he offered Mass every morning.[43]

"Four Minute Man"

Rabbi Israel Bettan was another ardent patriot—one whose deeds matched his words. He was also born in Lithuania, and in 1907, at age eighteen, he immigrated with his parents to the United States, where the family settled in Brooklyn, New York. The young man worked hard to acculturate himself. Bettan graduated from the University of Cincinnati with a bachelor's degree in 1910, and five years later, a Doctor of Divinity. In the interim, he was ordained a rabbi in 1912. Upon completion of his studies, he accepted a position as rabbi at Temple B'nai Israel in Charleston, West Virginia. While there, he was very active in local civic affairs. Although short of stature (Bettan was 5' 4" and weighed 150 pounds), he soon discovered that he had a genuine talent for public speaking—remarkably powerful, persuasive speech, all the more so considering that he was only a decade in America.[44]

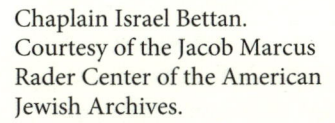

Chaplain Israel Bettan.
Courtesy of the Jacob Marcus Rader Center of the American Jewish Archives.

After war was declared by the United States in April 1917, Rabbi Bettan volunteered to speak as a "Four Minute Man" under the auspices of George Creel's Committee on Public Information. As such, he and others like him gave short speeches in local movie theaters just prior to the show, in order to encourage the purchase of War Bonds. On one occasion, after apologizing to the audience for the interruption, Bettan asked them to match the sacrifice of the young American soldiers "selected" to serve their country: "You have called and they have answered like men. They are now calling upon you to loan to your government . . . so that they, who have offered at your bidding . . . their lives to their country, may be adequately equipped and protected." Raising the specter of German domination, he continued with a rhetorical flourish: "Now which do we prefer, our own Liberty Bonds or German bondage?" Bettan's short talk swiftly reached its climax, concluding with a stirring challenge: "Buy Liberty Bonds to show the boys in the trenches who will lay down their lives that you and I may live and enjoy freedom and prosperity, to show these heroic defenders of the nation that you and I are men and women worth fighting for."[45]

In late 1917, after Bettan had delivered one of his "four minute" talks at the Burlew Theater in Charleston, an article appeared in the *Gazette* that described it as "one of the most patriotic speeches" ever heard, after which the audience "rocked the building with applause." The article went on to allude to the speaker's foreign birth and subsequent accomplishments:

> The speaker himself is the significant thing. Here is a man, alien born, who saw in the Statue of Liberty a real symbol, who divorced the fragmentary recollections of a mother country for the genuine realities of the one of his adoption. In about one decade he has accomplished more than millions of men do in a lifetime; he became educated in the strictest sense of the word; he did not just glance through life's book, but he paused at its commas and stopped at its periods. His speech showed the clarity of his thought, his English the last word in triumph over a foreign tongue; his loyalty was expressed in his sincerity and his sympathy for the cause was manifested in the unmistakable pathos in his voice. . . . How in contrast was this figure in that big theater to many alien sympathizers with a foreign foe, yet natives of this country![46]

Bettan also aided the war effort by speaking at larger bond rallies, crisscrossing West Virginia, often sharing the stage with clergymen of different faiths. In Huntington on April 23, 1918, he appeared with Bishop P. J. Donahue, a Catholic, and Rev. J. E. Scott, a Methodist minister, referring to the group as the "ecclesiastical triumvirate." Bettan told the audience of twelve hundred:

> Today more than ever before, Jew and non-Jew, Catholic and Protestant, we are Americans all. A great and grave national crisis is facing us, and we feel ourselves drawn closer together, like members of one family, ready to defend with our lives our national home, our family hearth, our undying family traditions which alone have made us one and forever unconquerable.

Calling out Prussianism and Kaiserism as the cause of the current troubles, he challenged his audience:

> We must determine with a determination that is strong and steadfast to persevere in this our great undertaking until victory has crowned our efforts and the world is forever set free from the curse of Kaiserism and the menace of militarism—yes a grim determination that fight we shall and win we must.[47]

His speech was well-received and an article that appeared the following day lavished praise on the young man:

> Rabbi Bettan's visualization of the world crisis as it relates to all free peoples was masterful to a degree which compelled the most serious reflection, and eloquent and moving to the point which brought not only the most vociferous forms of enthusiasm, but which also beguiled many of those who heard him to unrestrained tears. Rabbi Bettan has great patriotic vision, great eloquence and great love for American ideals.[48]

During the summer of 1916, Bettan had attended some brief training at Plattsburg, New York, and despite his obvious contribution to the war effort through his public speaking, he was convinced that it was not enough. He felt that it was his duty to serve in uniform, and in particular as a chaplain, to look after the spiritual needs of the Jewish soldiers. On September 16, 1918, he was commissioned as a Chaplain (1st Lt.), sailed for France in October, and upon arrival, he was ordered to report to the headquarters of the 26th Division.[49]

24 SKY PILOTS

Chaplain Malcolm E. Peabody, *seated, center*, Harvard Medical School Unit, Red Cross. Courtesy of Schlesinger Library, Radcliff Institute, Harvard University.

Learning a Chaplain's Work

Anticipating the need for experienced medical personnel, individual medical doctors volunteered, as well as several medical schools, which organized and sent to France complete surgical hospital teams to serve alongside the British. One of these units was Base Hospital No. 5, otherwise known as the Harvard Medical School Unit, which was formed by the likes of famed surgeon Harvey Cushing. It was logical for Cushing to look within the Harvard family for a chaplain to join the unit. The young man he selected was Malcolm Endicott Peabody, scion of an old New England family. Peabody was born in Danvers, Massachusetts, on June 12, 1888, to Endicott and Fannie Peabody. His father was the founder of the prestigious Groton School. Malcolm was a graduate of Harvard College and attended Trinity College, Cambridge, England, for what would have been his senior year. Peabody served as Headmaster at the Baguio School for American Boys in the Philippines from 1911 to 1913, at which time he undoubtedly became acquainted with Bishop Brent. Upon his graduation from the Episcopal Theological Seminary in 1916, he was ordained a deacon and married Mary Parkman. The following year Peabody was ordained an Episcopal priest, and shortly after the birth of his first child, Marietta, he took a leave of absence as Curate of Grace Episcopal Church in Lawrence and joined the Harvard Unit. Peabody was appointed as a temporary Red Cross chaplain, without actual rank or a commission.[50]

The Harvard Unit sailed for France in May 1917 aboard the *Saxonia* and arrived first in Falmouth, England. It promptly crossed the Channel to France to its first location at Dannes Camiers in the British Zone. The hospital was one of a group of five, and part of a larger English general hospital complex, composed mostly of tents with some wooden huts, and referred to as "under canvas." Peabody's primary duty was to serve as "spiritual guide" to several hundred wounded patients and the more than one hundred medical personnel, including doctors and nurses. The only problem for the young clergyman was that he "knew nothing about the job." Worse, he had to face the challenge "practically alone," without any guidance. He did work with preeminent medical men like Cushing, but, in looking back on the experience, he felt that he "would have done better if [he] had been better qualified" as a minister. One perk or "privilege" that Peabody seemed to enjoy, to the exclusion of the rest of the officers, was secretarial help. Harvey Cushing facetiously described it as a "privilege only for padres."[51]

Peabody had nothing but praise for the fortitude of the British soldiers who were patients:

> The Tommies are too marvelously wonderful and brace me up no end. Always most respectful and glad to see you, they are never anything else but "quite well, thank you sir." . . . You see they all expected to get killed when they "went over the top" and because they have only lost an arm or a leg, it is a theme for endless congratulation. . . . Death is so part of the day's work that life seems the off chance and worth seas of pain to win back. . . . What may be depressing business, therefore, becomes the most inspiring of jobs because every Tommie gives you a boost. He loves having you come, appreciates a simple prayer, and never uses bad language.[52]

In November 1917, the hospital moved to a Red Cross base hospital located in the Casino in Boulogne. Peabody described the building, with its dark and poorly ventilated wards, as "a most lordly mansion which it was no doubt in the old, old days, but today, bereft of its ancient glory and with a 'history' of three years as a military hospital behind it, much of its charm has fled." At least the facility was inside and out of the cold. However, he still had to deal with hundreds of patients and the continued threat of nightly bombing raids. Peabody stuck with the job, and after more than a year in France, through bloody Passchendaele and the 1918 German Spring Offensive, both of which generated enormous numbers of casualties, he was able to look back with an honest assessment. "The hardest part for me had been the relentless ministry in the hospital," he wrote, adding, "It was also the most rewarding." He also composed a memorandum about the duties of a base hospital chaplain based upon his own experience. In his opinion, the two principal functions of the chaplain were first and foremost to be a "religious leader" to "everyone in the unit regardless of creed." Secondly, a chaplain must be a "general utility man [where] no job was too boring or trivial to command his attention."[53] That attitude would hold him in good stead in the days ahead.

Another clergyman sponsored by the American Red Cross was the Rev. Ernest de Fremery Miel from Hartford, Connecticut. The forty-nine-year-old rector of Trinity Episcopal Church took a leave from his pulpit and joined the Red Cross in May 1917. Miel, who took on several assignments while in France, served as a Red Cross field chaplain with the 101st Sanitary Train from August 25 through December 11, 1918, where he conducted religious services, and occasionally for the 101st Machine Gun Battalion. His son Charles ("Duke") Miel left his studies at Trinity College in Hartford and was a member of Company B.[54]

Another Early Bird

Many young men and women wanted to serve without delay. In fact, some individuals had enlisted in other armies just to do something. They drove ambulances, flew airplanes, staffed hospitals as doctors and nurses, and even soldiered. Legalities aside, there was a practical side to their actions, in that when the United States did actually join the fight, they had skill sets that would ultimately prove useful. In 1916 and early 1917, many colleges and universities, as well as major hospitals, formed self-contained surgical hospitals and ambulance companies. The American Red Cross and the American Field Service (AFS) also sponsored large numbers of ambulance companies for service in France. For the most part, many of these hospitals and ambulance units were ultimately integrated into the United States Army as it increased its presence and the war ground on.

The driving force behind the AFS was Abram Piatt Andrew from Gloucester, Massachusetts. Andrew had first sought a position at the American Military Hospital at Neuilly, France, in late 1914, shortly after the war began in Europe. The 1893 graduate of Princeton was anxious to do his bit; however, once in France, he proved restless, and not content to do "jitney work" as he called it. He agitated for and developed the model for frontline ambulance units by stationing his ambulances at the aid stations (*postes de secours*) instead of waiting at the hospital for the inevitable call. Thus, time was saved, not to mention lives and limbs. The French were happy; his superiors at the American Military Hospital (now American Ambulance) were not. He officially broke with that organization in late August 1916, and he formed his own. Thus, the American Field Service was born.[55]

One of these "early birds" was Chauncey Allen Adams, who joined the AFS as an ambulance driver. Born in Eaton in the Province of Quebec, Canada, Adams received his bachelor's degree from McGill University in 1902. Following graduation, he travelled extensively in Europe and Asia, under the aegis of the YMCA, during which time he served as International Secretary in Colombo, Ceylon, from 1905 to 1907. Adams immigrated to the United States in 1907, and he married Marion Fairbanks the following year. For two years, he served as the YMCA Secretary in St. Johnsbury, Vermont. Adams became a naturalized citizen in 1911, the same year that he was ordained a Congregational minister. His first assignments were at the Congregational Churches in Irasburg, and later at Danville, Vermont, where he was pastor at both.

Adams took a leave of absence from his pulpit at the Danville Congregational Church, and he went to France with the AFS in May 1917. Shortly thereafter, the minister received plaudits from the Vermont Congregational State Conference for the "patriotic offer of yourself for the arduous and dangerous work of ambulance driver." He served with the AFS until June 28, 1918, at which time he received a commission in the United States Army as a Chaplain (1st Lt.). Fittingly, Adams was assigned to the 101st Ammunition Train, which was made up mostly of Vermont National Guardsmen.[56]

A Foot in the Door

Prior to their assignment to the Yankee Division, many chaplains like Harrison Ray Anderson had considerable experience, albeit in rear areas, where they felt that, somehow, they were not making a difference. Ray Anderson was born in Manhattan, Kansas, on January 24, 1893. The Anderson family can trace its roots to seventeenth-century Ulster, from which sprang a long line of Presbyterian ministers, railroad pioneers, and educators. In addition to being a minister, Ray's grandfather, John A. Anderson, served first as a chaplain in the 3rd Regiment California Volunteer Infantry during the Civil War, and later as President of Kansas State Agricultural College (now Kansas State University). Rev. Anderson was also an ardent Unionist, and in 1861, at the outbreak of the Civil War, he offered a motion to the

General Assembly of the Presbyterian Church calling for unwavering loyalty to the federal government. Many felt that this was the catalyst that split the denomination, when a Southern faction, unable or unwilling to comply, withdrew from the Presbyterian Church as a result. He also served several terms in the U.S. House of Representatives, where he drafted the bill which established what would become the Department of Agriculture.[57]

Following his graduation from Kansas State University in 1911, Ray worked the next three years on his family's orange farm near Santa Barbara, California. He returned east to attend McCormick Theological Seminary in Chicago, graduating on April 26, 1917. While in Chicago, he served as a seminarian at the Fourth Presbyterian Church, where he became close to the pastor, Dr. John Timothy Stone, whom he addressed affectionately as "Dominie." After his ordination in Manhattan, Kansas, on May 2, in short order, he applied for an Army chaplaincy, married his sweetheart, Margaret Ann Blanchard, and on October 18, 1917, became Pastor of the First Presbyterian Church in Ellsworth, Kansas.

Four months later, Anderson passed his chaplaincy exam and was ordered to Camp Pike in Little Rock, Arkansas, where he was assigned to the 521st Battalion, an African-American unit led by white officers and noncoms that was a part of the 23rd Engineer Regiment. On April 1, he said good-bye to Margaret, who had come to Camp Pike to see him off. The young man had a hard time parting. "It just seemed to me that I tore a chunk of my old heart out and parted with it when she left me," he told his mother, "but then God will take care of her." As a man of God, Ray's faith was strong, and he offered reassurance: "He will take care of you and me and will bring us together again in His own good time. I am learning to trust Him these days. I need Him so, and I have just thrown my life completely upon Him to use me and all I have."[58]

The battalion sailed from Hoboken, New Jersey, on the *Agamemnon*, a seized German liner, on April 7. He landed in Brest twelve days later. While in France, the battalion built railroads and bridges. Anderson's principal duties were to conduct worship services and to provide for off-duty recreation. In addition, he spent his afternoons visiting the sick in the hospital, and he also conducted funeral services. Yet, he found something was lacking. Anderson told his father that he had stuck with his initial assignment, basically to get his foot in the door, as it offered a way to get to France in a hurry. Shortly after he arrived there, he wrote to Maj. Gen. Harbord and to Bishop Brent seeking an opportunity to serve with a combat division. Harbord could not help the young man, but the Chief Chaplain told him that while there were no openings at the moment, the office would keep him in mind.[59]

A Question of Faith and Morals

Following his graduation from Trinity College in Hartford, Connecticut, Henry Boyd Edwards did graduate studies at Columbia University. He went on to the General Theological Seminary in New York City, graduating in 1910. Edwards was ordained later that year at Christ Church in Cincinnati, Ohio, where he served as an assistant until 1913, when he became Rector at St. Michael's Episcopal Church in Milton, Massachusetts. There, he joined the Massachusetts National Guard and served on the Mexican border in 1916, while on a leave of absence from his pulpit. When America entered the war in Europe in April 1917, he took another leave of absence. Edwards received a commission in the Army as a Chaplain (1st Lt.) on July 25, 1917, and he was assigned to the 101st Engineer Regiment. He would serve with that unit throughout the war.[60]

Not the least of the many duties that Chaplain Edwards was charged with was looking after the morals of the regiment. Thus when it was brought to his attention that a certain officer was consorting with prostitutes, the chaplain raised the issue quite forcefully at an officers' meeting at Doulaincourt. Without naming the officer, Edwards "laid into" him, concluding with the admonition that "there must be none [of this] in this regiment." Well over six feet tall, the chaplain was already an imposing figure, and his remarks made a definite impression. A fellow officer, who was present, commented that Edwards was "a great man and whoever he is after better watch out." On a lighter note, another officer remarked on the length of Chaplain Edwards's legs. "We . . . used them to measure deep shell holes by having him stand in the bottom of the excavation," he said, and "anything of great length was compared to the good parson's legs."[61]

Boyd Edwards's attitude toward sexual morality was right in line with that of Bishop Brent. While attending a conference in London in May of 1918, the subject of which was venereal disease, Brent told the assembly that "this is the moment of the ages when we can take hold of this horrible thing in such a way as to make it a cleaner and better world." The bishop would play an influential role in Pershing's near obsessive concern for the rate of venereal disease among American forces in Europe. Aside from the moral side of the issue, there was also a very real readiness problem if large numbers of soldiers are incapacitated, as was the case with the British and the French. General Pershing asked for, and scrutinized, the daily venereal disease reports for any substantial changes, holding commanders personally responsible. When one man in the 101st Engineers was found to have contracted a venereal disease, he was brought up on charges, found guilty, and docked one-third of his pay for three months.[62]

While prostitution and venereal disease were very real problems confronting all commanders, as well as the chaplains, unfounded rumors also entered the mix. In early January 1918, it came to General Edwards's attention that certain individuals had overblown the problem within the Yankee Division, despite favorable reports by both the division chaplain and the division surgeon. In fact the chaplain had reported that "the moral environment and health of the troops are much better than in the United States." Clarence Edwards placed the blame squarely upon "Bishop Brent and all the other scare people," who, although sincere, had "an absolutely wrong idea of the facts." The rumors persisted, fueled by a report of the proceedings of a Methodist-Episcopal conference, coupled with the "misplaced zeal" of the YMCA, to the effect that more than a thousand Yankee Division soldiers were being "arrested every day for drunkenness." The chaplains told him that, as a result of the rumors, "their mail is flooded with letters from mothers to save their boys from these awful women."[63]

Chaplain O'Connor, who was out and about with the troops on a regular basis, was adamant about their good character, and he branded such rumors as "absolutely false." He elaborated: "I can assure all the good mothers and friends of our soldier boys that there is not the slightest foundation for all these stories," he wrote, "and I can further assure them that while their boys are away from them they have less temptations and are a great deal better off morally than when at home." Chaplain Dewart echoed these assurances. "The men simply are corkers," he told his wife, "there is practically no drunkenness or immorality in the regiment." In fact, some chaplains, both Protestant and Catholic, took steps to form an organization called the "White Knights" whose members had pledged themselves to purity.[64]

CHAPTER TWO

Early Days

"Some Country for Rain"

Upon its arrival in France, the Yankee Division was divided into two parts. The bulk of the division was taken by train to the Fourth Training Area, centered on Neufchâteau in Lorraine, in the northeastern part of France. The men soon had to contend with a harsh winter, many without proper clothing and gear. For the most part, the enlisted men were billeted in barns and sheds, where no fires were allowed, assuming they could have found sufficient seasoned firewood, which was scarce. Wet shoes froze overnight. Moreover, there was an appalling lack of proper sanitation, and endless acres of thick, gooey mud.[1]

The three artillery regiments, along with the 101st Ammunition Train, were taken to Coëtquidan (humorously referred to by the gunners as "quit your kidd'n"), an old Napoleonic Era artillery camp near Rennes in Brittany, there to begin their formal training under the tutelage of the French. The 101st Field Artillery arrived first, followed in order by the 102nd Field Artillery, and finally the 103rd Field Artillery. As the first batteries arrived, the men soon discovered a woeful lack of facilities, but with a good deal of effort on their part, together with forceful and effective demands by Colonel John H. Sherburne upon both the French and American higher commands, the camp began to take shape. The Yankees were assisted in their efforts by French soldiers (*poilu*) and German prisoners.[2]

Barracks were erected, although they were drafty, and there were no stoves in them at first, but at least they kept the men relatively dry at night. This was important, since the rainy season had begun. "It is some country for rain," exclaimed Chaplain Murray Dewart, soon after his arrival. Wood was scarce and coal expensive. As was the case near Neufchâteau, mud was everywhere, a thick, gooey sort, making walking difficult, not to mention driving the limited number of motor vehicles, often stuck hub-deep in it. Running water and sanitation were also attended to, although hot showers were only available to each regiment on a rotating basis. Field kitchens arrived a month later, and the food improved in quantity if not quality, as the men no longer had to eat the French rations. Finally, the artillery arrived with no guns, horses, or ammunition, so drills had to wait. Some men with time on their hands visited the nearby villages of Guer and St. Malo de Beignon to partake of the local applejack at the cafes. Chaplain Dewart was worried, needlessly as it so happened, that there would be problems.[3]

All of the chaplains who initially went to France with the Yankee Division in September and October of 1917, many of whom had already served as chaplains of their local National Guard or Militia units (some had even accompanied them to the border with Mexico in 1916–17), received no formal training in a chaplain school. Such training simply did not exist at that time. Many of these chaplains were already familiar to the troops, so that important barrier was overcome. Besides, as ordained clergy, each was practiced in the core functions of his ministry—conducting religious services, visiting the sick, and counseling the troubled. The rest, by long Army tradition, was in the hands of the regimental commander.

As the sole chaplain to the roughly fifteen hundred men in the 101st Field Artillery Regiment, Murray Dewart soon found out that his basic duties had greatly expanded once the division arrived in France. For starters, he would serve as statistician, graves registrar, athletic and entertainment officer, mess officer, postmaster, and censor. The last job alone could consume hours. It wasn't just the big tasks. Dewart, an inveterate pipe smoker, pleaded with the folks back home to send him American tobacco products, most of which he then distributed to the men. He also acted as an errand boy for both the officers and enlisted, traveling to nearby Rennes, or even to St. Nazaire, to do banking and to buy small personal items. This was all in addition to his worship services, Bible and French classes, and his visitation of the sick. He didn't mind, though. He told his wife, Mitty: "I am tickled to death to have it all to do as I want to be so busy that the time will pass so quickly and keep my mind from dwelling on how much I want to go home."[4]

Prior to leaving for France, Dewart was one of five Yankee chaplains provided with a truck to aid him in his ministry. The problem was that, once it arrived in France, his hardly ever ran and was constantly under repair. Earlier, each of the other chaplains had wisely traded their Rush truck for a more reliable Ford. Alas, Dewart did not, since he had felt sorry for the salesman who had begged him not to exchange it as the others had. Rennes was 25 to 30 miles away, and unless he could catch a ride with Malcolm Stackpole, whose truck did run, he was reduced to taking a three-and-one-half-hour ride on a narrow gage railroad, which some of the doughboys likened to the "Toonerville Trolley." For Dewart, he dreaded "the stupid trip to and fro."[5]

However, it was the evolution in the performance of some of the chaplain's core functions, now dictated by conditions in France, that changed in ways perhaps not contemplated by these men before they left the United States. For Murray Dewart, the change began shortly after his arrival at Coëtquidon. The initial lack of facilities there forced him to conduct his Sunday service out of doors, most often in the pouring rain. Later, a meningitis outbreak in the camp resulted in a quarantine, as well as further restrictions on large gatherings indoors. Through it all, he continued to visit the sick, whether contagious or not. Dewart gradually overcame his nervousness at preaching to his congregation, and he acknowledged a change for the better. His presence among the men and availability to serve them made a difference. "The men are much more appreciative of the chaplain here than they were on the Border," he wrote in November 1917, "I think they all feel very friendly toward me." As evidence of that fact, he added: "Almost every day one or more tell me about how he is getting good from the services."[6]

The chaplain had his share of colds, a touch of the flu ("grippe"), hives, and he spent two weeks in the hospital with the mumps. Through it all, Murray Dewart retained his optimism and sense of humor. "I am in the hospital with mumps," he told his wife on New Year's Day 1918, "my face is as big as a bath tub . . . [and] . . . I am trying to keep myself very warm so the mumps won't go down to some parts where in adults it sometimes goes." He was not afraid to poke fun at himself, as when he mistakenly took a large swallow of what he thought was cough medicine, which turned out to be a strong gargle solution made of "sulpho-naphthol and glycerine," and he promptly lost his dinner. If, as the saying goes, "absence makes the heart grow fonder," Murray applied that thought to his own situation. "Just think," he told his wife Mitty, "how we are finding out how much we love each other and need each other, and all our future lives will be happier for it."[7]

In the larger picture, all of the chaplains continued to work together for the good of the division, and they drew lessons from each other. On Sunday, October 7, shortly after the division arrived in France, Chaplains O'Connor and Rollins, accompanied by members of the band, conducted a joint service for the men of the 101st Infantry in a small field outside of Rebeuville. On Sunday, November 4, 1917, Murray Dewart hurried from his service to look in on Malcolm Stackpole's service, "to see how it goes." For his part, at Coëtquidon, Malcolm Stackpole, Chaplain of the 102nd Field Artillery Regiment, conducted regular Sunday services accompanied by members of the band. For Catholics, of which there were a good many in the regiment, no doubt with Fr. Farrell of the 103rd Field Artillery, he made arrangements so that they could attend Mass on Sundays. In Rolampont, the Catholic members of the 101st Engineers had the good fortune to find out the pastor of the local church had previously served a French parish in Boston. Chaplain Edwards conducted Sunday services for the remaining members of the regiment in the village square.[8]

When the men of the 102nd Field Artillery Regiment sat down to Thanksgiving dinner on November 29, both Markham Stackpole, the Regimental Chaplain, and his counterpart in the 103rd Field Artillery, Billy Farrell, were among the officers present for the occasion. A Thanksgiving Day football match between the 101st Infantry and the 101st Engineers was refereed by Chaplain George S. L. Connor, a former team captain at Holy Cross College. On Christmas Eve, Chaplain Dewart celebrated the occasion with a religious service complete with trumpeters playing carols. Closer to Neufchâteau, the men of the 102nd Machine Gun Battalion enjoyed a breakfast of pork chops and fixings, followed by a Christmas service by Chaplain Rollins in a Y hut.[9]

Fr. Mike Takes the Initiative

Michael O'Connor, still chaplain for the 101st Infantry Regiment, along with his fellow chaplain and Holy Cross grad, George S. L. Connor, made regular visits with the men in the division several days a week to see to their temporal and spiritual welfare. He called it "Fording around." Fr. Mike felt that it was important that the men, regardless of denomination, have regular Sunday services available, as well as the ability to talk to a clergyman whenever they felt the need. As a result, in the 101st Infantry, every Sunday the men were marched to local churches, with the aid of some band members, Catholics to one for Mass, and Protestants to another for a service conducted by Chaplain Rollins. He also saw the need for more recreational opportunities to keep the men occupied. The shortage of chaplains in the division, especially Catholic priests, was acute, particularly in some units where the regular Protestant chaplain reported that one-half the men were Catholic and would benefit from a priest. On his own initiative, during a visit to Paris on regimental business, O'Connor paid a call on Walter N. Kernan, the director of the Knights of Columbus in France. The determined priest "bombarded" Kernan until the latter released four "worthy gentlemen" to accompany the chaplain back to the regiment to work with the men and at the two hospitals serving the division. In addition, O'Connor was also able to obtain from Kernan "a sum of money to be used in providing places of recreation for the men."[10]

Fr. Mike was not alone in taking the initiative. During the dead of winter, when Harris E. Starr and E. L. Wismer, two New Haven clergymen then serving in the YMCA, found out that the men of the 102nd Infantry Regiment had not been paid in months, they emptied the Y storehouse and "gave away the entire stock." Generosity proved to be a two-way street when the men of the 102nd Infantry took up a collection and sent Chaplain Petty to Paris to buy toys for the local "half-orphaned" children.[11]

Life Underground

In February 1918, the division had reached the point in its training where it was taken by train and truck to the Chemin des Dames, there to be gradually inserted into the front line alongside French units to complete the next phase. At this time, the artillery regiments and their supporting units rejoined the rest of the division. This was classic trench warfare, where the men were taken on raids, and the artillery were given the chance to fire under actual combat conditions. The three artillery regiments, fresh from training in Brittany, arrived in the Chemin des Dames Sector via a cold, two- to three-day train trip, mainly in the now familiar "forty and eights" or, as they were sometimes referred to, "side door Pullmans." The new sector took its name from the ancient road that the ladies of the court used to traverse the ridges between Soissons and Reims. The regiments detrained during the night at a remote station west of Soissons, through which the weary men then marched on the way to their new assignment. The once lovely, ancient cathedral city was nearly unrecognizable due to years of constant artillery bombardment, a fact that the artillerymen could not help but notice.[12]

While in the sector, the men lived mostly underground in caves and quarries (*carrière*) of various sizes carved out of the soft limestone. Many had been fitted up by their French and German predecessors as barracks, hospitals, and stables, complete with electricity. Some soldiers whiled away their free time carving their names in the soft cave walls. Murray Dewart himself gave way to a "youthful impulse" and did the same. "Someday," he wrote, "one of the boys can come over here and see them." Living in this nether world had its advantages, despite the damp and an occasional booby trap, as it was safe from artillery and aerial observation. "Surprised by the grandeur" was how one soldier described an underground chapel, called Our Lady of Victory, situated in a cave previously occupied by the Germans, where "the altar and statues were all carved on the walls" by the French. Fr. O'Connor said Mass there on the Division's first Sunday in the sector, and Col. Edward L. Logan, commander of the 101st Infantry, was the altar server.[13]

"Off to the Front." Chaplain Rollins delivers a sermon in Jeanne d'Arc Square, Neufchâteau. Courtesy of the Military History Institute.

However, as the Yankees soon found out, they were not alone, as they shared their quarters with large rats and other vermin. If that was not enough, some of these caves held grisly surprises, as some doughboys from the 103rd Infantry found while exploring one. There, according to their chaplain, Paul Dwight Moody, they found several dead German soldiers, four of them playing cards at a table, where, frozen in time, "three had fallen back in their chairs. The fourth had pitched forward on the table, where the cards were still lying. One man had reached for a bottle; it was lying on the floor, but his fingers were still curved to clutch it." All had apparently died from a massive concussion from an artillery blast near their underground shelter.[14]

On the other hand, separated from the carnage and devastation above ground, despite the numerous vermin below, the caves provided many soldiers with a sublime religious experience. "Most impressive to me," wrote Doc Hesselgrave, "were the religious services held in the candle-lighted cave in which the boys participated with enthusiasm, interest and devotion, such as only the circumstances under which we lived and served could have brought about." Another soldier described the emotional experience of attending Mass in a cave, the altar a "pile of hewn rocks," with hymns

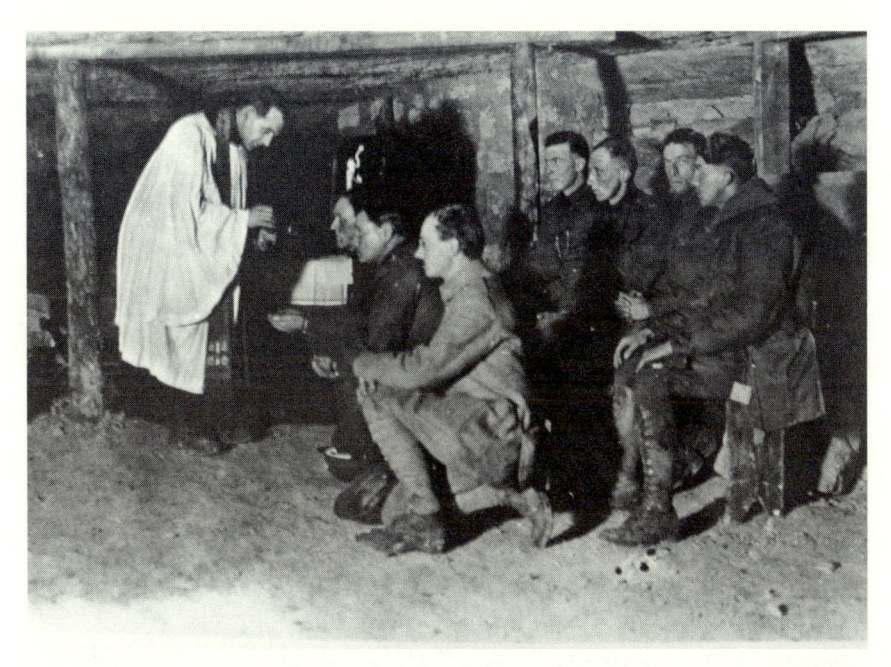

Chaplain Rollins conducting church services in a dugout. Courtesy of St. Michael's Episcopal Church, Marblehead, MA.

sung "in a subdued tone, but . . . with such fervor." Afterwards, he said that the men "appeared more devout," and that "the experience in that cave brought tears in every eye."[15]

Chaplain Lyman Rollins, who shared the trials and tribulations with the men of the 101st Infantry, described life in the dugouts. In a letter to a young parishioner back in Marblehead, Massachusetts, he wrote:

> I am writing this in my dugout which is 30 or 40 feet under the ground, so dark, damp and cold with rats, bugs and smells thrown in. We sleep with our clothes on and sometimes with our boots and a gas mask either around our necks or close to our heads. We keep pretty close to them over here. I have not had my clothes off for so long that I can hardly remember when it was. But of course we change them often enough to keep from getting the cooties and even then we get them. I have had my head clipped for the same reason. So you can imagine that I am some sight.

Rollins went on to say that he also conducted religious services in a dugout complete with vestments and a portable altar. "It is rather strange to be here under ground and hear the big guns booming away," he added.[16]

Lyman Rollins was born in Concord, New Hampshire, on April 21, 1881. He received a degree from Bates College in 1906, and he was ordained a Baptist minister at the Curtis Memorial Church in Concord. Later, he would attend Newton Theological School (1911) and the Episcopal Theological School, from which he graduated in 1912. In the spring of 1915, he was assigned to St. Michael's Episcopal in Marblehead, Massachusetts. He served as chaplain with the 5th Massachusetts Infantry on the Mexican border in 1916, and later, after war was declared, he sailed to France with the 101st Infantry Regiment. Though somewhat slight of stature, Rollins was extremely brave, and the epitome of Bishop Brent's ideal chaplain. Like most chaplains, he was imbued with an ecumenical spirit, and he was often heard to say, "I feel I am as much a chaplain of the Jews and Catholics as the Protestants of my regiment."[17]

ALL FOR THE GOOD OF THE REGIMENT

Regimental headquarters for the 101st Field Artillery was located near Chassemy, with the forward command post at Vailly.[18] Its six batteries were immediately scattered over a wide area throughout the sector. Dewart considered it his personal mission to look out for "his boys," and he had been doing so with many, if not most, of them since they all had served together on the Mexican border in 1916. There, he had developed a reputation for going after "something for his men . . . with a directness, persistency and informality which often shocked the officers with whom he had to deal . . . [and] . . . he always succeeded in reaching his goal."[19] As a case in point, he was told by his commanding officer that his place was back at headquarters, but that was not the way he saw things. He insisted that his place was with his men, and his superiors relented, if only a little. Dewart was told one day a week was acceptable. That was all he needed, and he took that opening and quickly increased it to daily visits. It was an essential step along the way of his evolution as a wartime chaplain, and he was not to be denied.

Neither shellfire nor the distance separating the various batteries deterred Murray Dewart from visiting each and every one of them on a regular basis, despite the "cold and inclement weather." The men worked seven days a week, so "filling the pews" on Sunday was "impossible." Moreover, large concentrations of men were discouraged due to the likelihood that they would draw enemy artillery fire. Whether on foot or on horseback, the Chaplain gradually brought the religious services to the men, albeit in smaller groups, often several times a day, in some cases outdoors and at other times, out of the rough elements in caves or barracks. He told his wife that he was "like an itinerant preacher making the circuit most of the time." A typical service involved a short sermon, followed by a conversation with individual soldiers, and then making a list of their various errands for him to do. At one such service, the ceiling of the cave was so low that both he and the men had to sit on bunks and odd pieces of wood while he, "preached them a little sermon and we sang a hymn and I said a prayer."[20]

At the same time that he was describing the sights and scenes of his front line experiences, Dewart assured his wife that he was not in, nor would he court, danger. "I am in no particular danger at all," he told her. He continued to run errands for the men, and each Thursday, Chaplain Boyd Edwards drove him to the nearest town in his Ford.[21]

"THE HERO PRIEST"

Fr. Osias J. Boucher was born in Saint Madeleine, Quebec, Canada, on August 17, 1880. He was the son of Charles and Sophie Boucher, and he immigrated with them to the United States at the age of twelve. Boucher studied for the priesthood both in Canada and the United States, and he was ordained in Fall River, Massachusetts, on June 10, 1911. Prior to the war, he was a curate at several parishes in that diocese, the last being at St. Anthony of Padua in New Bedford. Sponsored by the Knights of Columbus, he served with the 2nd Battalion of the 101st Infantry Regiment from October 1917 through March 1919, when the division came home. Boucher described himself as the "toughest looking chaplain in France." Although he was not a commissioned officer, as was the case with many others who were sponsored by outside organizations, he wore a regular doughboy uniform and shared the hardships and risks with the men. He would win the coveted Croix de Guerre for his actions in the Chemin des Dames sector.[22]

For the priest, the voyage to France proved eventful, from a close encounter with a mine, which the ship missed "by a few feet," to a German submarine chased away by some well-placed shots by the deck gunners. To make matters worse, he was seasick for most of the trip, in spite of calm waters. Nevertheless, he arrived safely and spent some time in Paris before joining his unit at the front. In a letter to his bishop, he described a continual fog in Paris, much like London, and shortages of many goods. "But in time of war one must expect that and still worse than that," he observed.[23]

Like Chaplain Rollins, Boucher described his living quarters: "We are living here like rats and with these dirty fellows, under the ground about 20 meters in the bowels of the earth in a damp and narrow hole." His health was good, and he was happy to be with the troops. "I am in the first line," he told his bishop, "and every night I pay a visit to the advance post to see my boys, who are always pleased to see the priest." In fact, Boucher considered it his "duty to be always with them." He also looked out for their spiritual welfare, offering Mass and communion regularly, at times twice a day—once in the rear area, and again at the front line. Boucher went on to describe life in the front lines:

> At the front, life is very enervating, because when you hear shells bursting around you; the cannons continually roaring and vomiting iron and gas; and when you see above your head these treacherous airplanes always ready to drop bombs on you and finally expecting a gas attack at any moment, and this gas is a very terrible weapon. . . . However I am cheerful and pleased, because these boys of ours are a great consolation and comfort to me, by their good conduct and faithfulness to their religious duties.[24]

The morning of February 23 was chosen for the 101st Infantry Regiment to participate with the French 64th Infantry Regiment and a detachment of engineers in a large joint raid on the German observation positions located at Chevregny and the Moulin Rouge just across the Ailette River and L'Oise à L'Aisne Canal. Twenty-three volunteers from Companies E and H, together with two of their junior officers, Second Lieutenants William Koob and George H. Davis, respectively, and their chaplain, Osias Boucher, joined their French counterparts. All in all, one hundred men took part. The raid, the purpose of which was to destroy the German observation positions and to seize prisoners, was scheduled to start at precisely 6:00 A.M. The artillery preparation beforehand was also a joint effort, but it would be short—five minutes, to be exact. The early hour had been chosen to coincide with the time that the Germans relieved the watch. The coordinated infantry follow-up would be crucial to the mission's success.

At 5:55 A.M. all six batteries of the 101st Field Artillery Regiment opened up on the German positions. At the same time, the 103rd Field Artillery Regiment joined in, as batteries E and F laid a "standing barrage" on the Boche concrete machine gun emplacements. This was undoubtedly effective, as the infantry would later report no fire coming from those locations. At 6:00 A.M. the fire mission changed. A rolling barrage (reportedly the first by an American unit) was laid down by batteries A, B, and C of the 101st Field Artillery, along with four French batteries. This created a "curtain of fire" rolling forward toward the objective at the rate of 100 meters every three minutes. The infantry followed along behind this protective shield. After a while, the artillery shifted to a box barrage (again, the first by American artillery), in order to hem the defenders in. Batteries D, E, and F of the 101st Field Artillery, along with three French batteries carried out that mission.[25]

The infantry raiders jumped off at the point called Albia, where the L'Oise à L'Aisne Canal, which runs south away from the Ailette River, enters a tunnel on its way to the Aisne River. After crossing the canal, the Yankees were split into two groups. Lieutenant Davis and the men of Company H, under the command of a French lieutenant by the name of Thomas, went to the left, accompanied by a detachment of French engineers, which carried sections of bridge in order to span the Ailette in place of the destroyed one. Upon arriving at the river, the party was greeted with sufficient German fire to prevent the laying of the temporary bridge at that point. In response, the soldiers spread out to the left and right and returned fire. All, however, was for naught, as the portable bridge sections proved to be too short, and further attempts to cross would be futile. During this foray, Leo J. Lipsie, an automatic rifleman from Company H, kept watch over a dugout where some Germans had taken refuge. The patient doughboy out-waited and out-witted them, and he took them all prisoners as they ultimately emerged from their lair. Soon, the enemy fire slackened as the Germans withdrew from their positions. The respite was short-lived, as German artillery soon began to rain down a barrage, first on their own forward positions, then gradually creeping forward toward the attackers. Lt. Thomas ordered his portion of the raiding party to fall back, and they all arrived safely at the jump-off position at 7:10 A.M.[26]

Meanwhile, once across the canal, the second party, including Lieutenant Koob and the men from Company E, headed northeast along the road to the Ailette River, under the overall command of a French lieutenant by the name of Dufihol. This group broke into three smaller parties and followed the rolling barrage. The Yankees advanced close to the curtain of fire, too close, in fact, for the comfort of their French companions. The French well knew from long experience that shell bursts, regardless of their source, cannot distinguish friend from foe. However, the Americans had confidence in their own artillery, which was not misplaced that morning. These groups continued to advance beyond the river, achieving a penetration of about 750 yards. At one point, the doughboys chased a group of fleeing Boche through their trenches all the while "yelling like Indians." They captured numerous German prisoners before they were ordered by Lt. Dufihol to return to the jump-off place as a heavy enemy barrage began to rain down on them.[27] During the withdrawal, a Company E man was wounded, and Chaplain Boucher remained behind and attended to the young man while under fire.

At a ceremony at Chassemy on March 6, 1918, sixteen members of the 101st Infantry, including Fr. Boucher, were the first Yankee Division men awarded the Croix de Guerre by the French, on account of their exploits during that raid.[28] The priest downplayed his role:

> I received with them the same decoration because I had been with them in time of danger and because I went to give Extreme Unction to a wounded one of mine on the battlefield, while the Boches were shelling very heavily. However, to be frank, I can assure you, that I was anything but brave that time, so much I was afraid. But being a priest, I went and performed my priestly duty toward that dear good Catholic boy.[29]

Although Private Thomas A. Leahy of Company E, 101st Infantry was not a participant on that raid, since some of the members had been drawn from his company, he had heard the results firsthand. In a letter to his mother six weeks later, he attributed the success to Fr. Boucher's visit to the company the night before and to Divine intervention. "I think God was with them in this particular instance," he said, due to the fact that the priest had "prayed for our boys' success, both from a spiritual and also a military view, and our Dear Lord must have answered his prayers, this 'kindly priest,' for it was a success."[30]

The "Saving Element"

The service organizations, principally the YMCA and the Knights of Columbus, as well as the Salvation Army, Red Cross, and the Jewish Welfare Board, Bishop Brent's "saving element," played important roles in the lives of the doughboys, both at and away from the front, some both materially and spiritually. The latter function was important, since the Army was only slowly recruiting, training, and bringing chaplains on line. Many who volunteered in the first two organizations were also clergymen like Robert C. Campbell from Warren, Massachusetts. He had arrived in France in January 1918, and by February, he was already operating among the front line troops. Campbell described his duties to a friend back home:

> You would be surprised to see the kind of work we do some days. I have been given charge of a little group of men and we do all kinds of things. How would you like to start out in an auto truck without any

cover on a cold morning in a snow storm, ride 26 miles, clear away the snow and lay over the floor for a YMCA tent and ride back home the same way at dusk in the evening?[31]

The two distinct roles these men played were often conflated in the soldier's mind depending upon his overall experiences, thus coloring his opinion. The often crowded YMCA hut was an oasis away from the squalor and chaos of the front—a place to write home, enjoy a conversation or a game with others, or to sip a cup of coffee or hot chocolate and to eat a doughnut. One soldier thought the particular YMCA hut he was frequenting in the Toul sector was good. He pointed out that it was a place "where the boys can get paper and envelopes and buy lots of little things, such as candy, oranges, cookies and tobacco." Still another soldier, an infantryman from Monson, Massachusetts, heaped praise upon the YMCA, which, he opined, "is the greatest thing that ever happened over here." He added: "When we were advancing, they were there with supplies of tobacco and candy and the latest newspapers. One YM man went over the top with us without any rifle or firearms of any kind." James Harrison Dankert, also in the 104th Infantry, put it more simply: "The YM here is a 'pippin.'"[32]

It might seem strange, however, that the praise was not universal. Moreover, each soldier seemed to develop an individual bias or preference; many had a bad experience with one or another of the organizations which colored their attitudes. One of those was Charles M. Streeter of Battery B, 103rd Field Artillery. The artilleryman was in the Troyon Sector following the St. Mihiel offensive. Creature comforts were impossible to come by. But for his mess sergeant, who was able to get a very limited supply of candy and tobacco, which he sold to them in small quantities, those articles would have been nonexistent. The soldier felt that the YMCA had very definitely dropped the ball. "At last, I have a little writing paper," he wrote, with some feeling of exasperation, "so I am writing." He went on: "We have plenty of time to write letters, and we can mail them all right, but it is almost impossible to get paper, especially envelopes." Communication with the folks at home was a high priority with the doughboy, so this deficiency was serious. "The YMCA, which claims to do so much for us, is doing absolutely nothing," he fumed, "and the men are disgusted with it." He explained his current situation: "We are situated where there is absolutely no place to buy anything, and it is such a place that the Y should work, instead of at training camps and big cities, where things can be gotten elsewhere. It is a wonder what they have done with all the money they have collected."[33]

Another soldier, Everett E. Taylor, originally from Company A, 101st Infantry, and who was then on detached duty, was just as blunt with his negative comments. "I am sending you a card the YMCA people are giving to us boys," he wrote in a letter to his mother, "and it is the only thing that they give away in France!" He went on to explain: "They are charging enormous prices for tobacco and other things and there is no need of doing so. A small cake of candy which we can get in the stores at home for ten cents is selling for twenty and thirty cents!" For one soldier, his primary complaint was the lack of YMCA huts or canteens near the front lines. This was important to the perpetually broke doughboys, who looked forward to purchasing the "essential" items like tobacco and cigarettes at reasonable prices. "Once in a while, a 'Y' man will come up with his little Ford," wrote Fritz Potter, "and if you are lucky you may be able to buy one package of cigarettes." In contrast to the YMCA, the motto of the Knights of Columbus was, "Everybody Welcome; Everything Free."[34]

Shortly after his return from France, 1st Lt. James Y. Rodger was interviewed about his service overseas. Among the organizations he singled out for praise were the Red Cross, Knights of Columbus, and the YMCA; however, it was the last that evoked his lengthier comments. "My observation in France was that it did admirable work and it did it on a tremendous scale," he said. Dr. Rodger added, "in a great organization embodying perhaps 5,000 workers, there must be some imperfections, but we must judge by general results, and not by the complaints of a disgruntled few." The officer emphasized his point: "I have no patience with those who would discredit a great organization for the faults of a few."[35]

Doc Hesselgrave would undoubtedly have sympathized with those soldiers' complaints, for he worked hard to set up Y huts or tents, in particular with the 101st Machine Gun Battalion, to which he had more or less attached himself. He followed that unit wherever its orders took it. He didn't just try to provide useful items like tobacco, sweets, stationery, etc.; rather, he also looked after their entertainment. In addition to supplying creature comforts, many YMCA facilities did double duty, serving as a canteen one day, and as a chapel the following Sunday.

Filling a Need

The need for chaplains of all denominations grew apace with the burgeoning AEF. Bishops were asked to encourage priests to serve these young soldiers as chaplains, particularly overseas. Bishop John J. Nilan of the Diocese of Hartford asked for volunteers from among the priests under his direction.[36] Fr. Anselm Joseph Mayotte, then assistant at St. Mary's Church in Putnam, Connecticut, was one of more than forty who answered the call. Mayotte, the son of Albert Mayotte, a blacksmith, and Mathilde Bon-

Chaplain Anselm J. Mayotte. Courtesy of the Aspinock Historical Society of Putnam.

neau, was born in St. Dominique, Quebec, Canada, on December 11, 1888. While he was still a youth, his family immigrated to the Quinebaug section of Thompson, Connecticut, in the "Quiet Corner" of the state, where it literally touches Massachusetts.

Anselm attended Bartlett High School in nearby Webster, Massachusetts. Early on, it became apparent that he was destined for the Church, and in the fall of 1906, he left Bartlett and enrolled at St. Thomas Seminary in Hartford, where he spent the next five years. His religious education was rounded off with three years of study at St. Sulpice in Paris, followed by two years at St. Bernard Seminary in Rochester, New York. Mayotte was ordained at the Cathedral in Hartford by Bishop Nilan on June 10, 1916. He served several months as an Assistant at Sacred Heart Church in New Haven, and then he settled in at St. Mary's in January 1917. There he assumed the additional duty of principal of the parish school. Mayotte was in Putnam at the time that war with Germany was declared, and he answered another call, when he joined the Army as a chaplain. While the members of the parish were proud that their curate left to become a chaplain, he had become a popular figure and would be missed.[37]

Fr. Mayotte was commissioned a Chaplain (1st Lt.) on February 1, 1918, and he sailed for France as a casual—that is, as an individual and not with any particular regiment. He described the voyage as "uneventful and monotonous" with lifeboat drills every morning and evening. One officer aboard jokingly referred to the drills as "rehearsing for your funeral." Mayotte and another priest did manage to say Mass and to hear confessions, the latter taking place in the ship's post office. Upon his arrival in France, he first attended an eight-week officer training course, most likely at Gondrecourt, followed by a special ten-day course for chaplains at Neuilly-sur-Suize near Chaumont. On May 3, he was assigned to the 102nd Infantry Regiment, by then serving in the Toul Sector. While in training, he noted the fall off in religious fervor among the French people. "Religion has lost its hold," he observed, "even among the soldiers." Not so with the Americans. "Our soldiers are certainly teaching the French a lesson in Christian Faith," he opined, "they fill the churches."[38]

Winding Down

The quality of mercy was often extended to the enemy. On the evening of March 11, a large German Gotha bomber was shot down by antiaircraft on its way to Paris. The plane crash landed in the vicinity of the Supply Company of 104th Infantry. Several soldiers rushed over to the wreck and found the crew in various stages of medical distress. The injured were carried to a nearby cave where first aid was rendered. Although one died, the remaining flyers were taken to the hospital in Chaplain Danker's car. He had happened along and offered the use of his car to transport the Germans to a field hospital. The chaplain made the men comfortable and he took them away. At Missy on Friday, March 15, a fire "completely destroyed" the wooden hut occupied by many of the officers of the 101st Engineers, including Chaplain Edwards. Not only did the fire destroy all of their clothing and personal effects, but also "a considerable sum of money" that the enlisted men had left with the chaplain for safekeeping.[39]

While in the Chemin des Dames, as the 3rd Battalion, 104th Infantry returned from its turn in the front lines, Fr. de Valles remembered that it was almost St. Patrick's Day, a big event celebrated annually by the town of New Bedford and its citizens. Given the numbers of Irish-Americans in the regiment, he set about to organize an appropriate event. Starting the day before, he heard confessions, and on Sunday, March 17, he celebrated Mass on an altar made up of two empty ammunition boxes. That afternoon there was a baseball game, the first of the season, but the best was last, an entertainment in the cave that served as a barracks. The priest described the scene:

> The cave barracks was filled to its utmost capacity. The orchestra seats were nature's own on the hard soil of Mother Earth. Dim candle lights with an abundance of cigarette smoke and the noise of the buzzing planes overhead gave this St. Patrick's Night Entertainment a never to be forgotten touch of interest. I've stood in many difficult pulpits before, and on many platforms, but I shall never forget the rickety box on which I had to announce the different numbers of the programme every one of which was heartily applauded with real New Bedford spirit. At 10:00 P.M. the affair was over and how we did scatter in the darkness of the surrounding hills and valleys.[40]

For the men of the Yankee Division, the time spent training in the Chemin des Dames had been a valuable learning experience. Osias Boucher looked back on the previous six weeks: "These long and enervating days passed in the trenches were some experience to me, a peaceful minister of Jesus Christ. I have seen there all the terrible weapons that the modern way of waging war has invented, and I can assure you that they are anything but mild when we see the destruction they do accomplish." He went on to describe his own experiences: "I spent all my time with my battalion, eating, sleeping and learning with these brave boys of mine. . . . I came out of the trenches dirty and covered with mud from foot to ears, for the only way to avoid being wounded from shells is to lay low in the mud of the trench."[41]

By the end of his stay in the Chemin des Dames, Murray Dewart had completed his transformation. He reflected about the change in a letter to Mitty:

> It's a funny feeling to go around preaching any minute of the day. I am preaching (if you call it that) now almost every day somewhere.

Chaplains O'Connor and Rollins conduct the first YD funeral in February 1918 near Vailly in the Chemin des Dames Sector. Courtesy of the Military History Institute.

The men seemed to listen awfully well. You can appreciate how I feel about being asked to preach without a moment's notice, I fancy, after you have endured twelve years' experience as the wife of a nervous old fussy body.[42]

Earlier, he had told his wife that he was getting used to the shell fire, comparing it to his preaching back home. "I've been so everlastingly scared to death standing in front of congregations that I am almost used to the sensation," he confessed, adding confidently, "I defy them to scare me more." He felt that his chaplaincy made a difference in the lives of the men he served. As with all good chaplains, he had discovered the universal truth that "the men appreciate the chaplain's visits to them at the front especially." Murray Dewart had a way of looking past the bravado and the coarse language so prevalent among front line soldiers, and of getting right into the heart of the man himself, and the artillerymen were receptive to his message of faith and love, even amidst the clamor of war. They loved their chaplain.[43]

Chaplain de Valles also reflected about his recent experiences in a memorandum written for the folks back home in New Bedford:

People will perhaps wonder that we can get used to the whizz bangs and explosions and even jest under shell fire. Six months ago, a thunder storm would upset my nerves. Should anyone have then told me that for 36 days I could be able to promenade the front line trenches under shell fire and distribute cigarettes, tobacco, magazines, and jokes to the men in line at the guns, I could not believe such a thing possible. Environment counts for a great deal, and we are accustomed to the daily attacks of the Boche, and so much so that when Fritz does rest quietly a whole day, we don't believe we are at war. The "Sammies" are just anxious to spring at them (the Boche) and finish the game à la American in the "step lively" fashion, but we must wait a while yet before we give the world the real great sample of Yankee Spirit in the Great War.[44]

Harry Wright of the 104th Infantry had nothing but praise for the courage of Fr. de Valles. Earlier, he and a small group of soldiers had gathered in a grove of trees on Sunday, March 10, as the intrepid priest offered Mass "with shells bursting over our heads and around us."[45]

What had initially been scheduled as a month-long training period in the Chemin des Dames had been extended another two weeks. By mid-March the division was ordered away from the sector to begin a joint training exercise with the 42nd ("Rainbow") Division. At this time, the Germans unleashed a large gas attack, which hit the 102nd Infantry the hardest. In addition, much of the division baggage was lost as some shells destroyed a train depot where it was being collected.[46]

CHAPTER THREE

Toul Sector

"Getting Down On the Germans"

For six months, the Yankee Division had been under the tutelage of the French, from whom the doughboys learned the elements of trench warfare, with an emphasis on raids and patrols. It was, by and large, defensive warfare—that is, static—except for an occasional large-scale attack that generally resulted in incremental gains, if any. Pershing felt that it was time to conduct an exercise utilizing his pet theory commonly referred to as "open warfare," which relied upon the mass movement of overwhelming numbers of American soldiers, armed with rifles and bayonets, swiftly breaking through the line onto open ground where movement was easier. In the end, it proved to be beyond the AEF's ability to effectively implement.

As a result, the 26th and 42nd ("Rainbow") Divisions (both National Guard) received orders to conduct a joint exercise in March 1918, following the completion of their most recent stage of training. Accordingly, commencing March 18, the various elements of the Yankee Division made their way to Soissons, Braine, or Mercin-Pommiers, there to board trains for a one-day journey to either Bar-sur-Aube or Brienne-le-Château, another town on the River Aube, famous for a military school attended by the young Napoleon. Once fully assembled, the division would begin a four-day march, which itself would be an exercise in troop movement. Eventually, the plan was to conduct an open warfare exercise with the Rainbow Division.[1] However, the German High Command had other ideas.

Beginning March 21, 1918, almost simultaneous with the movement of the Yankee Division, the relatively stable situation along the Allied front from Flanders to the Aisne-Marne Sector near Château-Thierry suddenly began to unravel in the face of a massive German offensive, consisting of a series of well-coordinated attacks up and down the line starting with "Operation Michael" (March 21), followed in short order by "George" (April 9), and "Blücher-Yorck" (April 27). Two smaller attacks followed in June and July. The Germans had reason to be optimistic that these attacks would succeed—since Russia had left the war, she was now free to move dozens of her experienced divisions to the western front, at a time when the American forces in France were still small and not yet seriously battle-tested. Previously hard-won ground was lost in huge swaths as the German juggernaut rolled swiftly forward.[2]

As the gunners of the 101st Field Artillery Regiment detrained at Brienne-le-Château on March 21, they were unaware of the new German offensive. Following three days of rest, on March 24, the unit marched a short distance to the village of La Chaise, arriving there later that day. As part of the Headquarters Company, Murray Dewart was offered a room in the beautiful château, the home of a widowed marchioness, which had stood empty for the past two months. However, he opted for more cozy lodgings in a small home next door, occupied by two spinsters. There he found no rich furnishings and antiques or hardwood floors; rather, clean-scrubbed pine boards. The ladies were "ghastly poor but clean," he noted, "and how they could cook!"

Since it was Palm Sunday, Murray Dewart conducted a service on the grounds of the château that same afternoon. Music was provided by the regimental band, and the service was well-attended by members of the Headquarters Company, along with Batteries A and B. Dewart praised the men for their "magnificent record" in the Chemin des Dames, on which he said they could look back with "justified pride." He then noted how apropos that it was Palm Sunday, the day Jesus returned to Jerusalem and ultimately to his death, which he faced with resignation for the sake of all men. Jesus "always pours out his life for others," he told them, and like Him, "men of this regiment now are offering to do that very thing." He then built upon that theme: "God is alive in [you]. . . We all have capacities to do rotten things, but when you realize how near you are to doing the very supreme thing that Jesus did . . . you won't be so willing to slide along the easy way. . . ."[3]

For the next several days, the artillerymen continued to march and eventually arrived at the small village of Rimaucourt on March 29 (Good Friday), with the expectation that they would rest from their exertions. That was not to be. As a result of the massive German offensive, the joint exercise between the 26th and 42nd Divisions was abruptly cancelled. The Yankee infantry was rushed in French trucks to the Toul Sector, there to take over a long stretch of trenches previously held by the French, with the help of the American 1st Division. The French would then be free to help meet the German attack, while the 1st Division staged an attack at Cantigny in the Montdidier Sector.[4]

The 101st Field Artillery Regiment received orders to immediately proceed to Vignot in the Toul Sector. What for the gunners, up to that point, had been a leisurely series of road marches, at once became forced marches, which set a grueling pace for the men and animals over the next four days, that, according to the chaplain, "strewed dead horses along the road and exhausted every man in the regiment." In a similar vein, Horatio Rogers of Battery A recalled the misery of those four straight days of cold, drenching rain, with only an occasional break of sun; of long forced marches through heavy mud; and the sight of dead horses and abandoned wagons.[5]

In a letter to his wife summarizing recent events, Murray Dewart was incredulous that the Germans had any punch left. "It's hard to believe that the Germans are driving harder than ever," he wrote. "They shot up the place we just left [La Chaise] about an hour after we left it." As a result of his experiences, Dewart had begun to reach the point that all effective soldiers reach, that is, the demonization of the enemy. "Darn them anyway... I am getting quite down on the Germans," he exclaimed.[6]

On the Road to Toul

Unit by unit, the Yankee Division, strung out along the French road net, began to arrive in the Toul Sector on a cold, drizzly March 31 (Easter Sunday). Along the route, the soldiers took little note as they passed by the many little churches that dotted the French countryside, some abandoned or empty, as their priests were away serving with the French Army.[7] Chaplain Dewart was about to conduct an impromptu Easter service near Colombey-les-Belles, where the 101st Field Artillery had stopped for the day, when he made the following observation to correspondent Bert Ford:

> About this time I would be mounting my pulpit at home. I couldn't help thinking just now, as we passed that little church down there, of the contrast. Here we are up against the real thing at last; the thing we trained for on the border—mud and rain and cold and fog, and cannonading in the distance, entering a sector on the Great Western Front at an hour when churches at home are thronged with worshippers in their Easter finery. I can fancy myself part of the scene. I can see the faces and the vestry choir and fancy the fragrance of incense and flowers. Some difference.[8]

Those "little churches" were not always in the best of repair, but that did not deter the chaplains from using them to conduct services from time to time, if they were available. John H. Sherburne, former regimental commander of the 101st Field Artillery, recalled one such church in the Toul

Sector and the memorable service conducted therein by Chaplain Dewart. "One Sunday morning in June, in a French church, its roof torn off by German shells," he recalled, "he [Dewart] called his men together and administered Holy Communion." No doubt calling to mind the comfort to be found in ritual, he added, "I shall never forget it."[9]

Neither rain nor mud kept a chaplain from his duties. That same drizzly Easter Sunday, Chaplain Walton Danker came across the Supply Company of the 104th Infantry Regiment, which was traveling in advance of the artillery, as it slowly made its way toward the town of Vignot. When he stopped to visit, one of the men asked him if he would mind conducting an impromptu service. Clearly moved, the chaplain obliged, and the group adjourned to a soggy nearby field. As the brief service ended, the sun broke through the clouds. Danker pointed to the sky and told his small congregation: "Boys, I think that God is pleased." At the same time, Chaplain de Valles conducted a simple service from the tailgate of a truck.[10]

A Sector of Their Own

By all accounts, the trenches in the Toul Sector were the worst on the entire western front, knee deep in putrid water and mud that stuck to boots like glue. Although it was said to be a "quiet" sector (or as the French said, a "*bon secteur*"), after the Yankees arrived, it was anything but quiet, beginning with a massive artillery bombardment of both the 1st and 26th Divisions as the former moved out of the line and the latter took its place. Adding to the division's problems, the sector was dominated by Mont Sec, long a German stronghold and observation point. Thus roads, critical to the movement of supplies and the evacuation of the wounded, became death traps for the unwary or unlucky. The Yankees gave them names like "Hell's Half Acre," "Suicide Bend," and the notorious "Dead Man's Curve" near Beaumont.[11] The Germans relentlessly tested the National Guardsmen, right from the start at Apremont, and later at Seicheprey, Xivray-et-Marvoisin, and Humbert Plantation. The Yankees pushed right back with a large raid on the night of May 30/31.

At this time, there were some changes among the officers of the division, among which was the promotion of Michael J. O'Connor to Division Chaplain. Some of the Yankees found shelter in huts and dugouts, many of their own construction, where billets in the small villages were not available. Chaplain Rollins was known for his straight talk and his quick wit. One Sunday while in the Toul Sector, Rollins was using an underground dugout for services that coincided with a German shelling. One doughboy, who was walking outside and not attending the service, dove head-first down the dugout stairs in an attempt to dodge the shells, and to his utter surprise, he landed in a pool of water at the bottom. Shocked and chagrined, he uttered the Lord's name, right in the middle of Chaplain Rollins's sermon. Without missing a beat, the nimble-witted padre told the young soldier: "Greetings. You've come to the right place." Seeing his predicament, the equally nimble soldier muttered that he had meant the exclamation as a "prayer."[12]

Apremont (Bois Brûlé)

The first real test for the division came on April 10, 1918, when the Germans staged a large raid near Apremont. There, the line was held by the 104th Infantry Regiment, men from western Massachusetts. Like most others, the attack began early in the morning, following a heavy artillery exchange, when eight hundred elite German troopers surged toward the American lines. The fighting lasted all that day, and after a lull on April 11, it resumed the next day with the same intensity over the course of another two days. It was fierce, vicious, hand to hand combat, ebbing and flowing, with a section of trench lost here and there, ultimately to be regained. The after-action report prepared for GHQ at Chaumont alluded to the intense fighting and observed, among other things, that "the action seemed to depend more on the individuality of the men than on organization." In other words, it was something of a melee.[13]

All throughout the fighting, Captain Walton S. Danker, one of the regimental chaplains, "attended the sick and wounded and bestowed the last rites to the dead," and he saw to the removal of their bodies. Danker remained in the front line trenches encouraging the troops during the intense fighting. As a result of his efforts during that fight, Chaplain Walton Danker was awarded the Silver Star by the United States Army, and for his "particularly meritorious devotion, the most complete spirit of sacrifice and duty," the French awarded him the Croix de Guerre with gilt star.[14]

For his part, Chaplain de Valles spent those four days, amidst the shellfire, coming and going from the aid station, where he assisted the medical staff, to the front line where he distributed cigarettes and chocolate bars, to No Man's Land where he ministered to the wounded and dying. The intrepid priest was seemingly everywhere at once. At one point during the fighting, when de Valles heard that a wounded man was stuck in the barbed wire, he crawled out to him and dragged him back to the aid station operated by the 103rd Ambulance Company located just behind the lines at St. Agnant.[15]

Since casualties were mounting, the priest went next to the 104th Field

Chaplain John B. de Valles, *left,* receives the Croix de Guerre at Chassemy, March 6, 1918. Courtesy of the Diocese of Fall River Archives.

Hospital operating further back at Vignot. The chaplain was just leaving the YMCA hut there, where the band was rehearsing, when he was met by Major Sydney C. Hardwick, the regimental medical officer, also bent on the same mission, who told him that volunteer litter bearers were urgently needed to assist those of the 103rd Ambulance Company. Both men returned to the hut, whereupon the priest gave the band members a short pep talk. As a result, the entire band volunteered for the duty, and bandleader Ralph M. Dawes and fifteen members were chosen from the lot. De Valles and the volunteers were taken back to the front lines by truck. The litter bearer's work was strenuous and exhausting, as some carries involved a two-hour round trip to the ambulance head, over broken ground littered with the detritus of war. When their arms and hands could no longer hold a stretcher, the litter bearers looped signal wire around their wrists, which soon tore into their own flesh. Yet they carried on. The final tally from the fighting was more than 200 wounded, many of them severely.[16]

De Valles would later be awarded the Distinguished Service Cross for his actions at Apremont. His citation read in part: "Chaplain de Valles repeatedly exposed himself to heavy artillery and machine-gun fire in order to assist in the removal of the wounded from exposed points in advance of the lines. He worked long periods of time with stretcher bearers in carrying wounded men to safety." To many of his "boys," de Valles was the "Angel of the Trenches," owing to his disregard for danger and his dogged determination to bring aid and comfort to as many of them as he was able. One soldier commented about the priest's recent actions: "He's as game as they make them and every inch a soldier." The French also recognized his gallantry and awarded him the Croix de Guerre for "Extraordinary heroism and exceptional devotion to his duty. Under uninterrupted enemy fire, [he] did not cease to care for the wounded and to encourage to renewed efforts the men worn out by hard fighting." At one point during the fighting, the exhausted priest's emotions got the better of him after seeing some of the dead and wounded, when he was heard to utter, "Kill the bastards!"[17]

In an interview with correspondent Bert Ford just after the fighting, the chaplain recalled his actions:

> First you recoil and get scared blue, and then you forget all about yourself when you see men dead and wounded around you. It was hell. That's the only name for it while the shelling was at its height. . . . If anybody told me then I could face and survive what I went through today I wouldn't have believed him. The noise was maddening. Shells dropped everywhere, hurling earth and stones and shrapnel.

His actions aside, the modest priest told the reporter that the soldiers should be the real focus. "All glory goes to the men in the ranks," he said, "That's where you find the real heroes."[18]

When it was all over, both chaplains collected the personal effects of the dead and saw to their proper burial in a plot prepared by Danker near Vignot. Later, a joint religious service was conducted there.[19] In addition to Chaplains Danker, de Valles, and their companions, on Sunday, April 28, the entire 104th Infantry Regiment was awarded the Croix de Guerre, the first time in history that an American unit received a foreign decoration.[20]

The "Fighting Chaplains"—Seicheprey

For days, Yankee observers had noted considerable activity toward their front, particularly in front of their lightly held forward positions at the town of Seicheprey and the nearby Bois de Remières. Two companies of Connecticut National Guardsmen, along with some scattered machine gun positions, were all that stood between the Germans and the main Yankee line about a mile behind, then on Beaumont Ridge. The alignment was consistent with a typical "defense in depth" strategy, with the forward positions used as a tripwire to warn of an all-out attack and, hopefully, to slow it down. Colonel John Henry Parker, the commander of the 102nd infantry was understandably concerned, and he requested and received permission to adjust his position. Nevertheless, the Germans chose the precise moment when Companies B and C had just settled in, having relieved Companies G and E, to launch a massive, all-out raid.[21]

The fighting began with an enormous early morning barrage all along the Yankee front, from side to side and front to rear, isolating the forward companies and severing virtually all land lines to the rear. When the barrage let up, three thousand well-armed Storm Troopers (*Stosstruppen*) and others surged forward, advancing out of the woods in the midst of a heavy morning fog to attack the Yankee positions. The vastly outnumbered Connecticut men fought back with grit and courage, with rifles, fists, and virtually anything they could grab. For many, it was a fight to the death against overwhelming odds. Despite enemy artillery fire to the rear of Seicheprey, which was intended to deter any relief, some infantry companies were sent forward to assist their beleaguered comrades, resulting in yet more casualties. For its part, Yankee artillery began to fire back hoping to hold back the attack. In fact, casualties were so heavy that early that morning, the 104th Ambulance Company sent word to other companies to assist with the evacuation of wounded. Meanwhile, back on Beaumont Ridge, with communications virtually nonexistent, except for scattered reports from some intrepid runners, the division command could not be sure if the raid was, in fact, a general attack. Amid all the ensuing chaos, Chaplains O'Connor and Boucher volunteered to cook and serve hot chow to the fighting men, at a time when both their spiritual and temporal needs required attention.[22]

Eventually, the Germans began an orderly withdrawal. Unfortunately, word that the German raiding party was withdrawing did not give specifics as to their precise position, and some friendly rounds landed among the friendly troops remaining in Seicheprey, adding insult to injury. As a result, with typical doughboy humor, the heavy guns from the batteries of the 103rd Field Artillery were dubbed "The Kaiser's Own" by some of the infantry. The Germans left with approximately 180 prisoners, an embarrassment for the defenders to be sure, but the raid resulted in heavy casualties on both sides. The doughty Yankees gave as good as they got. When it was all over, Chaplain Rollins conducted a burial service.[23]

Two of the division chaplains distinguished themselves by their conduct during the fighting. The first, Father William J. ("Billy") Farrell of Dorchester, Massachusetts, the regimental chaplain of the 103rd Field Artillery, became known as the "Fighting Chaplain." Farrell grew up in South Boston and graduated from Boston College in 1898. He studied for the priesthood at St. John's Seminary in Brighton. After ordination, Farrell served various area parishes in Lexington, South Lawrence, and, just prior to the war, at St. Bernard's in West Newton. As a member of the Massachusetts National

Chaplain William J. Farrell. Reprinted from Kernan, *History of the 103rd Field Artillery*.

Guard, Fr. Farrell was sent to France as chaplain of the 103rd Field Artillery Regiment, and he was commissioned as a Chaplain (1st Lt.) on October 6, 1917. One doughboy wrote home that, "Father Farrell has been right in the thick of the fight with us." This was no exaggeration. At Seicheprey, when German fire landed on one of the batteries, Farrell helped to evacuate the wounded. In fact, he literally carried Cpl. Myron D. Dickinson of Battery F on his shoulders to the dressing station at Beaumont. Nearby, at another point during the fighting, he drove an ambulance full of wounded through a hail of fire at the notorious "Dead Man's Curve." After all the wounded of his unit were evacuated, he volunteered to deliver ammunition to an artillery section, where he, himself, was wounded by shrapnel and had to be evacuated.[24]

Kenneth N. Burnham of Battery C, 103rd Field Artillery, described Fr. Farrell as "one of the most beloved of all our superiors." Later, during a visit to the battery in May 1918, the chaplain made a humorous reference to the wounds he had received a month earlier while "administering to some of his boys" and at the same time making no mention of the part he played in the fighting. Burnham ends his letter with an observation about Fr. Farrell, stating that, "he's all right!" Another artilleryman told his mother, "Father Farrell has been right in the thick of the fight with us." The French honored his bravery with the Croix de Guerre for his actions at Seicheprey, noting that he was "a very brave chaplain who displayed the most profound contempt for danger."[25]

In the meantime, as Chaplain Farrell was performing his heroics on Beaumont Ridge, 1st Lt. Orville Anderson Petty, one of the chaplains of the 102nd Infantry, was performing heroics of his own, albeit closer to the point of attack. The forty-three-year-old Cadiz, Ohio, native was one of several New Haven pastors who had enlisted in the Connecticut National Guard as chaplains. In fact, Petty had already seen service with the 2nd Connecticut Infantry Regiment when it was sent to the Mexican border in 1916. The son of Asbury F. and Sarah Kyle Petty, he received his undergraduate degree from Muskingum College in 1898. Petty furthered his studies at Colorado College, and he obtained a Ph.D. from the University of Chicago in 1915. In the interim, Petty was ordained a Congregational minister in 1901, and he served as pastor in Greeley, Colorado, and Aurora, Illinois, prior to his coming to New Haven. At the time of his enlistment, he had been serving as pastor of the Plymouth Church (formerly College Street Church) since 1911. He was so well-regarded, that his congregation granted him an unlimited leave of absence and continued his salary. As the Yankee Division took shape, Petty and several officers, including Chaplain Harris E. Starr, formed a recruiting party and traveled all over southern Connecticut looking for volunteers to bring the 2nd Regiment up to strength.[26]

Petty performed his soldierly ministry in the midst of the carnage wrought by the fierce barrage and counter barrage, where death and destruction were everywhere, and where in desperation, rocks and fists became the only weapons. He was cited in the General Orders and recommended for the Distinguished Service Cross. His citation read, in part:

> he carried relief to the wounded on the extreme firing line repeatedly, and working himself to the point of exhaustion in evacuating dead and wounded and set an example of coolness and courage beyond all praise in every part of the field of action, from the most advanced firing line to the cemetery where he buried dead under heavy artillery fire.

Petty was ultimately awarded the Silver Star for his actions.[27]

New Blood

As Chaplain Mayotte made his way to the headquarters of the 102nd Infantry Regiment, he may well have asked himself what he was doing there.

Chaplain Orville A. Petty receives the Silver Star. Courtesy of the Military History Institute.

It was his first time in the combat zone, and as he got closer to the front, Mayotte "began to hear the continuous roar of the cannon." He was able to poke fun at himself, though, remarking that he "felt like a pacifist for a while." Moreover, the "steel helmet which had seemed so large and cumbersome," when he was first issued it in the rear area, "now seemed ridiculously small." He wrote that the men flocked to the Sunday Masses in all the little local churches; however, on a more sobering note, he observed that many of the soldiers, by now well inured to the sights and sounds of battle, had become "reckless" and, as a result, they became casualties by "sheer carelessness." Although warmly welcomed to the regiment by Colonel John Henry Parker, Mayotte's stay would be short. In early June, he received word that he would soon be transferred to the 2nd Division, specifically to the 12th Field Artillery Regiment. As the less senior Catholic chaplain of the two assigned to the 102nd Infantry, he had to make way for a Protestant one. By then, he himself was well used to the "noise and danger," which was as it should be; otherwise, he wrote, "no man could stand this life and remain sane." On June 15, 1918, he left the Yankee Division and joined his new regiment.[28]

Hickey's Raid

Planning for the first large American raid had been in the works for about a month. Approximately four hundred men from the 101st Infantry Regiment would cross No Man's Land, the object of which was to obtain German prisoners. The raid was scheduled for the evening and early morning hours of May 30/31. On the day before the raid, Chaplain Farrell said Mass, followed by a Protestant Communion service conducted by Chaplain Rollins. Each clergyman gave a sermon on "courage." While those who were to take part prepared their equipment, some artillerymen from the 101st Artillery Regiment, many from the same towns as the infantrymen, wandered over to their area and paid them a visit. Prior to jump off by the infantry, the Yankee artillery was ordered to soften up the position with gas and high explosives. Meanwhile, their commander, Col. John H. Sherburne, placed a call to headquarters to voice his concerns. Earlier that day, he had observed the terrain and took note of the prevailing winds. Knowing full well the potentially lethal effects of the gas shells to be used, he feared that the gas was likely to drift back upon the raiders, with catastrophic results. The recently assigned artillery brigade commander brushed aside Sherburne's concerns. "It was too late," he opined, and besides, the plan conformed to the current French standards then being utilized. "Carry out your fire mission," he ordered.[29]

At the appointed hour, the preparatory barrage commenced. As the men made their way in the dark, across the debris-littered ground, a faint odor of gas could be detected, becoming stronger as they got closer to the German lines. The doughboys pressed on. Chaplain Lyman Rollins went along with his men, "just in case." The raiders reached the enemy lines only to find them virtually abandoned, save one teenaged soldier. Seizing him, they started back. However, something was very wrong. As Col. Sherburne had anticipated, the men increasingly began to suffer the ill-effects of the gas. Litter bearers were alerted, but for some, the damage was done. Over the course of the next several hours more and more men began to develop signs of gas poisoning. In fact, virtually all of the raiders suffered some ill-effects, including Chaplain Rollins, but most later recovered. Some died horrible, lingering deaths in the division field hospitals, literally drowning as their lungs filled with fluid. In the aftermath, the French and American armies developed revised tables for the firing of gas shells and wind direction.[30]

On June 8, 1918, Rollins was cited in the General Orders "for gallantry in action May 30–31, 1918 during a raid into the enemy's lines to the Rupt-de-Mad." From the Chaplain's perspective, his actions were anything but

"Home on Leave."
Chaplain Lyman Rollins.
Courtesy of St. Michael's
Episcopal Church,
Marblehead, MA.

extraordinary. He was simply doing what he felt strongly was his duty—it was his place to share the dangers of the front line with his men. They, in turn, were extremely proud of him. Capt. James T. Duane, a company commander in the 101st Infantry, summed up these feelings in his memoir: "They were all praise for the little chaplain from New England, who went over the top with 'his boys' and came back with them. It was their opinion that their Regiment had some sky pilot." He added that, "it's mine, too."[31]

Shortly after the raid, Rollins returned to the United States, more than likely to share his experiences with the students in the Army Chaplain School at Camp Taylor, Kentucky. His original orders had called for him to return earlier; however, he prevailed upon his superiors in Chaumont to delay his departure until after Hickey's Raid, so that he could take part as planned, since he had been an "enthusiastic" participant in all the rehearsals. In any event, it appears that he spent parts of June and July 1918 in Kentucky, after which he returned to France and his beloved 101st Infantry Regiment.[32]

"No Greater Love"

The Yankee chaplain corps was not without its losses. Only a month before, Chaplain Walton S. Danker, along with other members of the regiment, had been decorated with the Croix de Guerre. Danker, the Protestant chaplain of the 104th Infantry Regiment, gave his life in the line of duty near Royaumeix, in the Toul Sector, on Sunday, June 16, 1918, at 8:55 A.M. While a large group of soldiers was milling about waiting for both Protestant and Catholic church services to begin, the Germans began a heavy bombardment of the town. The shelling should have come as no real surprise, as the Yankees had come to learn early on in the Chemin des Dames. There, following a similar Sunday shelling, Lt. Donald S. Dinsmore of the 103rd Field Artillery wryly observed: "The Boches are no respecters of the Sabbath."[33]

Corp. Harry Lamb of Company A, 104th Infantry was standing guard that night, his post about one hundred yards from the church. "Everything went smoothly until Sunday morning. Then 'John Boche' sent over some big shells into our town. First they sent over about five shells which didn't amount to much—sort of range finders." As the shelling increased in intensity, it became apparent that the town itself was the target, and men began rushing to escape. Corp. Lamb continued his account: "Then about fifteen minutes later they sent over a second set of them. These landed about in the middle of the town near the church. The boys were coming out of church when the second batch came over. God, wasn't it awful!"

Twenty-two of the waiting troops were wounded and eight killed outright, many by direct hits. A hastily manned aid station was established. Lamb was obviously moved by the sight and hastened to help carry the wounded to the medics. "I never in all my life saw such a sight," he recalled. "I always thought I couldn't stand the sight of blood, but I stood it that morning. I even helped the first aid fellows by washing the faces of the poor fellows that were wounded. One fellow had a wound on his back and wanted a pillow. Well, I gave him my blouse; he needed it more than I did."[34]

Emerging from a dugout shelter in the midst of the artillery barrage, Reverend Danker was struck in the back by a shell fragment and mortally wounded. His companion, Col. George Shelton, was also wounded, and the latter's orderly was killed. Shelton refused treatment until the more serious cases were dealt with. The chaplain had been on his way to conduct

Chaplain Walton S. Danker. Reprinted from Sibley, *With the Yankee Division in France*.

religious services that morning.[35] Pvt. Willard S. Smith of the 104th Infantry had been sitting in the YMCA hut awaiting the Protestant service that morning when the shelling started. He and a companion helped carry the wounded to an aid station. As he and his fellow litter bearer approached the other wounded, he came upon Chaplain Danker. He noted the events of that day in his diary:

> It was plain to see the chaplain was in bad shape. His face was ashen gray and I suppose he was in shock. He kept asking for water, but everyone was busy—his wound had been dressed—so I looked around and saw a French water can, the kind with the cover chained on. I managed to twist the cover off, poured it full and gave him a drink. I'm glad I was there to do it.

Danker died two days later in a field hospital and was buried the next day in the military cemetery at Ménil-la-Tour. He was thought to be the first American chaplain to die at the front, however, it was later learned that just three days before Lt. Wilbur S. Sewell, a Methodist minister, had also been killed.[36]

That same morning, the Division Chaplain, Michael O'Connor, barely escaped serious injury himself. He and several officers, including Capt. Harry D. Cormerais and Col. John Logan, had assembled in the latter's dugout at Bernecourt, when a large shell burst outside and metal fragments flew through the open window, seriously wounding Cormerais and slightly wounding another occupant. The shell fragments just missed Col. Logan, who had risen from his chair, thus inadvertently stepping out of the path, as well as Fr. O'Connor, who had averted injury when he moved away from the window seconds before the blast.[37]

On June 19, the morning rain gave way to afternoon sunshine, when a well-attended and moving ceremony was conducted by the Catholic chaplain, John B. de Valles. Reverend Danker's brother William, also a minister, and who had recently arrived in France, was one of the pall bearers. As taps was sounded, the bare-headed troops, officer and enlisted alike, gave way to emotion. Once again, Private Smith gives us a firsthand account: "Through the mist in my lashes I saw tears running down the cheeks of nearly every man. Soldiers, all hard, calloused, yet not so hard but what they wept unashamed as the clear, sad notes of the soldier's requiem died away." Major Stillman F. Westbrook called it, "without exception the most impressive service I have ever attended."[38]

Ready to Move On

The activity in the Toul Sector was more or less routine, punctuated by several intense bursts of violence. Virtually every unit was involved at least once in some fighting during the division's two-and-one-half month stay there. The next sector would make the Toul Sector seem like a *"bon secteur."* For Osias Boucher of the 101st Infantry, the men of his battalion were gaining confidence every day and ready for whatever the Germans would throw at them. They attended services regularly, and each of them, he said, was "as good a soldier as they are a good Catholic." The chaplain went on to describe just how far "his boys" had come: "Their spirit is the very best and their morale is excellent. There is no sign of weakening in them; on the contrary, they look to be better soldiers every day. Their main qualities [are] cheerfulness, courage and endurance. We are still in our lively sector, witnessing daily duels of artillery and avoiding to be nailed by the numerous shells falling all around us. Yet we cannot complain. We always say that the worst is yet to come and we are all ready to face it when it comes."[39]

CHAPTER FOUR

Aisne-Marne

"Hell Is before Us"

While the initial German spring offensive showed promise, each separate thrust ground to a halt as French or British resistance stiffened. However, that all changed on May 27, 1918, in the Champagne-Marne region, when a massive German push rolled back French and British defenders on a wide front stretching from Soissons to Reims. In a matter of days, the Germans had opened a pocket that stretched almost to the Marne, its axis pointed straight at Paris. The untried 2nd Division, composed of one brigade of Marines and one of Army troops, was called upon to stem what looked like an overwhelming tidal surge. Amazingly, though untested, the fresh, eager, often reckless young Americans did just that. The brutal month-long fight came, nevertheless, with a large price tag.[1]

Late June 1918 found the Yankee Division on the move. Some units travelled by truck, but most rode the "side door Pullmans," the famous "40 and 8's." Rumors abounded that the division would soon be in Paris to take part in the July 4th celebrations. Hopes ran high, as the trains reached the outskirts of the "City of Light," only to be dashed as it soon became apparent that it would be once more into the fight. Over the course of the next few days, unit by unit, they made their way back toward Château-Thierry to relieve the 2nd Division. As the columns passed each other, tired, hungry, battle-weary soldiers and Marines greeted their relievers. Some Marines called the National Guardsmen "Boy Scouts." Most, however, were happy to quickly impart some hard-learned lessons and grateful for a cup of hot coffee from the Yankee rolling kitchens. All of them were simply relieved to be out of that hell hole that had bled them of all but their fighting spirit. As for the men of the 101st Machine Gun Battalion, Doc Hesselgrave observed that whatever the future might bring, they were in good spirits and ready to take on the Boche. "All carried their present burdens with light hearts and unreserved gaiety," he wrote. Lt. Col. Chase of the 101st Engineers had a more sober view. After getting his first look at the new sector,

Chaplain O'Connor offers mass for the 101st Infantry near Etrépilly in July 1918, using the tailgate of an ambulance for an altar. Courtesy of the Military History Institute.

he observed: "A busy front and no trenches. Hell is before us but we will come through."[2]

By coincidence, Anselm Mayotte had been transferred to the 12th Field Artillery Regiment in the 2nd Division on June 15, just in time to take part in the heroic, month-long effort to blunt the German offensive at Belleau Wood and nearby Vaux, as the panicked French *poilu* retreated toward Paris. Although he was still a relatively new chaplain, Mayotte took to his assignment like a veteran. Despite the near daily shelling and other enemy activities, he remained with the men. "I am living in a tent in the woods and like this open air life very much," he wrote, "Of course, there are many hardships and privations, but I do not mind these because by sharing these with the men, I find is the best way to gain their confidence and sympathy." He said Mass in the open air and heard confessions. Each day, he visited on horseback all six batteries in his regiment. This commitment to the troops was at the essence of his duty. Soon he would write: "The one desire of the soldiers is to be at the front. It is my desire too, and in spite of the dangers and hardships, I hope to be at the front until the end. That is where the chaplain can do his best work."[3]

New Arrivals

Little by little, new chaplains were being assigned to the Yankee Division. One of these men was Harrison Ray Anderson, who had almost given up any hope of a transfer. Returning from his visit to the hospital one day, he received orders to report to the 103rd Infantry Regiment of the 26th Division. Ray wasted no time complying. On the way to his new assignment, he stopped at Chaumont, headquarters of the AEF chaplaincy, where he met with the Rev. Paul D. Moody, himself formerly the chaplain of the 103rd Infantry, and who was then serving on the Board of Chaplains. Anderson would be replacing Moody, who told him that the regiment was "the finest in the service." It did not take Anderson long to echo Moody's assessment. As he visited the various units astride his horse, "Dick," to whom he referred as his "splendid Assistant Chaplain," he quickly came to know the doughboys. Each chaplain viewed his job, and its inherent dangers, from his own perspective. In an effort to allay his mother's concerns, he reassured her: "I am not one of those chaplains who thinks it is his duty to show his men how brave he is. I am here for another purpose than that and while I do not think I am a coward, yet I will take every precaution."[4]

Anderson was clearly in his element. He expressed his feelings in a long letter to his father:

> I have been with them a little while now . . . and they are the most wonderful men in the world. They are not afraid of anything and I am proud to become one of them. . . . I have the finest regiment in France. They belong to the best Division too. . . . [The men] are

Chaplain Harrison Ray Anderson. Courtesy of the Fourth Presbyterian Church, Chicago, IL.

young, strong, cheerful, swearing and kicking all the time, yet always ready for a fight. I love them and will give them my shirt anytime.

Although most of the officers and men were New Englanders, he found several from other parts of the country. While Ray missed his family, he told them:

I thank God that I'm here. I am so happy here . . . because it is the place I should be. I could have stayed with my old regiment and grown fat and returned to you as one who did not give all he had for his Country. That was the temptation. Well, I chose to come here and I've left the easy thing behind to enter in here where men are needed.[5]

Ray had arrived at his new assignment in late June 1918, just as the Yankee Division was in the process of relieving the 2nd Division. He settled into the town of La-Voie-du-Châtel, where the 104th Ambulance Company was operating a dressing station. The area that the 103rd Infantry inherited was full of evidence of the recent battle. The worst part of it came that first night after it arrived in the sector, when members of the regiment tried to dig foxholes in the dark so as to provide some shelter. To their horror and disgust, they found the ground swarming with maggots and hastily buried bodies. Exhausted from their fruitless efforts, many came to the inescapable conclusion that there was nowhere without buried flesh and simply bedded down amidst the remains.[6]

The young chaplain got to work right away, establishing a canteen a few miles behind the front, where the soldiers could get "tobacco and canned fruit," and he also assisted in the burials of the dead Marines. Later, after the hard fighting had begun, Anderson "worked in the dressing station with the surgeons." In the meantime, as the divisions changed places and the Yankees were establishing their lines, the fighting must have seemed upside down, what with nighttime raids and the concealed movements of men and materiel during the day. "Where I am we fight at night and sleep during the day," Anderson told his mother. "As soon as dark comes the world wakes up and everything comes to life. Wagons filled with food go by. Men march; cannons roar. Then daylight comes and everything looks deserted. It's a queer game."[7]

Also joining the division was Allen Evans, Jr., the son of Allen Evans, Sr., a prominent architect, and his wife, Rebecca Chaulkey Lewis. He was born in Haverford, Pennsylvania, at the family home, literally on the very land his mother's ancestors had purchased from William Penn. Evans graduated from Yale University in 1914, and he went on to study at the Philadelphia Divinity School, where he received his Doctor of Sacred Theology in 1917. He attended a training camp at Plattsburg, New York, in 1915 and 1916, and later, in April 1918, he reported to the Army Chaplain School at Camp Taylor, Kentucky, where, upon graduation, he was commissioned a Chaplain (1st Lt.) on May 30. The newly minted chaplain arrived in France on June 22, and he was assigned to the 104th Infantry Regiment, just in time for the fighting around Château-Thierry. He joined Father de Valles and would remain with that regiment for the duration of the war.[8]

The Burial Detail

For upwards of a month, the bodies of dozens of dead, both Marine and Boche, lay scattered throughout Belleau Wood, others only hastily buried. Shortly after assuming control over the sector, General Edwards approached General Omar Bundy, his classmate at West Point, then in command of the Second Division, and offered to assume responsibility for a burial detail, thus relieving the tired Marines of that sad and gruesome duty. Bundy agreed. The task was assigned to the 101st Engineers, in particular, Company D, led by Capt. Carroll Swan. Sometime after midnight on the night of July 6/7, 1918, half of the company was transported by truck to a drop off point a mile or so from the edge of Belleau Wood, where, in the inky blackness, the soldiers set forth on their grim task. When the men reached the designated position, the burial detail was confronted with the overwhelming smell of death, so much so, that many engineers had to don their gas masks.[9]

For that reason, among others, for many enlisted men, the burial detail was the most difficult task of all. The work was often complicated by the effectiveness of artillery, which made short work of flesh and bone. Not only were the soldiers assaulted by the smell of decay, they often found body parts in trees. The body, or what was left of it, was generally gathered up and buried in a blanket, or in some instances, a wooden box made by the company mechanic. The grave was marked with a cross and the doughboy's dog tag and helmet. Robert Graves, a British officer who led several burial details, vomiting during the carry each time, described the process of retrieval:

> After the first day or two the corpses swelled and stank.... Those we could not get in continued to swell until the wall of the stomach collapsed, either naturally or when punctured by a bullet; a disgusting

smell would float across. The colour of the dead faces changed from white to yellow-grey, to red, to purple, to green, to black, to slimy.

Another soldier described the bodies as having the "consistency of Camembert cheese," covered with flies and maggots. Worse yet, legs and arms pulled away from the torso when they attempted to lift them.[10] One can just imagine the overpowering aversion that had to be overcome that night by those engineers assigned to the burial detail.

Corporal Elmer Buswell of Company D was a member of Capt. Swan's party, and he detailed the grim experience in his diary: "We . . . started hiking through the woods down to the front where the dead men lay. . . . None of us had ever been over the place before and the ground [was] full of shell holes, barb wires and shells come over and breaking all around us . . . It was a very nerve wracking job."[11] By mid-afternoon the following day, the party had buried nine Marines and forty-three Germans. Then, Capt. Swan ordered a halt to work, and he told the men to carefully make their way back. It was at that moment that he saw "the tall form of Chaplain Edwards coming through the woods" all alone. The Chaplain had heard about the burial detail, and he had walked all the way to pay his respects to the dead. The two officers visited every grave, where a cross and a tag had been placed. Swan mused: "It was a strange sight, we two standing there uncovered in the bright sunlight a few hundred yards from the enemy who had killed these men, the good parson with the open Book saying the last words and a prayer over these brave Americans. . . ." The captain was unstinting in his praise of Edwards and the other chaplains: "Just realize these conditions—our proximity to the enemy, the hasty burials, the shelling going on, the dangerous task of the Chaplain getting there. Then, perhaps, you can realize what kind of fellows our Army Chaplains are. . . ."[12]

Attack, Attack!

The Germans made one last attempt to cross the Marne near Château-Thierry on July 15. They failed, due in large measure to the heroic stand taken by units of the 3rd Division, which earned its well-deserved nickname, "Rock of the Marne." After three days defending the final German onslaught, it was time for the Americans to go on the attack. As chaplain of the 101st Infantry Regiment, during the fight near Château-Thierry, Father Mike stood along the road that stormy night of July 17/18, and as the men of the regiment passed by, he blessed them and gave them general absolution. Knowing that he did not have time to hear all of their individual confessions, he told them as they passed him that they should whisper an Act of Contrition. The very next day, he was out among the dead and wounded, many of whom he had blessed the night before. For his part, that same evening, Osias Boucher, also with the 101st Infantry, held a service in a barn attached to a battalion headquarters at Taffourney Farm. He offered a pep talk, and for the Catholics, general absolution. For all of his boys, regardless of denomination, he offered a simple prayer with a double meaning. "All for One (the One God)," he proclaimed, "and one for all." James T. Duane, a company commander who was present at the service, himself had words of praise for the doughty chaplain: "Father Boucher was a very much loved man, for he lived in the front lines with the boys continually, and the boys of his battalion never went on raids or attacks without him."[13]

On the morning of July 18, the torrential rain slowed and over the next several days the troops enjoyed warm, brilliant sunshine. Spearheading the fight for the Yankee Division was the 52nd Brigade, composed of the 103rd and 104th Infantry Regiments. Two days later, the balance of the division joined in a concerted push. For a week, the division slogged forward against a well-entrenched enemy, experienced in defense. The Germans fought one day, and slowly slipped back to another position at night, ready to start the process all over again the following day. Each day, despite heavy casualties, the Yankees pushed on, nest by nest, until all had been silenced or where their occupants had slipped away. During that first day, the 102nd and 103rd Field Artillery Regiments were firing in support of the 103rd and 104th Infantry Regiments. The dressing station where the wounded were brought for triage and transport was located at La Voie-du-Châtel. It was there that Chaplains Markham W. Stackpole and William J. Farrell went to help out. The latter passed out cigarettes, and both men offered words of encouragement as the wounded awaited ambulances.[14]

It was a bruising, bloody contest, and the casualty figures were extremely high. Most accounts of the next several days describe the grimly determined lines of khaki-clad doughboys, bayonets fixed, advancing through waving, golden wheat fields, at the same time ditching their packs, blankets, and "extra" gear in an effort to lighten the load in the steamy summer heat. They also describe the deadly, scythe-like effects of the German machine guns, hidden in nests strategically placed in the fields of grain and in the verges of the wooded areas beyond, pounding and tearing at the flesh and bone of the young soldiers. Captain Stanhope Bayne-Jones, the newly appointed Regimental Surgeon of the 103rd Infantry, witnessed the effects firsthand. "Our men showed a bravery and endurance that has not been surpassed," he recounted. "They advanced across open wheatfields in the face of machine gun nests, hidden in the woods, or a little beyond through shelling and through gas—through every sort of terror and hardship to get at the German, and kill him." "Our men fought like wolves," echoed Lt. Col. Horace Hobbs, "as could easily be seen by our dead as they lay in the edge of woods or in wheat fields with their rifles . . . still in their hands."[15] There was plenty of work for the chaplains to do.

The high number of casualties was not due to the inexperience and eagerness of the doughboys alone. In point of fact, it was due in large measure to the inexperience of large-unit commanders and conflicts over doctrine. The American division, which contained elements of infantry and artillery, was large and powerful by all standard measures. However, as Pershing envisioned it, the ordinary infantryman, armed with his rifle and bayonet, charging en masse, should always carry the day. At best, such an attack would follow an initial barrage or a rolling barrage. In the words of one historian, these "unimaginative" tactics merely traded "bodies for bullets."[16] It would be a bold corps or division commander, indeed, who dared to challenge the Commander in Chief in this viewpoint.

The fact is that, given the size of the battlefield, and the then-current doctrinal thinking and state of weaponry, as well as the relatively primitive and unreliable communication systems, open warfare was simply not practical. It was a myth. When the infantry advanced beyond the effective range of the artillery, it was vulnerable to enemy artillery and machine gun fire. Some forward-thinking division-level commanders, like Charles Summerall, an artilleryman by experience, and John A. Lejeune, a Marine and commander of the 2nd Division, recognized that the answer lay in the closer coordination of artillery and infantry, so that when those limits were reached, the infantry would simply halt and wait for the artillery to catch up. Even Major General Hunter Liggett, First Army commander, eventually came around to that way of thinking. They were glaring exceptions. Pershing never did, even long after the war was over.[17]

For the Yankee Division, constant attack was the order of the day issued by Generals Jean Degoutte and Hunter Liggett. General Edwards, the division commander, was under intense pressure to attack without letup. Conscious of the growing casualty numbers, at one point he requested a brief halt in order to bring his artillery forward. The request was denied. Thus the Yankee artillery was almost always playing the exhausting game of catch up, as described by Corporal Frederick W. ("Fritz") Potter of Battery A, 101st Field Artillery. "[The] Boche . . . retreated before us so fast that it was impossible at times for us to keep up with them," he wrote, "We would haul up our guns, get into action, and before we knew it they would be out of range, and we would have to advance again."[18]

Such was the case during the Aisne-Marne Offensive. On the night of

July 20/21, the 101st Field Artillery, while in support of the 52nd Infantry Brigade, temporarily stopped firing, since it did not know the positions of the infantry, which was constantly moving ahead. At daybreak the following morning, the regiment was ordered forward once again, its destination, the village of Etrepilly. Along the way, the gunners viewed the full effects of modern war. Corporal Potter told of seeing, "piles of German ammunition, guns, and equipment of all kinds."[19]

Sometimes a chaplain's desire to get to the front lines could have unintended consequences. On the morning of July 21, 1918, Murray Dewart was ecstatic that his truck was finally repaired, and he was eager to join up with "his boys" in the 101st Field Artillery, who were moving forward to catch up with the infantry. That day, the chaplain loaded the truck with all of his equipment, and he and his driver took to the road, bound for Etrepilly. "It was easily the most interesting day of my life," he recalled, "to pass on to positions which had been under steady fire for weeks, with now no sounds at all; to pass on to positions yesterday in the possession of the Boche, today with only Boche equipment lying around trenches and dugouts." The Germans having left in a hurry, there were souvenirs everywhere, and the chaplain kept stopping to add "German belts, revolvers, knives, canned heat and such things" to his collection. "Of course, being in the truck, I went faster than the regiment," he recalled. "I was very eager to see it all." One road led to another, and as a result, he became hopelessly lost. At long last, as his truck reached the crest of a long hill, a group of French soldiers waved him to stop, and by means of words and frantic gestures, warned him that he was about to enter the German lines. Dewart had advanced well beyond the regiment, and he had inadvertently strayed into the French sector! Eventually, he found his regiment, but not before his truck finally gave out, again. Leaving the vehicle and his driver behind, the disappointed chaplain began the long walk back to the regiment. Luckily for him, along the way he met a friendly medical officer, and he persuaded him to lend him a mule-drawn ambulance to take him and his luggage back to headquarters.[20]

The Americans learned valuable lessons during the Aisne-Marne Offensive, but the price was high. By the same token, the hapless German machine gunners, ammunition all expended, also found out that hands raised and a shout of "kamerad" was not always a guarantee that any mercy would be shown. More often than not, a Yankee pistol shot summarily silenced the Boche gunner. Payback![21]

Every now and then a chaplain experienced a moment of inspiration amidst the carnage of war. Such was the case for Ray Anderson one evening toward sunset, as he and his burial detail returned to 2nd Battalion headquarters during the Aisne-Marne Offensive. Coming through a small town, they passed a small church where a shell had torn a huge hole in the side:

> The wall had fallen across the street and I had to climb over the stones to pass. As I did so, I glanced into the church and there was the Christ—above all the wreck and ruin Jesus remained untouched. He stood there (a statue of Him, of course) above it all. And I thought that after it is all over it must be just Jesus who must stand out above these ruined nations, else the war will have been in vain and this precious blood offering will be lost.[22]

On July 25 the bulk of the division was relieved. However, some elements, like the Sanitary Trains, were held for a day or two to assist in the transition to the 42nd Division. Still others, like the 101st Engineers, the entire 51st Artillery Brigade, and the 101st Ammunition Train stayed on another ten days, attached to the relieving divisions until early August in order to lend punch to the continuing attack as they took up the fight to push the Germans beyond the Vesle River. While the engineers were primarily called upon to maintain the roads and bridges so that the infantry and artillery could flow forward freely, they, themselves, were often called upon to pick up their weapons and serve as infantry. As they viewed the battlefield from both the front and the rear, their perspective was all-encompassing. Relief for those elements came between August 3 and 5, after a brutal fight at Sergy several days earlier. Since the beginning of the offensive on July 18, the 101st Field Artillery Regiment had lost 29 men killed, along with another 145 gassed or wounded. Many of their replacements would come from the Midwest.[23]

A "Man of Adamant"

Throughout the entire Aisne-Marne Offensive, Murray Dewart was seemingly everywhere at once. No matter what the danger, including a close call with a high-explosive shell, he felt that his place was with the men, particularly so, as the casualties in the regiment began to mount. That's what a chaplain did. Taking a page from Theodore Roosevelt, Murray simply outpaced "Black Care." All of his near manic energy was poured into this solemn duty, and it began to take its toll on him both physically and emotionally. Dewart would never ask to be relieved; it simply wasn't in him. He had grit. "The welfare and the comfort of the men in his command were uppermost in his mind at all times and no effort was too great and no place too dangerous for him," recalled a fellow chaplain. Brigadier

General John Sherburne, formerly Commanding Officer of the 101st Field Artillery and well acquainted with the doughty chaplain, recognized the warning signs, called Chaplain Paul D. Moody at General Headquarters, and asked for Dewart's relief. Sherburne told Moody: "[Murray's] life is too valuable to be thrown away. . . . He is literally working himself to death, on the go day and night. . . ." Moody immediately ordered Dewart to Chaumont, where a very contentious meeting took place between the two clergymen. In a tone bordering on insubordination, Murray adamantly refused to accept reassignment, arguing that his place was with his men, and that some of them would die without benefit of a chaplain if he was not there. Moody also saw the by now self-evident signs, and he would not back down. For once, Dewart lost the argument and bowed to the inevitable. He went on to serve as chaplain at the base hospital in Langres. The regularity of his duties there, away from the clamor of war, gave him a chance to renew both body and spirit. However, that is not to say that the chaplain failed to bring his characteristic energy and intensity to bear upon his new assignment. That would certainly not be Murray.[24]

There were other changes in the ranks of the Yankee chaplains at this time. H. Boyd Edwards of the 101st Engineers received some welcome assistance with the arrival of Father Libert, a new chaplain sponsored by the Knights of Columbus. Lucien Gaspard Libert was born near Kankakee, Illinois. His parents, Gaspard and Lea, who were both immigrants from Belgium, operated a farm near St. George. Lucien was the third of six children, although he was the oldest remaining son, his two older brothers having died in infancy. While he regularly helped out on his parents' farm, "he was never of rugged constitution." Libert attended St. Viator's College in nearby Bourbonnaise, and he was ordained a priest in Chicago on May 13, 1911. After assignments in Eagle Township, Canton, and Chicago, Illinois, he became pastor of the Catholic church in Martinton, where he was serving when the United States entered the war. Libert was the first priest in the Peoria Diocese to apply for a chaplaincy, but due to his age, he was repeatedly rejected. His persistence paid off when he learned that there was a need for a French-speaking chaplain, and he immediately applied for the job. Under the sponsorship of the Knights of Columbus, he left for France on June 16, 1918, as a Field Secretary and volunteer chaplain. Upon arrival in France, he was assigned to the headquarters of the 101st Engineer Regiment.[25]

Also at this time, the 101st Infantry Regiment was the beneficiary of another young chaplain, by the name of Burnham North Dell. The son of William and Florence Dell, he went on to study at Princeton University, where he was a member of the track team. However, it was on the tennis court where he really shone. He and a classmate, Dean Mathey, won the national intercollegiate doubles championship in 1910. Following his graduation in 1912, Dell continued his studies at Union Theological Seminary in New York, where he obtained a degree. After his ordination, Dell served first as assistant rector at St. George's Episcopal Church in New York, and later, in November 1917, at Emmanuel Episcopal Church in Boston. In the interim, on June 3, 1916, he married Margaret Hally Bissell at St. Peter's Church in Morristown, New Jersey. The bride was attended by the daughters of two former presidents, Cleveland and Taft. One of the groom's ushers was T. Guthrie Speers, another graduate of Princeton and the Union Theological Seminary, who, by coincidence, would later serve as a fellow chaplain in the 26th Division.[26]

Emmanuel Church served a large city population, with all its many interesting and challenging aspects. The rector, Dr. Elwood Worcester, met these challenges head-on. He began the Emmanuel Movement, in some respects the forerunner of Alcoholics Anonymous, treating those with drug and alcohol addictions while addressing as well the extreme poverty of many city residents. While at Emmanuel, Dell was assigned to the Health Work Department, to teach at the Vinton School, and to other parish duties as well. Dr. Worcester commented, "Mr. Dell has been with us but a short time but he has proved his value as a preacher and church worker and he has endeared himself to us by the sweetness of his disposition." In 1918, Dell took leave from Emmanuel and enlisted in the Army, and he was sent to the Chaplain School at Camp Taylor, Kentucky. Dell received his commission as a Chaplain (1st Lt.) on July 6, 1918, and by July 30 he was in France, where he was initially assigned to the 101st Infantry Regiment. He would later be transferred to the 102nd Infantry Regiment.[27]

After the Aisne-Marne fighting was done, Chaplain Ray Anderson looked back. "I have been through hell this past month, but for God," he lamented. Anderson continued: "There never will be a front as bad as the one we came out of. There never will be one so hard on the men and officers. I feel as though the hard part of the war is over so far as I am concerned. I have seen the worst and God has marvelously brought us through it all. I cannot thank Him enough for it all." When all was said and done, nearly five thousand Yankee doughboys had died or were wounded during their time in the sector.[28] Unfortunately for Anderson and the Yankee Division, despite the recent heavy number of casualties, his optimism was misplaced, as there would be far worse days to come.

On Sunday, August 4, 1918, in a park in the town of Ussy-sur-Marne, the 103rd Infantry held a memorial service for those members of the regiment who had died up to that point. The entire regiment was assembled, and the men listened to speeches by Brig. Gen. Charles H. Cole, Colonel Frank M. Hume, and Chaplain Anderson.[29]

"Second to None" (2ND Division)

If the men of the 2nd Division had any thoughts that they would be sent to a rear area after the brutal slugfest in June, they were soon disabused of that notion. The division was sent north to the opening of the German pocket near Soissons, where it would play a critical role in squeezing the Germans out as the Yankee Division and others pushed on the salient from the sides and bottom. However, problems abounded, as over the course of three or four days the various parts of the division were ordered north in a helter-skelter manner, many without the knowledge of its new commander, Maj. Gen. James Guthrie Harbord. Some units marched, while others rode in French camions driven by silent Annamite (Vietnamese) drivers to where the 2nd Division was slated to play a role in the Allied attack commencing July 18. It would not be fully assembled until literally the morning of the attack, and, in fact, many units were thrust into the battle on the run, soaking wet from the storm the night before, without having eaten for more than a day. Some, like the Marines, whose rolling kitchens had not caught up with them, were given permission to eat one day's reserve ration.[30]

Starting at 4:00 A. M. on July 14, the 12th Field Artillery began the move with a grueling 24-hour march. Hungry and exhausted, the artillerymen reached a woods near Villers-Cotterêts where they slept. Observing the activity during the following three days, Anselm Mayotte could tell something big was in the works. "The roads were filled with moving troops, cavalry, infantry, artillery, tanks and thousands and thousands of trucks," he wrote, "Never did the traffic cease night or day." When it came, the attack was massive and devastating. For the priest, he came to know war in all its awful aspects, which he described in a letter:

> Here it was that I saw awful sights—the dead lying everywhere, the ground plowed by shells, giant trees uprooted or broken asunder by shells as if they had been mere toothpicks, villages destroyed, here and there an aeroplane dashing to the ground, dead horses lying about. Above all this, the continual roar of thousands of cannon. Surely war is hell and no matter how horrible the descriptions may seem, they are not exaggerated.[31]

Persistence Pays

Working with the YMCA since January, Robert Campbell frequently served on the front lines, where he got to know many soldiers and to see and experience for himself firsthand just what they were experiencing. "My contact with the men has been wonderfully pleasant," he would write, adding, "I regret that the canteen in [the] YMCA work requires so much of my time. I have often wished I were an army chaplain." Campbell liked his work with the YMCA; however, it was not enough to match the sacrifice of other young men his age. Although he had been under fire and only recently returned from the hospital, having suffered the ill effects of a gas attack, he was worried that a new assignment would take him away from the front lines, and thoughts of resignation crossed his mind. "My experience as a YMCA worker has been very exceptional and has given me great satisfaction," he wrote to friends in Warren, Massachusetts, adding, "there have been some drawbacks to that work, however, and unless I could remain all the time at the extreme front, I would have none of it."[32] His would be a very common refrain among many of the younger Yankee Division chaplains.

Then, out of the blue, came word that, in answer to his prayers, he would be given a commission as a Chaplain (1st Lt.) on August 3. He was ordered to report to Chaumont, where he met with Bishop Brent and his fellow committeemen, Fr. Doherty and Rev. Moody, and got acquainted with them during a hundred-mile auto trip, presumably to his new assignment with the 101st Field Artillery Regiment. Campbell would join the regiment in early August just as it was completing its extended tour of duty, helping to chase the Germans back across the Vesle River. As chaplain to seventeen hundred men, Campbell would wear many hats, from morale officer to athletic director, spiritual guide, and mailman. He was assigned an orderly, a car and driver, and a "nice saddle horse." However, his biggest challenge would be to fill the large shoes of his predecessor, Murray Dewart, now on assignment at Langres.

One of Campbell's first tasks was to bury the dead and notify the relatives. He wrote of this very solemn duty:

> All matters pertaining to the dead are in my charge, providing for their burial, keeping records of how and where they died, and the location of the graves. It is my duty to write to their parents and notify them. I have quite a collection of pocket valuables which belong to those who have fallen, which I am to send to a certain place where they are forwarded to the relatives.

All in all, he was pleased to be where he was: "We will soon be in real action again and I will be right there with the boys. We are all willing to stand as much as necessary, but naturally we are anxious that the end of the war shall come very quickly." No doubt, Campbell heard from some of his parishioners from time to time about his absence, and he gently reminded them of the need for shared sacrifice: "I have no doubt that the church feels keenly the absence of the minister, but let us remember that the parents of the boys who are doing the fighting are glad to know that there is a chaplain in the ranks and on the battlefield at their side when he is needed most."[33]

More Incoming—Respite and Replacements

The 101st Infantry Regiment was ordered back to the area of Château-Thierry to begin the process of rest and refitting, along with more training in order to absorb the lessons of the recent battle. Osias Boucher reflected on the events of the past month:

> During these hard days I was priest, litter bearer, infirmarian and would have readily been a soldier, if I could have obtained a rifle, because those Boches did not even respect our Red Cross. We are at rest somewhere in France. Ah! You cannot imagine how we all appreciate this rest after having been so long at the firing line.

On another note, the humble chaplain was experiencing the Army bureaucracy at its most annoying:

> I am always well pleased with the work, although at times some who by their call should help you, try to make it hard. . . . I am working for God's glory and for the good . . . [of] . . . my boy's soul, so these little things do not affect me. I am not working for publicity; I do my work without tooting my horn, while my opponents always blow their horn in order that the little they are doing seems big.[34]

However, for Ray Anderson, with the 103rd Infantry Regiment, there was no real rest, as he sought out the dead for burial and wrote letters home to grieving kin. He had been the sole chaplain for a regiment of more than three thousand men. However, help was on the way, and he expected both a Catholic and another Protestant chaplain to join him, which would provide one chaplain for each of the three battalions. As evidence of Bishop Brent's success in bringing more chaplains to the front line troops, Ander-

Chaplain Albert G. Butzer, Sr. Courtesy of Albert G. Butzer III.

son was soon joined by Rev. Albert George Butzer, Sr., a Protestant, and Fr. Michael Nivard, a Catholic.[35]

A native of Buffalo, New York, Chaplain Butzer graduated from North Central College in Naperville, Illinois, after which he attended Union Theological Seminary. Butzer interrupted his studies and volunteered to serve in the Army as a chaplain. He received his commission as a Chaplain (1st Lt.) and was sent overseas in July 1918, where he was assigned to the 3rd Battalion, 103rd Infantry. Ray Anderson, now with the 2nd Battalion, would tell his father that the "new chaplain [Butzer] is a fine one."[36]

Father Michael Nivard traveled a somewhat longer route to the regiment. Born in Hoorn, Netherlands, the forty-three-year-old priest was older than many of his colleagues, but not lacking in spirit. Following ordination there on December 3, 1899, he came to the United States in 1901, where he served various parishes in Rhode Island, Michigan, and Wisconsin. At the time that he volunteered for service, he was a member of the Missionaries of the Sacred Heart, living in Sparta, Wisconsin. The chaplain was sponsored by the Knights of Columbus and went overseas on October 9, 1917. While under the auspices of the K of C, he ministered at the front in the Chemin des Dames and Toul Sectors. Like Chaplain Butzer, he received his commission on July 9, 1918, and, after some brief training at Neuilly-sur-Suise, he was likewise assigned to the 1st Battalion, 103rd Infantry, where he began his Army service with the Aisne-Marne Campaign.[37]

Joining the 104th Infantry Regiment in August was Charles K. Imbrie, who was assigned as chaplain to the 1st Battalion. Imbrie, whose parents were missionaries, was born in Tokyo, Japan. Upon his return to the United States, he attended the Lawrenceville School, followed by Princeton

Chaplain Michael Nivard. Reprinted from Cabot, *History of the 103rd U. S. Infantry.*

University. The young man worked as an apprentice in the shops of the Pennsylvania Railroad in Harrisburg, Pennsylvania, and later as a machine tool salesman. However, like his parents, his true calling was the ministry, and he enrolled at the Auburn Theological Seminary, in Auburn, New York, where, as a student, he served as assistant pastor at the First Presbyterian Church. Upon his ordination at the Lancaster Presbyterian Church in Lancaster, New York, on June 7, 1916, he was installed there as pastor.[38]

Like many young men his age, following the declaration of war with Germany, Imbrie wanted to participate in some form of war service. Not wishing to lose their minister so soon, but seeing his determination, the Church Elders arrived at a surprisingly creative plan, whereby Imbrie would continue to receive his minister's salary while at the same time working six days a week in a munitions factory. His wages from the outside work would be donated to the Lancaster Presbyterian Church War Fund to be distributed as the church saw fit. Six months later, Imbrie was not satisfied that he was doing enough, and he advised the Elders that it was very likely that he would soon be called upon to serve in the Army. "The call of our Country should have the right of way over any church or family ties," he told them. The final Session Minutes contain a brief notation, harking to the words of St. Paul, where the young minister simply wrote:

Chaplain Charles K. Imbrie.
Courtesy of the Lancaster (NY)
Presbyterian Church.

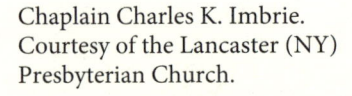

"Col. 2:5." ["For though I be absent in the flesh, yet am I with you in the spirit, joying and beholding your order, and the steadfastness of your faith in Christ."] Imbrie took a leave from his pulpit and reported to Camp Taylor on June 15. After the completion of Chaplain School, he was commissioned as a Chaplain (1st Lt.) on July 5, 1918. Imbrie sailed for France and was assigned to the 1st Battalion, 104th Infantry Regiment, where he would serve throughout the war.[39]

At this time, the 102nd Infantry Regiment was also the beneficiary of two chaplains, a Catholic and a Protestant, Chaplains Sherry and Speers, respectively. James Peter Sherry was born in Peabody, Massachusetts, and he attended local schools there. He was a graduate of St. Charles College in Baltimore, Maryland. Sherry was ordained a priest on November 30, 1912, following his graduation from St. John's Seminary in Brighton. The priest served as an assistant, first at St. Patrick's Church in Roxbury, followed by St. Thomas Church in Jamaica Plain, where he was serving at the time of his enlistment. Although his commission as a Chaplain (1st Lt.) dated from January 1918, his overseas service began in March, when he was assigned to the 303rd Stevedore Regiment. Following a brief stay in an Army hospital, he joined the 102nd Infantry Regiment as a chaplain on July 21, 1918.[40] Shortly thereafter, he would be joined by Guthrie Speers.

Thomas Guthrie Speers ("Guthrie") was born in Atlantic Highlands, New Jersey, on August 27, 1890, the second of six sons born to James Milliken Speers and Nellie Carter. The senior Speers had emigrated from Northern Ireland and rose to become a very prosperous merchant. He was also active in the Presbyterian Church, serving, at one time, as President of the Board of Foreign Missions. Guthrie was educated at Princeton University, where he graduated Phi Beta Kappa, and at the Union Theological Seminary. In 1915, Guthrie took a year to travel the world with the Board of Missions, and upon his return and ordination, he worked for a year with Dr. Henry Sloan Coffin at the Madison Avenue Presbyterian Church, and the following year in "Hell's Kitchen" at Christ Church. Later, he became Associate Pastor at the University Place Presbyterian Church, assisting Dr. George Alexander.[41]

When the United States entered the war in Europe, the young minister resigned his pulpit, and he, along with four of his brothers, joined the war effort. Although he described himself as a "semi-pacifist," Speers came to realize that the issue was not all "black and white." Long after the war, Speers told an interviewer, that, in a general sense, "it seemed . . . that the ideals that Woodrow Wilson was holding forth, made it a little more important to go on with his ideals into the war, than to let those ideals be dashed to the ground." Specifically, he and his college roommate wanted to be chaplains because "all the young fellas were going to the war, and we just naturally felt that he felt that we ought to try to be ministers to them. If they were going to be away, and if they were going to be in odd situations, they needed chaplains, and we wanted to be the ones. . . ." Guthrie applied and was commissioned as a Chaplain (1st Lt.) on July 6, 1918, following training at Camp Taylor, Kentucky. Speers was immediately sent to France and assigned to the 102nd Infantry Regiment.[42]

Bishop Brent Giveth and He Taketh Away

As the AEF forces expanded in France, ultimately reaching nearly two million men, there was a need for experienced chaplains to serve the newly arrived divisions. Naturally, the Board of Chaplains at Chaumont looked to the well-established divisions like the 26th to meet this need. In August 1918, Brent sought to reassign Chaplains Petty and Rollins, and to place them at Base Section No. 2 and with the 3rd Division respectively.[43] Anticipating that Major General Edwards, who had been long acquainted with Brent through his activities in the Philippines, would issue a protest, the bishop sought to calm the waters in a diplomatic letter to the sometimes volatile general:

Your Chaplains have developed such gifts that we are looking to them for leadership . . . to take the most responsible positions that we have in the Army . . . I know how hard it is for the men themselves to be taken from their first love and how difficult it is for the Commanding General to have efficient men removed, but it is a compliment to you and to your Division that when responsible positions stand in need of capable men we find them in the 26th Division.[44]

Rollins, who had just returned from a brief assignment in the United States, followed his orders, but he missed his former outfit. While he had been well received by the officers of his new division, he told General Edwards, "it is not home," and "I am counting the days till I may return to the 26th." He added, with emphasis, "anywhere in the 26th."[45] Both men would eventually return to the Yankee Division.

Chapter Five

St. Mihiel and Troyon

St. Mihiel, the Prelude

The Battle of St. Mihiel, which began on September 12, 1918, was the debut of the newly formed American First Army. The focus of the American attack was a roughly triangular pocket, approximately two hundred square miles in area, with its apex at the town of the same name. It was well fortified by the Germans, who had occupied the area since 1914. To date, the French had been unable to dislodge them. An American Army of approximately 500,000 men, together with 110,000 French, would attack simultaneously from two separate sides, converging, and thus hopefully trapping the enemy. For the first time, American tank units would participate on a large scale in the attack. Coincidently, the German High Command had come to realize that the salient was a luxury they could ill afford, and it had ordered the withdrawal of its forces. That process had barely begun when the attack came.[1]

Making its way toward St. Mihiel from the training area at Châtillon-sur-Seine, the Yankee Division travelled by night and hid out in the woods by day so as to avoid the prying eyes of the Germans, particularly their aircraft. The 104th Infantry Regiment paused briefly along the way at the town Guerpont, near Bar-le-Duc, where Chaplain Allen Evans, Jr., conducted an open-air baptismal service. The summer weather quickly gave way to the wet and cold of fall in eastern France. Chaplain Robert Campbell, Jr., now with the 101st Field Artillery Regiment, described the march to the jump-off positions for the St. Mihiel attack: "The rain had been pouring down for about a week and it seemed as if the drive would be impossible. The mud was deep and it was difficult to draw guns through the woods and over the hills. The boys were soaked through on account of the mud and water."[2]

Victory

Heavy rain poured down on man and beast alike. Horses neighed and snorted in their traces, and men quietly cursed, as they stumbled into each other in the dark, occasionally slipping on the muddy ground, while they made their way to the jumping-off places. Brave engineers were already out in the wire creating gaps for the infantry to pour through in the daylight. Still with the 12th Field Artillery Regiment, Anselm Mayotte moved into the sector with the 1st Battalion. On the night of September 11, his unit received orders to move into position for the attack of the St. Mihiel salient, and he described the scene:

> The night was dark and rainy and a chill wind was blowing from the north. All that could be heard was the splash, splash of the horses' feet in the mud. In some places they had mud and water up to their knees. Although I wore a waterproof trench coat, before we reached our destination I was drenched to the skin. My feet were fairly dry, but when I got off my horse I was in mud and water up to my ankles.

In the dark, he had some difficulty finding his dugout; however, if he had any notion of sleep, he was soon disabused of it, for the whole space was already taken up by sleeping men. He could do nothing but wait for the initial artillery preparation.[3]

Then, at precisely 1:00 A.M., and for the next seven hours, the sound of three-thousand artillery pieces firing rent the otherwise still air. At 8:00 A.M., behind a rolling barrage, the Yankee Division, along with the French Second Colonial Division, attacked from the northwestern side of the salient, over high, broken ground. Three hours earlier, the bulk of the American forces, including the 2nd Division, had already begun their attack from the southeast side, over more level, but swampier ground. Anselm Mayotte offered his description of the start of the battle, beginning with the artillery barrage. "It was as if hell had suddenly broken loose upon the earth," he wrote. At the sound of the guns, he went outside, where he observed the sky lit up on all sides, "by bright flashes." It was, he said, "a horribly beautiful sight." Later that morning, after the infantry had gone over to top, Mayotte went to a dressing station, where he assisted with the wounded.[4]

By the second day, it was clear that the Battle of St. Mihiel had been a resounding success by most measures, though by no means as difficult or as costly as contemplated. Casualties in the Yankee Division for the main attack and the mop up were relatively light—479 dead and wounded, mainly in the 103rd and 104th Infantry Regiments.[5]

The high point of the attack occurred during the night of September 12/13, when the 102nd Infantry Regiment made a dramatic, last-minute march across the Heights of the Meuse, under command of the intrepid Colonel Hiram Bearss. He and his Connecticut Yankees handily beat the

1st Division to an early morning rendezvous, the purpose of which was to close the St. Mihiel salient at Vigneulles. During the night march, the soldiers were greeted with an awesome sight as they reached the eastern slope of the Heights. There on the Woëvre Plain below, they could see numerous fires marking all the scattered villages. However, what appeared at first to be the burning of the villages themselves was, for the most part, the retreating Germans burning their stockpiles of ammunition and supplies. Many of those who took part in the night march, as well as others, would comment upon that haunting scene.

One of those men was Chaplain Robert Campbell, Jr., with the 101st Field Artillery, which had followed close on the heels of Colonel Bearss and his men. He, too, told of the wake of destruction left by the retreating enemy all along the Grande Tranchée de Calonne:

> I wish you could have accompanied me and taken a glimpse of the surrounding countryside over which one may look from the plateau taken by the Americans. The march was hard on the horses and they lay all along the road. Many dead Germans, including Austrians, were to be seen on either side of the road. Such a sight has never become common to me, and each new case is just as horrible as the first I looked upon. I only saw one dead American. . . . As the Germans retreated they burned the towns behind them and it was indeed an awful spectacle when darkness came on.

At the same time, the young minister was aware that his absence left his congregation back in Warren without a guiding hand. "I regret that I could not be with you when a number of occasions arose calling for my presence," he confessed, "but you will be pleased to learn that my work here is much appreciated."[6]

Elsewhere on the Battlefield

The task assigned to the 103rd Infantry Regiment was made difficult by the terrain, which was not only hilly, but also littered with old tangles of barbed wire and pitted with old trenches and shell craters. Their mission was to drive the Germans off of the Heights of the Meuse and to seize the towns of Billy-sur-les-Côtes and Vieville-sur-les-Côtes at the eastern base of the escarpment. Both towns were major supply hubs for the enemy, which attempted to destroy its storehouses there as it retreated across the Woëvre Plain toward Metz. Ray Anderson, 2nd Battalion chaplain in the 103rd Infantry Regiment, who accompanied the troops as they pressed the attack forward on September 12, wrote that at noon the following day, he "stood on a high hill and watched the Hun retreat back toward Germany across a plain of 18 miles burning 7 villages as he went," adding that, "it is a sign of what is coming."[7]

As the regiment moved down from the Heights to occupy the towns, which were virtually destroyed, the Yankees found, much to their delight, that in addition to weapons and other matériel, the Germans had failed to destroy a substantial amount of stores. It was a windfall for the tired men as they discovered canned food, kegs of beer, and other luxury items in abundance. The chaplain described the scene:

> I wish you could have seen the boys as they entered these German towns full of German supplies and provisions. They were hungry and tired and cold and it didn't take them long to fill up on German food. Even Ray enjoyed the largesse. He sent a box of German cigars to his father as a souvenir that he had "rescued from a burning village." "I don't suppose they will be very good smoking," he warned his father, "but they will no doubt prove interesting to you and your friends."

All was not fun, as two weeks later, the chaplain "hiked a long way . . . through rain and mud to bury a boy who was killed . . . by a shell."[8]

The men of the Company G, 2nd Battalion, 104th Infantry had hardly caught their breath when they were ordered to send out a patrol to take and hold St. Hilaire and Waddonville out on the Woëvre Plain. As usual, Chaplain de Valles accompanied the leading file of men; however, he was clearly showing the effects of ill health. His assistant observed that "he still had spirit [but] he looked very tired, his face was thin, with a sallow complexion." He was continuing under a doctor's care, and should not have gone, but as with all of the Yankee chaplains, he felt that, as long as he could muster the strength, his place was with "his boys." Arriving just after midnight, the small force, finding no enemy there, bedded down for the night. The morning was a different story. Just as the men had started breakfast, they were attacked by a strong force of about two hundred. After a sharp, one-hour fight, the enemy was driven away, leaving behind dead and wounded, along with several prisoners. The chaplain had a close call when a German soldier was shot and killed just as he was about to toss a grenade into the dugout occupied by the priest. The men were ordered to withdraw from St. Hilaire, as the position was too exposed. The Germans returned in even greater force and reoccupied it later that day. De Valles returned from the patrol "sick and exhausted."[9]

"Outward Bums and Inward Saints"

Following the victory at St. Mihiel, the Yankee Division settled in on the Heights of the Meuse with some units occupying the small villages at the immediate base; many men made good use of the huts and dugouts formerly used by the enemy. While some of these places may have been "luxurious" by doughboy standards, many were infested with fleas, lice, and other vermin. In a letter to his wife, Lt. Col. Horace P. Hobbs, the Division Inspector General, offered an assessment of the battle just ended. "We have driven the enemy from all the high ground on this side of the salient," he exulted. He then continued, describing the view: "There is low flat marshy country which he [the Boche] can live and is entirely commanded by our artillery. The enemy can only beat it for Metz and that is what he is doing, all who have escaped."[10]

Hobbs's assessment was only partly accurate. True, the panoramic view east from the Heights took in the large Woëvre Plain, an area dotted with small villages connected by poor roads, all interlaced with streams and swampy patches. However, it was also a critically important area for the Germans, as it served as a buffer between the Allied forces and Metz. True, also, American artillery had the ability to cover quite a lot of the plain below, but that was true as well for the Germans, who now were able to fire back on their former positions. Moreover, for the next several weeks, patrols and raiding parties from each side, seeking intelligence and prisoners, briefly occupied and then abandoned or were driven from these villages. One such village was St. Hilaire.[11]

On the night of September 17/18, following some artillery preparation, a patrol from the 2nd Battalion, 102nd Infantry conducted a small raid on the town of St. Hilaire, then occupied by the Germans. Chaplain James Sherry accompanied the force. As they approached the village, the chaplain boosted another soldier up a tree to see if he could locate the positions of the machine gun and artillery piece that were firing on the party. Although the raid was not deemed a total success, since no prisoners were taken, Sherry and several others were later commended in the General Orders for their bravery "in the face of intense artillery and machine gun fire." The commendation went on to state that, "these troops caused much havoc and execution among the enemy, forcing him to evacuate the town." The brigade commander, Brig. Gen. George H. Shelton, referred to the "spirit and dash" shown by the participants.[12]

For some men, the time spent in the Troyon Sector was a period of reflection. Ray Anderson was now living in an abandoned German dugout (or mine, as he called it), forty feet underground and therefore safe and sound, "for there are no shells large enough to bother" him. In a letter home to the Rev. John Timothy Stone, his former mentor at the Fourth Presbyterian Church in Chicago, he told of his newfound appreciation for the men that he soldiered with: "I wish you could know my men; they are outward 'bums,' and inward saints and all heroes. I never knew God made such wonderful fellows before. . . . I understand a lot more myself since all this happened." He added, no doubt with a humorous touch, that he was going to a nearby dugout, where many of his men lived, to preach a sermon, "within sight and shooting of the Germans," and it will be "the deepest sermon I ever preached!" Anderson confessed to Dr. Stone that "my task isn't easy, but I love it." To his father he wrote: "We are being careful as can be, only we are doing our bit for God and country and you. I would rather be killed doing this than die a man who had been disloyal."[13] The words may have explained his motives, but they surely missed the mark if they were intended to allay any parental concerns.

During the division's stay in the Troyon Sector following St. Mihiel, a small incident seriously tested cordial Franco-American relations when Doc Hesselgrave located an abandoned German piano near the town of Deuxnouds-aux-Bois. The enterprising "Y" man quickly secured a truck and the help of a number of doughboys from the 101st Machine Gun Battalion to load it. He was excited by the find, as he knew it would make a great addition to the Y hut. Unfortunately, just as the Yankees were hoisting the piano onto the truck, a large group of *poilu* happened on the scene, saw what was happening, and insisted that the instrument was by rights theirs. What followed in short order was a heated exchange beside the vehicle. Shouts and imprecations in both French and English filled the air, culminating with a threat by the angry Frenchmen to shoot the unarmed Yanks. Ultimately, discretion yielded to greater numbers. The doughboys relented, and our Allies made off with the piano. Hesselgrave succinctly described the incident: "Our boys had the piano almost loaded on the truck before they were discovered by the French, who claimed the trophy, and threatened to shoot if the instrument were not returned. Overpowering numbers and the French language defeated our well-intentioned efforts."[14]

Marchéville–Riaville Raid—A Diversion

The major American effort in the Meuse-Argonne was scheduled to commence on September 26, 1918, and the Yankee Division would not be used as one of the leading divisions in the main attack. Rather, it was chosen to stage a large diversionary raid on the towns of Marchéville and Riaville, both well out on the Woëvre Plain. The idea was to convince the German high command that the real object of the Allied attack was a drive toward Metz. If successful, the raid would force the Germans to keep a number of its divisions facing the Yankees and not the attack west of the Meuse. Two battalions of infantry, drawn one each from the 102nd and 103rd Infantry Regiments, along with selected men from the 101st Engineers and other support troops, would once again serve under the overall command of Col. Hiram Bearss, the no-nonsense Marine who had taken command of the 102nd Infantry at the start of the St. Mihiel attack. In support of the raid, several field artillery units were moved to the eastern base of the Heights of the Meuse.[15]

During the initial stages of the attack, the swampy ground was covered by a thick fog as Bearss's force made its way toward the twin objectives. The fog provided good cover, but at the same time caused many to lose their sense of direction. Obstacles presented themselves early on, principally the Longeau River, swollen from recent rains. It had to be crossed, and the engineers had brought along some logs to span the stream. Impatient to move forward, and not wanting to fall victim to the machine gun fire spraying the advance, many Yankees, weighted down with their equipment, plunged right into the cold, waist-deep water and crossed to the other side.[16] Resistance stiffened, particularly on the left, as the men worked their way closer to the twin towns.

Major Roy Hanson and the 1st Battalion, 103rd Infantry came within sight of Riaville, but despite a valiant attempt, they were unable to force their way into the town. There were simply too many machine guns in concrete emplacements, and Hanson was unable to obtain sufficient effective fire from the Yankee batteries. Major Hanson ordered his men back to a nearby trench while he sought some artillery support. He commenced a second futile attack, again stymied due to ineffective artillery support against the machine guns and mortars. On the other hand, Bearss and his battalion drove the enemy from Marchéville in tough, house-to-house fighting and established positions on the other side of the town. From his command post in a building within the town, Bearss directed the fight for the balance of the day, bombarded by heavy artillery fire and fending off repeated counterattacks by nearby troops as well as a large German force which had approached Marchéville from St. Hilaire (at that time back under enemy control). Ultimately this force, and the supporting artillery fire, proved to be too strong for the smaller Yankee one, which began to incur serious casualties.[17]

Toward evening, Bearss recognized the gravity of his situation as his command post was nearly surrounded. Earlier, he had given orders for some of his force to withdraw behind a stone wall and trench near a château at the southern edge of town. It was at this time that the engineers

Chaplain Thomas Guthrie Speers, Sr. Reprinted from the *New York Sun*, December 29, 1918. Courtesy of Thomas Guthrie Speers III.

became infantry as they were ordered to help hold that position. During the early evening, with the approval of Division Headquarters, Bearss gave the order to conduct a fighting withdrawal. All the way back to the starting point, Hanson, Bearss, and their men withdrew in leapfrog fashion, carrying most of their wounded as the Boche artillery fire intensified and the Yankee gunners responded in kind. Colonel Bearss asked a valiant Company A from the 102nd Machine Gun Battalion to be the rear guard. That unit alone suffered thirty percent of the casualties, including five dead, seventeen wounded, and another four missing, presumed captured.[18]

Guthrie Speers had elected to accompany the forward elements of the attacking force into Marchéville and to remain with it throughout the entire engagement, including the withdrawal under fire, where he carried a wounded officer to safety. Years later, Speers recalled the incident:

> Just as we were leaving [Marchéville], a young officer was shot in the leg and now couldn't move, so I picked him up and carried him with the fireman's carry.... We started down an old trench and finally came out into the open, still under fire, but whenever we could, we got down behind something. You'd be surprised what seemed to be a protection. By and by, I found four or five fellas from our outfit who were also going back, and they picked up some of the boards that were put in the bottom of trenches to avoid the mud and made a kind of a stretcher out of it and they carried this fella from then on to the First Aid Station....

Capt. Joseph H. Dunn was in charge of the aid station. Ignoring a direct order to withdraw, Dr. Dunn and his two assistants, Capt. Reuben G. Hamilton and Lt. Henry Christianson, remained on duty, treating and evacuating the wounded while under intense artillery fire until a new station could be established further to the rear.[19]

When it was all over, Guthrie and another soldier, an ambulance sergeant, sat side by side in a trench, exhausted, shells still flying overhead, casually eating some biscuits. Both young men were tired and dirty, and their hands were covered with dried blood from their recent efforts helping with the wounded, none of which served to curb their appetites. The other soldier turned to Guthrie, and he poked a little fun at the chaplain: "What would your mother say if she saw you eating a biscuit with your hands like that?" He added, no doubt harking back to his own childhood: "When you were a kid did your mother use to spit on her handkerchief and wipe some stain off your face?" Guthrie started to answer, but stopped short, and both men had a good laugh, which served to relieve the tension.[20]

For his efforts, Speers was awarded the Distinguished Service Cross. His citation read in part: "He was continually aiding and cheering the wounded and particularly distinguished himself by carrying a wounded officer to a dressing station through heavy artillery and machine gun barrage." He would also be awarded the Croix de Guerre with Palm. In the aftermath, Chaplain H. Boyd Edwards led a burial detail.[21]

More New Blood

The push to get more chaplains to France was steady, especially for those who could speak French. The bishop of Burlington asked for volunteers, and Arthur Joseph LeVeer answered the call. LeVeer was born in Bloomfield, Vermont, on February 3, 1886. He was the son of Peter LeVeer, a railroad section boss, and Mathilda Gagné, both of whom had emigrated from Canada. He was one of eleven children, eight of whom survived infancy. After attending local schools and college in Canada, LeVeer enrolled at St. Mary's Seminary in Baltimore. Following his ordination in June 1915, he served the Diocese of Burlington as an assistant at *Notre Dame des Victoires* in St. Johnsbury.[22]

In July of 1918, LeVeer received a call from the Bishop of Burlington, who asked if he would be willing to serve as an Army chaplain. He answered affirmatively, and following a brief application and selection process, he was commissioned as a Chaplain (1st Lt.) on August 7, 1918. He sailed for Liverpool, England, from New York aboard the S.S. *Megantic* on September 8. Three weeks later, after presenting himself at AEF Headquar-

Chaplain Arthur J. LeVeer. Courtesy of the Diocese of Burlington.

ters in Chaumont, he attended a three-day chaplain's school in a château in nearby Neuilly-sur-Suise and awaited his assignment. That was not long in coming. On September 29, he was ordered to report directly to General Edwards's headquarters, where he was assigned to the 102nd Machine Gun Battalion. He reached battalion headquarters at Longeau Farm on the evening of October 2, where he soon got his "first taste of life in European mud under shell fire."[23]

The 101st Machine Gun Battalion diary entry for September 22, noted the addition of Earl R. Taggart as chaplain. Taggart spent his early years in Bethany, Missouri, and in Independence, Kansas. He came east in 1908, where he was employed by the War Department in Washington, D.C., as a stenographer. At the same time, he attended George Washington University from which he graduated in 1917. Taggart was ordained that same year as a minister of the Disciples of Christ at the National City Christian Church. Earl enlisted in the Army on June 15, 1918, and he was promptly sent to Chaplain School at Camp Taylor. Upon graduation, Taggart was commissioned as a Chaplain (1st Lt.) and sent to France, arriving there on September 2. He reported to Chaumont and was soon assigned to the 101st Machine Gun Battalion. On October 15, shortly after Taggart's assignment, Doc Hesselgrave left his duties with the battalion and reported to Y Headquarters in Verdun, where he would become Divisional Secretary. There, he assumed responsibility for all Y activity in the division sector.[24]

Meanwhile, in October, the Chaplain School moved to bigger quarters near Tours, at the Château d'Aux at Louplande.[25]

Chapter Six

Verdun

It was early October, and the Yankee Division, now relieved by elements of the 79th Division and the 2nd Dismounted Cavalry (French) Division, gathered itself together and made its way slowly, wearily to a new sector. The experience of the 102nd Machine Gun Battalion was typical. On October 4, after being relieved at Longeau Farm, the unit withdrew to Troyon, where they remained several days. The machine gunners started north again on October 8 to Casernes de Bevaux, a cluster of French barracks just outside Verdun. There, in the words of Chaplain Arthur LeVeer, "for the first time I got in touch with the spiritual side of my battalion of 800 men." He said Mass and heard confessions of men both from his battalion, as well as those from the 101st Machine Gun Battalion, which did not have a Catholic chaplain. After several more days, the unit moved on to Samogneux and more fighting. There, LeVeer helped with the wounded at a nearby dressing station.[1]

Chaplain Robert Campbell of the 101st Field Artillery told of his journey north to Verdun:

> We did not come by trains, but by long night marches. One night we covered over 18 miles. The whole regiment stretches out over two miles. It causes an awful rattle with a dull echo as the guns, wagons, horses' hoofs, and groups of men move over the road. The nights are pitch dark and cold. The sky is illuminated constantly by the flashes of guns which thunder away incessantly.

In spite of the dangers from occasional shelling and fragments of anti-aircraft shells sprinkling down upon the column, Campbell found the night marches "extremely fascinating."[2]

Neptune Sector

Even when the shells were not flying, a World War I battlefield was a dangerous place, littered with booby traps and unexploded ordnance. In addition to the rusting barbed wire, unburied or partially buried bodies, and the sucking mud, there were shell holes full of slimy, stagnant water, and all was overlain with persistent, toxic mustard gas. Whether you carried a weapon or a litter, if you touched it or inhaled it, either way, you suffered its effects. It simply could not be helped. The Heights of the Meuse, east of the river and north of Verdun, had been fought over virtually from the beginning of the war. The Germans and the French suffered nearly three-quarters of a million casualties in one six-month period alone, from February through September 1916. This critical ground was likened to a hinge that the Germans were determined to hold, and where the Allies needed to dislodge them in order to protect the flank of the American advance to the west of the Meuse.[3]

There were few trees still standing. Forests, so-called, were, for the most part, merely reference points on a map. It was difficult to get one's bearings with so few landmarks, as the respective trench systems zigged and zagged, nearly touching at some points. Besides the littered ground, there was a stench in the air of cordite, gas, and death. The last was present everywhere, with bones and body parts lying on or just below the surface, putrefying. The doughboys found shelter in dugouts previously occupied by French and German soldiers, or in shell holes and shallow trenches and hastily dug foxholes, with a poncho pulled over them for a cover.[4]

That was the scene on the ground when the Yankee Division made its way to what was referred to as the Neptune Sector in early October 1918. The scene on the ground was coupled with rain and cold, all compounded by the raging influenza epidemic. The division was under-strength to begin with, especially in the 101st and 102nd Infantry Regiments. It was a critical sector for Pershing's attack proper in the Meuse-Argonne, which began well on September 26, but frustratingly bogged down by the time the Yankees had reached the fight two weeks later. Once settled in the sector, the Yankee Division joined the French II Colonial Division, old friends from St. Mihiel, as well as the American 29th and 33rd Divisions, already there and finding the going very tough.[5] The sector was important, since it kept the Germans, who were well entrenched on the ridge, from firing on the flank of the main American attack. All the Yankees knew was that their final battle would be "uphill" in more ways than one.

General Edwards established his forward headquarters in a dugout at Bras-sur-Meuse, as did the 101st Field Signal Battalion as well as the chaplains for the 101st Engineers. Shelling by the Germans was regular and fairly accurate. On October 19, Chaplain H. Boyd Edwards had a close call when a shell landed just outside his dugout, wounding two passing orderlies, but, luckily, leaving the chaplain unharmed.[6]

The preparations for the upcoming battle were massive and very evident to the artillerymen as they reached their destination. Robert Campbell told of "hundreds of big guns, stacks of ammunition, thousands of men and horses [and] all along the hills, wagons and equipment." He went on:

> The roads are literally blocked with traffic moving both ways in solid lines. It is hard on the horses which lie all along either side of the roadway where they have dropped dead or incapacitated so that it is necessary to shoot them. In one spot alone I saw six. These horses are rolled into shell holes and covered over.[7]

The 103rd Infantry arrived in the new sector tired and under-strength. "The men are tired and worn out with constant fighting," Ray Anderson told his father, "but we still have a few good licks in us and will deliver them. . . ." He was proud of his division, and more so of his regiment, which he called "one of the finest in the American army." He, too, was tired of the fighting and looked forward to peace. Chaplain or not, Ray's blood was up. He wrote: "My what a wonderful day when all this mad war will be over, and yet as much as I want peace, I do not want it until this hellish gang that has caused it shall have been brought to see the awfulness of it all."[8]

On October 14, shortly after the 104th Infantry Regiment arrived in the sector, it was ordered to conduct what amounted to a futile and costly attack in the Bois de Haumont. The French tanks slated to assist in the attack never materialized, and the results were predictable. It was at this time that Chaplain de Valles confessed to his assistant, Connell Albertine, that he had been having some health issues and had been advised to report to one of the division hospitals for treatment. "If I don't get any relief from this medicine I am taking, I will go," he told him, "but I want to stay with the boys as long as I can." With the orders for the regiment to move forward, Fr. de Valles simply put his own health concerns on hold and stayed. "The boys always felt quite safe as long as Father de Valles was near," declared Albertine. "He was certainly a great inspiration to all of them."[9]

One of the duties of a chaplain was to conduct religious services, often under very difficult circumstances. Like all chaplains, Guthrie Speers felt it was too dangerous to gather a large body of men together at any one time, so smaller services were in order. The biggest job he found was meeting with the individual soldiers, person to person. "Getting to know them," he recalled, "making them feel that somebody cared; getting in touch with their particular needs or any family situations that you could help in." That's what made his job, in his words, "wonderful."[10]

The Last Rose of Summer

As the division settled into the new sector, there were the inevitable changes. On October 13, 1918, Chaplain Farrell was transferred from the 103rd Field Artillery to the 104th Infantry. He was assigned to the 2nd Battalion, perhaps in light of Chaplain de Valles's deteriorating health. Billy Farrell was much beloved and sorely missed by the gunners, so his replacement had some big shoes to fill. By some accounts, some of the men in the 103rd Field Artillery treated the new chaplain as an interloper. That man was Father John Francis Tucker from Wilmington, Delaware. As a young man, he stopped using his first name, preferring instead to use "Francis," or the more formal, "J. Francis." At the time of his appointment as Chaplain (1st Lt.), effective September 10, 1918, he had been teaching at the Salesianum School in Wilmington. The newly appointed chaplain was a member of the Oblates of St. Francis de Sales. He was born in Wilmington on January 8, 1889, the son of William and Mary Tucker. Following studies in the United States and in Rome, he was ordained on October 11, 1911. Tucker was of medium height and build, and by all accounts took to his job with a lot of energy and worked hard to overcome any residual resentment in the outfit. Fellow chaplain and friend Malcolm E. Peabody described him as "a hustler and . . . a first class padre."[11]

Chaplain John Francis Tucker. Courtesy of the Oblates of St. Francis de Sales.

Chaplain Tucker sailed for France as a casual, aboard the *City of York*, along with the 127th Field Artillery Regiment (34th Division), and he arrived during the first week of October. Though the voyage was rough at times, he was a constant inspiration to the men. He was not an officer to "impress his importance" on the soldiers, and one of them told him later that "to find an officer who still remained a man was a wonderful thing." During one large Atlantic storm, as the vessel was being tossed about, Tucker calmly said Mass surrounded by kneeling men. He heard the men's confessions in his cabin and quieted their fears with his teasing. "We were always at home" there, recalled one man. He took his turn standing watch along with the other artillerymen on the "cold, slippery deck." Much later, near Verdun, during an attack, one man recalled seeing the priest standing on a slight rise above Battery D, 103rd Field Artillery, one minute shouting encouragement to the gunners, the next, waving an empty bottle and singing "The Last Rose of Summer."[12]

Sharing the Hardships and Dangers

By late October, the Yankee Division was fairly used up. It was badly in need of replacements and short on rations. Of more importance, the under-strength 101st and 102nd Infantry Regiments conducted a concerted attack on the Heights of the Meuse above Verdun, where the battle ebbed and flowed from October 23 through 28. Once again, Lyman Rollins had accompanied "his boys" in the attack that first day on Le Houppy Bois and the ridge known a Belleu Bois, and once again, he had been gassed. The chaplain was evacuated by ambulance along with Johnny Evers from Troy, New York. Evers was part of the famed Chicago Cubs infield that will always be associated with the phrase, "Tinkers to Evers to Chance." Evers was then serving in France with the Knights of Columbus. Later on, at home, he would tell the story about how, as the ambulance made its way to the aid station, Chaplain Rollins ripped the field medical card off of his person, jumped out of the vehicle, and beat it back to the regiment.[13]

The 101st Infantry finally achieved its objective after four brutal days of seesaw battle, while the largely Connecticut 102nd Infantry had a much tougher time; it was only partially successful in its attack on Hill 360 and in the nearby Bois d'Ormont. The former was a veritable bastion, bristling with upwards of twenty-five machine gun nests. The defenders could not be dislodged, despite costly, repeated attempts, even with assistance from the 104th Infantry on Sunday, October 27. In the aftermath of the attack, Chaplain de Valles, now in obvious pain, was out among the wounded and dying administering the Last Rites.[14]

Supporting the 101st Infantry in its effort was the 101st Machine Gun

Battalion. One of the casualties during the intense fighting on October 23 was Corporal Lawrence Crothers ("Red") Yerges of Company B. The young man, who was a department superintendant at American Hosiery Company in New Britain, had enlisted in August 1917. Yerges was popular with both his comrades in Company B and his classmates at Ohio State University, from which he graduated in 1915. While his company was supporting the advance of the 101st Infantry, from a position near the crest of a hill in Brabant Woods, it was subjected to heavy shell fire, and he was seriously wounded and later died at an evacuation hospital at Glorieux. Chaplain Earl Taggart, newly arrived at the 101st Machine Gun Battalion, took on one of a chaplain's chief duties—offering a measure of comfort to Yerges's bereaved family in Columbus, Ohio. "I visited his grave at Glorieux," Taggart wrote, "and can assure you that it is beautifully located and well-marked and will receive the best of care."[15]

Also in support of the 101st Infantry was the 101st Field Artillery Regiment.[16] At the start of the big attack, Chaplain Campbell made his way to the 2nd Battalion, 101st Field Artillery batteries to, in his word, "give a little courage and strength to the boys." He reasoned: "A minister in times of peace often questions whether or not his presence is really desired . . . but there is no doubt about it when he carries a smile to a place of peril in the hour of trial." On the night before, after "many days of rain, mud, and cold, penetrating air," the sky had glowed "blood red," which the chaplain took to be a sign. At daybreak, he was at a battery, ears stuffed with cotton, in anticipation of the coming artillery barrage. After the attack commenced, he went from gun to gun, loading the shells and pulling the lanyard. He was, he wrote later, "anxious to prove that he was willing to put his hand where he had put his heart, as much as he disliked to." The chaplain reasoned that the killing was necessary and justified, even calling to mind the Gospel parable of the thief in the night. Moreover, who, he asked, "will refuse to share the dangers and hardships and fire the guns with the boys?"

As the battle intensified, he wrote, "the shells came thicker, faster, and nearer, mingled with gas," and the men had to don their gas masks. The German gunners zeroed in on the battery and destroyed one of its guns. At that point, Campbell and two other men, one of whom was Capt. Charles S. Weeks, the son of Senator John Weeks, ran to a shallow trench, pulled a tarp over their heads to protect from fragments, and waited for the barrage to cease. It did, but only for a short while, and as it resumed, the whole "scene," he said was "indescribable."[17]

That day, the Germans supported their tenacious defense with a fierce, prolonged artillery bombardment, which included both gas and high explosives, lasting nearly a full day, and raining down upon the entire division front. Hunkered down with nearly two hundred men in a dugout that served as headquarters for the 2nd Battalion, 103rd Infantry, was Chaplain Ray Anderson, who described the "most awful day I ever lived." The shelling began at about 10:00 A.M. and increased in intensity throughout the day and continued all night, when sometime during the following morning, a large shell penetrated the shelter. Had the shelling not stopped shortly thereafter, Ray told his father, "I would have gone stark raving mad." He went on to describe the experience: "Something seemed to be almost breaking in the back of my head. Well, a lot of gas had come into the dugout and by Monday night some of the men were blind." Somehow, up to that point Ray had avoided the effects of the mustard gas, so he left the dugout to see if it was safe for the rest of the men to venture out. It was then that he was exposed to the full effects of the gas. He continued: "My eyes were slower in swelling, but Monday night I couldn't lie down, and I just about went wild and more from the mustard gas in my eyes. It was just like two red hot stove pokers being pushed into your brain." The following day, Anderson attended to some burials, and "after I had stood the blooming stuff in my eyes about as long as I could," he wrote, "I went back and spent the next ten days in the field hospital getting gas out of my eyes and throat."[18]

Through it all, the Yankee Division chaplains continued their sometimes grim tasks. On October 26, in the midst of the great fight, Father Peter Sherry led a burial detail in the Bois d'Ormont, as did Chaplain John H. Creighton three days later, both of them finding and reverently interring the dead of the 102nd Infantry.[19]

Chaplain John H. Creighton near Verdun, October 18, 1918. Reprinted from George and Cooper, *Pictorial History of the 26th Division*.

In at the Death

For some men, just being in France was not enough; they itched to get into the fight. John Joseph Mitty was born in Greenwich Village, New York, to Irish immigrants on January 20, 1884. His mother died when he was ten years old, followed by his father four years later. Mitty and his brothers were raised, first by an aunt, and later by foster parents. An excellent student, he attended Manhattan College for one year prior to entering St. Joseph's Seminary ("Dunwoodie") in Yonkers, New York. He was ordained in December 1906, and following ordination, he continued his studies at Catholic University and in Rome. After a short stint as a parish priest, he was assigned to teach at St. Joseph's Seminary, where he met another future chaplain, Father Francis Duffy, who taught philosophy there. At the outbreak of World War I, Mitty volunteered to serve as a chaplain.[20]

Mitty was sponsored by the Knights of Columbus and received his commission as a Chaplain (1st Lt.) in August 1917. He was initially assigned to the 49th Infantry Regiment. Mitty served with that regiment in Newport News, Virginia, and at Camp Merritt, New Jersey, before sailing for France on July 18, 1918. However, as the war was winding down by that time, it was unlikely that his regiment would see any action at the front. Fr. Mitty pleaded to be assigned to a fighting division, and, in answer to his prayer, he was sent to the 26th Division on October 28, 1918, just in time for the final push in the Meuse-Argonne. There he became a chaplain in the 101st Infantry Regiment, which was, in his words, "Irish and Catholic." He was pleased with his assignment, telling a friend:

> I joined them up at the Front, and was with them long enough to get a taste and a realization of actual warfare. Believe me, it is hell. I saw only a little, but that made me thank God with a full heart that peace had come, and my hat goes off to the men who have stood the gaff through it all. Our infantry boys are wonders and the artillerymen hand it to the dough-boys every time.[21]

Another later arrival to the Yankee Division was Malcolm Endicott Peabody. His past year as an "acting chaplain" with the Red Cross had left him with a sense that he needed to do something more. In September 1918, he applied for a chaplaincy in the United States Army, and on October 18 he was commissioned as a Chaplain (1st Lt.) and assigned to the 102nd Field Artillery Regiment in the Yankee Division. There he would replace Chaplain Markham Stackpole, who had been temporarily assigned that month, first to Base Section No. 1, and later the following month to Base Section No. 6. Peabody would serve as a chaplain of the 102nd Field Artillery for the balance of the war.[22]

Years later, as he recalled those final days of the war, Peabody wrote that as Chaplain of that unit,

> I bloomed by reason of the sense of being needed, and working in a job with which I had some familiarity. I joined the Regiment outside of Verdun, and found that to be under the bombs joined men together in a very powerful way, in this cockpit of the War which swallowed up untold numbers of troops. It was indeed a privilege to be "in at the death" as a real member of the fellowship of the committed.[23]

Sacrifice Knows No Rank

October was a difficult month for the Yankee Division in more ways than one. Even the commanding general was not immune from loss, and the war exacted a stiff price from General Edwards. It was Father Mike who wrote a letter of condolence to Edwards upon learning about the death of his daughter, an Army nurse in training at Camp Meade, and his only child. Young Bessie undoubtedly contracted influenza, and she had died from the pneumonia that accompanied it. The general's wife had attempted to cable her husband with the sad news, but the message could not be delivered. Some of Edwards's officers had seen a news dispatch and told him. Chaplain O'Connor expressed the sorrow of the entire division when he wrote:

> I know that a heart like yours, which has caused you to show such sympathy for afflicted parents and wounded soldiers, must feel deeply the grief that has come to you. Were it possible for the officers and men under your command to lighten this burden, every man of them would feel it an honor if his life could restore hers to you. But we are powerless; yet if there be consolation in knowing that there are thirty thousand hearts which desire to lessen your sorrow, the Twenty-sixth Division grieves with you.[24]

Bishop Brent was also quick to offer his prayers and condolences, and he consoled Edwards with the thought that: "You must think of your bonny daughter as still being all that she was when you last saw her. Her loyal, loving nature has not been harmed by death; on the contrary, it has been heightened, and when the time comes for you and her to meet in the other world, the unit that you had on earth will continue."[25]

To add insult to injury, within days of his personal loss, Edwards also received word that he had been relieved of his command by General Pershing, just weeks before the end of the war. Pershing, who had an intense dislike of Edwards, had long sought his relief, and he had even started to do so that previous July. He thought better of it then, perhaps because Edwards still had many powerful friends in Washington, in addition to the universal love and respect of his officers and men. So, Pershing bided his time, and using his loyal staff, made life difficult for Edwards. Not that Edwards was without his faults. On the contrary, he was opinionated, often critical of fellow officers, including his superiors, and sometimes ignored his orders. Yet, his division was performing well, and there was no excuse for Pershing's vindictive action at that stage of the war. As a result, division morale plummeted. Long after the war, Yankee Division veterans harbored resentment toward Pershing.[26]

Influenza

Just as deadly and effective was the influenza epidemic that raged throughout all the armies on the western front. Dirty, exhausted, and hungry, the men of the Yankee Division had to contend with the nearly constant cold and damp weather that had settled in, which left them vulnerable to influenza. They succumbed in droves, and the chaplains were no exception. Shortly after the first of November, Chaplain LeVeer began to feel "somewhat played out," and by November 6, he was taken to a field hospital with a 103 degree fever, and where, in his words, "I came very near cashing in." LeVeer was evacuated to the rear, and he gradually recovered. In the end, disease, mostly influenza, accounted for as many deaths as those resulting from the lethal weaponry.[27]

By early November, Chaplain O'Connor, along with several regimental chaplains, and the Division Surgeon, reported to Colonel Horace P. Hobbs, then Division Inspector General, that the men of the 101st and 102nd Infantry Regiments were "mentally and physically exhausted." Hobbs issued a report that the regiments were worn out and in a state of near panic. The findings of the report were found to be "greatly exaggerated," and worse, it triggered a sharp exchange between Hobbs and Brigadier General George H. Shelton that ultimately resulted in the latter's relief. Lack of replacements, as well as influenza and bronchitis, were large factors in the state of the troops. Moreover, once supplied, the restorative power of hot food and baths, which had been sadly lacking, was soon evident throughout the division.[28]

Distinguished Alumnus

The war continued to grind on, despite rumors of its impending end. On the night of November 7, 1918, the 313th Infantry ("Baltimore's Own"), 79th Division, was ordered forward once more in an attempt to force the Germans back off the high ground that they had long occupied east of the Meuse. The division, then relatively untested, had seen hard fighting at Montfaucon at the start of the Meuse-Argonne offensive. Now it was joined with the 26th Division as part of the French XVIIth Corps. Chaplain George Jonaitis had been transferred to the 79th Division from the Yankee Division just after St. Mihiel. On the eve of the big attack, he had heard eight hundred confessions of the Marylanders he served, and now nearly two months later, he was just as much a part of the 79th as he was of the 26th.[29]

Jonaitis had itched to get into the fight and now, on November 7, he was still in the thick of it. Jonaitis advanced with the men of his battalion that night. He was known as the "Smiling Chaplain," and he had made it a point to talk with the soldiers, sleep where they slept, and eat what they ate. Jonaitis shared all of their terrors and privations, and he had come through the fighting at the Aisne-Marne and St. Mihiel without injury. However, his luck ran out near Verdun that November night, just days before the Armistice, when he was struck by a shell fragment in his right arm. Jonaitis refused evacuation and remained on the line. The untreated wound became badly infected, and the priest lost the full use of his arm for the balance of his long life.[30]

Last Rites

On November 3, 1918, Chaplain Connor bid farewell to the Yankee Division when he assumed the job of Chief Chaplain of the 32nd Division. Shortly thereafter, he would be appointed as the Chief Chaplain of the Third Army Corps (1st, 2nd, and 32nd Divisions). After the Armistice he served in the Army of Occupation. His place with the 101st Train and Military Police was taken by Thomas F. Temple of New York. Fr. Temple was born in Ireland at Shannon Harbor, County Offaly, on August 26, 1890. As a young man, he immigrated to the United States, where he began studies for the priesthood at St. Joseph's Seminary, Dunwoodie in the Bronx. Temple was ordained at St. Patrick's Cathedral on June 4, 1914, and assigned as curate at Saint Peter's Church in Manhattan. In August 1918, he joined the Army and spent five weeks in training at Camp Taylor. At the end of the course, he received his commission as a Chaplain (1st Lt.), and he sailed for France on October 16.[31]

After spending a couple of days at the nearby aid station close to his battalion, Ray Anderson was transferred to the 101st Field Hospital at Vacherauville. He was grateful to the doctors there, who decided not to send him further to the rear, which would likely have taken him away from the Yankee Division. Understandably, the chaplain wanted to be back with his own outfit, and on November 8, like Chaplain Rollins, he took matters into his own hands when he "slipped away from the hospital one morning before the doctors came around." Anderson was back with his battalion that same day, literally hours before they went into action for the final push.[32]

Rumors of an end to hostilities circulated throughout the division, yet men continued to die. On November 9, at Ville-devant-Chaumont in the Neptune Sector, while attached to the 104th Infantry Regiment, Chaplain Farrell learned that one of the men had been seriously wounded. Dodging artillery shells and fierce machine gun fire, the chaplain made his way to the dying man, alternately crawling and running from shell hole to shell hole. Farrell reached the soldier, administered the Last Rites, and remained with him until the soldier had "gone west." For his conspicuous bravery, both at Seicheprey and at Verdun, the army awarded him the Distinguished Service Cross.[33]

The following day, a German plane dropped several bombs on the 101st Machine Gun Battalion area, doing only minimal damage, but occasioning several close calls, including the one that "landed near the infirmary and blew in all the canvas windows in the Chaplain's shack." Luckily, Earl Taggart was unhurt.[34]

On October 30, the 79th Division moved into the sector as the Yankee Division slipped to the right just north and northeast of the Bois des Caures and continued its attacks. Sometime after he had learned of the new division's arrival, Chaplain Evans went over to visit with his brother, only to find that he had been "horribly burned" by poison gas during a recent attack.[35]

Armistice

Monday, November 11, 1918, dawned like any other day on the western front, with one exception—virtually everyone knew that a cease fire would go into effect at 11:00 A.M. Yet, incredibly, men were ordered forward, some to their deaths. Chaplain de Valles accompanied his 2nd Battalion, 104th Infantry through a German barrage. He administered the Last Rites to a dying soldier, and with the help of some of the men, he scratched a shallow grave for him a short while later. De Valles, who, by now "looked like a walking corpse," strode among the troops, offering words of encouragement. Later, at the precise moment of the cease fire, an eerie, all-pervasive silence enveloped more than four hundred continuous miles of trench, a fact not instantly absorbed by men used to the constant white noise of war. It was a defining moment in each soldier's life, one that he would remember and could precisely recount until the day that he died. Robert Campbell, Jr., described the noise that followed the silence. "No Fourth of July celebration will ever approach it," he exclaimed.[36]

When it was all over, the men of the 2nd Battalion, 104th Infantry knelt in a prayer of thanksgiving with Chaplain de Valles, and then they began a day-long celebration. Later that evening, as Connell Albertine and de Valles were making their way back to battalion headquarters, it became obvious that the priest could not keep up. His health and strength had been failing for some time, but somehow, by sheer strength of will, he had remained with the battalion right to the end. The chaplain told his assistant to go on ahead and that he would catch up. He never did, as he was evacuated to a hospital "totally exhausted and very sick," although he did rally sufficiently to return briefly home with the division.[37]

Albert G. Butzer of the 103rd Infantry Regiment took time that evening to write to his parents back in Buffalo, New York. "We stopped fighting this morning at eleven o'clock, but it was a fight to the finish—no let up on either side until the clock pointed exactly to eleven, then both sides stopped instantly and since then there hasn't been a shot fired," he recounted. The chaplain added: "Seems just like going from hell to heaven." However, his work that day was not finished with the cessation of hostilities. As happy as everyone was that the war was over, there was the sad reality: "Eight of my boys were killed just a few hours before fighting stopped," the twenty-five-year-old minister told his parents, and he "spent all afternoon finding their bodies and bringing them to one place where we are going to erect a little cemetery for them."[38]

Ray Anderson, also a chaplain in the 103rd Infantry, expressed similar feelings in a letter to his former mentor back home in Chicago. "Well, Monday afternoon was awful because of the silence," he wrote. "Can you imagine hundreds of guns firing all around you and on you and then in a moment everything stopping. . . . It was hard to realize in the front lines that day." After reality set in, the chaplain reacted to it. "I think everybody did about what I did," he recalled. "First we prayed and thanked God. Then we shouted a bit and shot up some flares and then we tried to sleep." Like Al Butzer, his work was only just beginning. "The next two days I finished up burying our dead," he said. On one body he found a small Bible, and he was struck by the inscription on the inside cover. "I leave for France with the love of God in my heart and with my life cleansed from all sin," the soldier had written; "God keep those at home and God help me be a strong soldier." "Isn't that wonderful," Anderson marveled.[39]

Life's Lessons

During the month that the Yankee Division spent in the Neptune Sector near Verdun, its already depleted ranks suffered an additional 4,681 casualties in dead and wounded. This did not take into account the awful toll taken by the still-raging influenza pandemic. More than 80 percent of the battle casualties were incurred during the period October 14 through 31, which encompassed the futile attack by the 104th Infantry in the Bois de Haumont and the costly attacks by the 101st and 102nd Infantry Regiments at Belleu Bois and the Bois d'Ormont, respectively.[40] There was much for the chaplains to do for both the living and the dead. The "awful carnage" of war imparted its lessons to all who served.

Robert Campbell, Jr., came away with his own dichotomous impressions, which he explained to his parishioners back in Warren:

> A man's experience over here is marked by great extremes, moments of joy and sorrow, comfort and hardship, bright anticipation and cruel disappointments, intense love for one another, then bitter hatred for the enemy, and so on. War is surely a great evil, but a wonderful developer of certain traits of character. Let us hope it makes us better men and women and a better world than we ever knew.[41]

Malcolm Peabody expressed similar thoughts: "War is as bad as soldiers describe it to be, but it brings the very best out of you and challenges you to do your utmost in a great cause." For Ray Anderson, his experience was an important milestone on his spiritual journey: "It has been a privilege to suffer what little I have, because, through it all, I have come to understand Christ so much better, and to know how He suffered for us. I have learned to love Him more through it all." One Yankee doughboy summed it up best: "It was the grandest experience imaginable to have gone through," he said; however, "I can imagine nothing more horrible than to be compelled to go through it again."[42]

Chapter Seven

Going Home

One Step Closer to Home

From the moment that the Armistice was signed, there was talk that the Yankee Division would be part of the Army of Occupation. That notion was soon put to rest. The division was pretty well used up during its long and arduous tour of duty. Within days, the division began to collect itself, absorb the recently received replacements (too late to really help with the fighting), and bury its dead. Ray Anderson, who had returned from the hospital, emphasized the positive in a letter to his father written shortly after the Armistice:

> My work has just begun too. Today I have been burying. Tomorrow and the next day I will continue. Then my work in bringing the boys back to life is going to be so wonderful. I long to preach to them and clinch all the wonderful things that have happened in their lives. So the time will fly and some day we will start home.[1]

Over the next several months, many old hands would make their way back to the division. Rumors were rife about a date for sailing home; some thought that it might be as early as Christmas. It was not to be. Billets were arranged in the area of Montigny-le-Roi, many kilometers to the south, and in the days that followed the Armistice, the weary warriors trudged there through French villages festooned with the flags of both nations. The nights were cold, but the men did not mind now that they were leaving the war behind. "We have not yet stopped long enough to get the mud of the shell holes off of us, and we are a dirty looking command," wrote Horace Hobbs. He added: "It is bitterly cold today and the wind biting. . . . All the roads here in rear of the old lines are jammed with troops. . . ." Along the way, the artillery regiments turned in their guns and horses.[2]

It was also a time when anxious parents wrote for word of the fate of their sons, and it was the chaplain's duty to get answers as the fog of war slowly lifted. Ernest W. Gillingham's mother had received word that her son had been wounded on October 23, but nothing further. She addressed her desperate plea to Chaplain Speers, "as the anxiety and suspense are a great load." He answered her promptly with the news that her son's wounds were not serious. A much-relieved mother responded: "It has made me so happy that I feel more than sorry for the mothers who had sons that lost their arms and legs or life, that I pray that God will send them some blessings to try to make up for their loss."[3]

On Thanksgiving Day, Murray Dewart, who had just returned to the 101st Field Artillery from his temporary assignment, conducted an open-air service on the grounds of the château near the edge of Guerpont, at the end of which were read the names of those in the regiment who had fallen and would not return with the division. "His clamor to rejoin his beloved regiment was too strong to be denied," and this time, Chaplain Moody had given in. Over in nearby Is-en-Bassigny, the 103rd Infantry also celebrated Thanksgiving. The regiment had a new commanding officer, Col. P. A. Arnold, whom the men liked. Ray Anderson described him as one who "doesn't swear or drink or carouse with women," which was, in his words, "a delightful change over the old order." In addition to a fine dinner on linen cloth, accompanied by the regimental band, Anderson preached a sermon at services entitled: "Thanks be unto God who giveth the victory." He told his father that he meant, not only God's gift of a victory over Germany, and also over death for those who had survived and for those who had died in Christ, as well as victory in the coming days.[4]

Shortly before Christmas, it was announced that President Wilson, who was then in France, along with General Pershing, would visit the 26th Division at Montigny-le-Roi and eat dinner with some of the enlisted men. Preparations were made in all of the units, in anticipation of an inspection, or at the very least a drive by. Some men waited in formation along the roadside in the cold and the rain, only to be sorely disappointed. The men of the 101st Engineers were luckier than most, as they "stood to in billets from 11:30 to 3 o'clock but no President." Later that evening, the officers, including Chaplains Edwards and Libert, did have a large dinner. The enlisted men did also, thanks to a large check sent to Col. George W. Bunnell by the Welfare Association back home. The president did have dinner with some of the division officers, but not any enlisted men as had been expected. Among the officers in attendance were Chaplains O'Connor, Farrell, Rollins, and Speers.[5] Aside from the presidential visit, the chaplains were busy with Christmas services of their own.

One of the returnees was Arthur LeVeer, who, upon his discharge from Base Hospital No. 26, caught up with the 102nd Machine Gun Battalion at

Poulagny. There, as was the case with many French-speaking chaplains, LeVeer was called upon to take over the local Catholic parish while the regular pastor was serving in the French Army. He would be called upon to do so again, in the villages of Esnouveaux and Mansigny, as the battalion moved closer to Brest and the voyage home. Surprisingly, the ecumenical spirit did not always prevail between the Allies. Some, but not all, French pastors denied Protestant clergymen the use of their churches in order to hold services, even in inclement weather. While the weather did not stop religious services, one chaplain described the lack of heat in the churches as "the greatest inconvenience suffered in France."[6]

For his part, recently arrived Malcolm Peabody knew that he had made the right decision, and he compared his current job as chaplain with the 102nd Field Artillery with that of Red Cross chaplain. "Eighteen months in Europe today," he noted in his diary on November 22, "wish I had this job for at least one-half of it, for some [of it] just suits me. The other was a terrible . . . strain of talking to sick men convinced with knowledge that I was not doing much for the men." The day before he had observed: "A chaplain's job certainly puts everything up to a fellow's ingenuity and personal pep. He has to wait for 'long run' results too. I have at last got the point (aided by out of door health) where I am fairly content to grab the psychological moment."[7]

Influenza

The new battle to be waged was really against an old enemy—disease. The cold, wet weather, coupled with men not yet physically recovered from the ravages of their time in the line, left many doughboys vulnerable to the flu and the real killer, the pneumonia that accompanied it. Field hospitals were now treating this scourge, which just would not loosen its grip. Given the virulent nature of the disease, a general order was issued to treat locally and not to transport influenza cases. Malcolm Peabody contracted the flu shortly after the Armistice and recovered. He attributed his recovery to the regimental surgeon, who, as he put it, "allowed me to stay in my digs and did not transport me to a base hospital . . . where men were dying from lack of attention."[8]

Anselm Mayotte, now chaplain in the 12th Field Artillery (2nd Division), was part of the Army of Occupation, and he was not so fortunate. Shortly before Thanksgiving 1918, the chaplain and his unit were near Buchenhöfe, Germany, when he was taken to a hospital in Echternacht, Luxemburg, with full-blown flu symptoms. He died there of broncho-pneumonia on December 5, and following a Solemn High Mass at St. Wilibrordus Church, he was buried there the following day. His battery commander praised the intrepid priest:

> Padre was a brave and true soldier. Nothing was too hard for him to do if Duty called. In fact, I've seen him do things as a matter of course which I would stop and think about. And I am not considered a coward. Padre has left a place in our hearts which it will take a long time to fill if at all. His sense of humor and good nature can never be forgotten.... Padre gave his life for his country just as surely as if he had been killed in battle."[9]

At home, his courage and patriotism drew praise:

> He comforted hundreds of his men and ministered to them as they passed from the hell of battle to the Kingdom of Peace. The Prince of Peace has crowned this young priestly knight with the crown of patriotic glory. His name will be cherished and held in reverence by all who appreciate high virtue consecrated to noble purpose.[10]

Mayotte was awarded the Silver Star for his bravery.[11]

Israel Bettan and the Jewish Welfare Board

Israel Bettan reported to 26th Division Headquarters shortly after November 13, 1918, no doubt sorely disappointed that he had just missed out on the fighting. For more than a year, he had sought a commission and an assignment to a combat division. Washington "red tape" and an appalling lack of foresight made it seem like the need for Jewish chaplains had only recently been discovered, more than a year after the first troops began arriving in France in significant numbers. Were there no Jewish doughboys among them? Bettan felt that perhaps he and other rabbis could have done more, which was nonsense. Dr. Henry Englander, a friend from Hebrew Union College in Cincinnati, Ohio, told him so:

> I feel that you are unduly severe upon the rabbis, and particularly upon yourself.... But the fact remains that our Government should have given us adequate representation among its chaplains much more promptly than it did.... You know that you were ready and eager to go at least a year before you were sent.... But it was absolutely impossible for you to get across in any capacity whatsoever."[12]

The exchange with Dr. Englander exposed a more complicated or nuanced problem than at first met the eye. Certainly, the federal government was short-sighted; however, in Bettan's eyes, the doctrinal strains within Judaism itself—as between Orthodox and Reform, for example—were as much, if not more to blame for the paralysis of action, because the rift prevented the various factions from presenting a unified front on this very important issue. While in practice, both the YMCA and the Knights of Columbus served the temporal and spiritual needs of all doughboys regardless of faith, the fact is that there were faith-based underpinnings to each of these organizations. So, too, with the Jewish Welfare Board (JWB). The rub came, not with the temporal support by the JWB, which was very effective, but rather with the strictly Orthodox point of view that was imparted to Jewish soldiers through the religious tracts passed along to them, and no doubt by the "Acting Rabbis," chosen by the JWB to fill the need for chaplains. Moreover, the importance of the role of the JWB itself had been magnified during the war in the absence of Jewish chaplains. Even after the appointment of Jewish chaplains, the JWB continued to proselytize its Orthodox doctrine, thus undermining the authority of the Jewish chaplain in the performance of one of his core functions.[13]

Recognizing the problem, Rabbi Elkan Voorsanger and other Jewish chaplains, including Bettan, formed the Jewish Chaplains Association, which held a meeting at the headquarters of the Jewish Welfare Board in Paris on February 24, 1919. The end result was a six-part "Program for Cooperation" between the two organizations, clearly defining their respective roles and calling for regular communication. Perhaps the most important point of agreement was the recognition that "all religious work shall be directly and solely under [the chaplain's] jurisdiction." Clearly, this was a good start for future action. For his part, Dr. Englander saw the larger picture. "I see this same tragedy which you see in the Jewish ranks in the army, in all our American Jewish life," he told Bettan, adding, "I trust that it will not be long before we wake up."[14] Bettan fully agreed and would use this experience as a stepping stone toward a life-long effort to find common ground within Judaism wherever possible. Both men saw it as a necessity to ensure the growth and survival of that faith in America.

Shortly after that meeting in Paris, Chaplain Bettan was transferred to 3rd Army Headquarters, effective March 20. His orders had been changed to allow him to share Passover with the Yankee Division, as he had already planned. As with all of his assignments, Bettan brought all of his energy and enthusiasm to bear, earning a strong recommendation to serve as a corps chaplain. In his new assignment, he served as "Jewish Chaplain at large," with a congregation of roughly four thousand Jewish soldiers scattered throughout the area. The Senior Chaplain, Rev. Patrick R. Donifan, recognized the difficulties inherent in the assignment, and wrote that Bettan had been "untiring in his devotion to the spiritual welfare of these men."[15]

Bettan's assignment at 3rd Army Headquarters was scheduled to end on June 14; however, earlier he had obtained a leave of absence from his duties and traveled throughout Europe during the months of May and June. He then sailed home as an unassigned casual and was discharged at Camp Dix, New Jersey, on July 10, 1919.[16]

"The Old Lion Is Dead"

Theodore Roosevelt had led a full life. There were few things that he had not tried, and he had achieved nearly universal success at all of them. Though a rancher, a warrior, a historian, an adventurer, and a Nobel laureate, to name a few, any one of which would have been sufficient for most men, Roosevelt still thirsted for the power and prestige of the presidency. Once achieved, no one or nothing could quite compare to that experience. In his mind, neither his hand-picked successor, William Howard Taft, and certainly not Woodrow Wilson, could measure up when compared with him. Neither an African safari nor his defeat in 1912 could tamp down that fire. Not even a near-death experience on the Amazon, or the tragic death of his beloved aviator son Quentin in France, or even the bullet of a would-be assassin could keep him out of the political sphere. He was larger than life; a force of nature; seemingly indestructible. Many were sure he would be the Republican candidate in 1920. So it came as a shock when he died suddenly of a pulmonary embolism on January 6, 1919, in his sixty-first year.[17]

The nation mourned, as did the troops abroad. On Sunday, January 9, 1919, the 101st Engineer Regiment held a review at Moncé to commemorate Roosevelt's death. Chaplain H. Boyd Edwards delivered the address. Another of the many memorial services was that of the 103rd Field Artillery, held in the Catholic church in the town of Vicq at 5:30 on the evening of January 12. The unheated church was lit by candles and the walls covered with the flags of both countries. Fr. Tucker conducted the service, which consisted of a Bible reading and hymns sung by the assembled men, who were accompanied by the regimental band. Tucker's breath could be seen as he first read the War Department order and then delivered the address. The gravel-voiced padre chided the men for always asking, "When are we going home?" He issued a stern challenge: "You ought to be ashamed to go home and face your friends and families after the sort of lives you have been living over here. Theodore Roosevelt always stressed clean living in all walks of life and . . . his own life was an example of what a real man can and should be." Taps was played and the national anthem sung to close the service. One who was present that day called it a "splendid service, and one of the most impressive that I have ever heard anywhere."[18]

THE ECUMENICAL SPIRIT

By and large, a remarkable ecumenical spirit prevailed among the Yankee Division chaplains.[19] Bishop Brent had emphasized that he was looking for chaplains to meet the needs of all the men in their unit regardless of denomination. In many respects, we see young men, who like most young men of their generation, were eager to do their bit for the war. They were soldiers first, sharing the hard times and dangers, and they developed a mutual bond. Witness, for example, Fr. Farrell serving a gun in the Toul Sector, when several gunners were killed or wounded, and Robert Campbell, Jr., doing likewise at Verdun.

In a larger sense, a spirit of cooperation prevailed among the chaplains themselves, to the point that some actually shared religious services. Chaplains O'Connor and Rollins are usually cited as an example, but the same could be said for Malcolm Endicott Peabody and John Francis Tucker, Chaplains Danker and de Valles, as was the case with others. In general, though, a Catholic service would be followed the same day as a Protestant service, or vice versa. That was the case in the 101st Field Artillery on October 27. The unit did not have a Catholic chaplain, so Robert Campbell made arrangements for a priest to come and say Mass. After both Sunday services had ended, the priest approached Campbell, who "came to congratulate [him] for being chaplain over such a regiment and for [his] work among the boys." Later that same day, the Knights of Columbus man came to the regiment to distribute treats. "If they were all like him, I couldn't say enough for his organization," Campbell wrote, adding, "they are doing good work over here." He told his flock back home: "The Catholics of Warren and the non-Catholics also should do all they can to help them." Campbell was optimistic about the future and felt that, "this war has done much to wipe out sectarianism."[20]

Still, even among the best, some old suspicions still lingered. Like virtually all Yankee Division members, Ray Anderson wanted to sail home with the division. Due to a shortage of chaplains in France, the word was out that only one per regiment would be allowed to return, the rest being assigned elsewhere. As the most senior chaplain in the 103rd Infantry Regiment, he felt strongly that his denomination was not a factor and that he should be allowed to go home with it. He offered the following observation:

"The Division chaplain is a Roman Catholic and he may send a Roman Catholic home with the regiment. You can never tell about these fellows. So you see how it is. I am going to fight to get home. It is my right and if I don't get to go with these boys, it will break my heart." Nevertheless, he recognized that he was in the Army and would have to obey his orders.[21]

Even at this late date, there were still not enough chaplains to serve all denominations, particularly the Catholics in the division. In early January 1919, Corporal Frank Houlihan of Battery F, 101st Field Artillery, wrote to his mother: "We never got that chaplain we expected, but we may get one before we go home. Kelley, Lathopele, and myself are going to confession to the French priest in this village Saturday."[22] The regiment never did get the new Catholic chaplain.

Mortal Remains

Although it was the least agreeable of a chaplain's responsibilities, care of the dead was one that each chaplain took seriously, not only for the sake of the soldier, but also for his loved ones. Once in the midst of a particularly tough battle, General Edwards came across Fr. O'Connor, coat off, sleeves rolled up, digging a grave. When the General asked why he didn't leave the job to enlisted men, the priest replied, "They are busy fighting and I desire to bury certain bodies right away." After hearing the story, Bert Ford asked O'Connor about his actions. He told the correspondent, "The only comfort left for parents and relatives was the assurance that their boy had a prompt and proper burial."[23]

Chaplain O'Connor explained his view in greater depth in a letter sent from France late in the war. First, he told of the chaplain's duties in this regard:

> The chaplains gather all the data, his name, organization, description of place where buried, marking the grave by a cross or by a bottle with the name etc. on a slip of paper inside the bottle, or in place of these marks, something to tell who lies beneath. All this data is sent to the Graves Registration Bureau, representatives of which are usually on the ground, and it is their duty to look up the locations of these graves, and when the proper time comes after the battle, all the bodies are transferred to a central cemetery and properly marked.

Wherever possible, he said, all who are found in the same vicinity are buried side by side.

O'Connor continued:

Chaplain Robert Campbell, Jr., and burial detail near Verdun, November 1, 1918. Courtesy of the Library of Congress.

The duty of caring for the dead under such circumstances is not the pleasantest in the world, but if the chaplain did not take the responsibility and do things which, under ordinary conditions, he would never think of doing, his usefulness with the soldier amounts to little. It is his duty to see to it that those dear fellows have committal prayers with them in their solitude, yet there is no solitude.

He found that the French would frequently tend the graves and lay flowers on them. After St. Mihiel, at O'Connor's suggestion, each company that lost any men sent a detail to comb the battlefield and erect crosses for the fallen, with their names, and wherever possible to erect fences around the graves for higher visibility. The importance of this sad ritual to the doughboy is exemplified in the story of one soldier who traveled around France following the end of the fighting. At one cemetery, he saw the graves of some men he had served with in the 101st Infantry. He scribbled some notes, he said, "so as I might tell their folks just where their bodies lay."[24]

Robert Campbell, Jr., told of his own experiences:

I have had quite a few burials. One can never become accustomed to these things, and in my experience, the last occasion was just as sad as the first. On one occasion, when I had the burial of three men, a major of the Quartermaster's Department came along with a moving picture machine and took pictures of the whole proceeding, at the same time asking many questions about marking bodies and graves and making records. He said that these pictures were to be used by the government. It was one of the few burials I have had when the enemy failed to send over shells and shrapnel in generous quantities.[25]

Heading the Graves Registration Service was Chaplain Charles C. Pierce, who had come out of retirement in 1917. In March 1899, during the Philippine War, he served as chief of the Office of Identification and Morgue. The dead were initially buried near where they fell, usually in small groups of between three and fifteen, with the location meticulously noted by the chaplain. Recognizing the need of families for closure and a sense that their son's sacrifice was not in vain, the government assigned four thousand men to this service, which was a part of the Quartermaster Corps based at Tours. The center there became a large repository for maps and index cards showing the location of the graves. Many of these men worked in small groups in order to locate and gather up the remains of their fallen comrades and to remove them to the military cemeteries which were then being established.[26] This group worked all over Europe where American soldiers fought and died, but their work was carried out mainly in northern and eastern France.

The disposition of the soldier's remains was always on the minds of his parents. Was he buried "single," as opposed to a mass grave, one parent asked Chaplain Speers. No detail was "too small or trivial." Another, who had lost two sons, felt it best to leave well enough alone and let his boy lie in France, for after all, he told Speers, "all the land in the world belongs to God." Besides, he added, "How do I know I don't get a Frenchman?" Mr. and Mrs. Miller from Brownville, Nebraska, whose son Gale of Company B, 102nd Infantry, was killed by a shell burst on October 26 north of Verdun, felt the same way.[27]

To perform this important task, France was divided into twelve districts, and the solemn task begun. The first of eight cemeteries was dedicated on May 30, 1919, at Suresnes, near Versailles. The American government offered the families of deceased soldiers the option to have their loved ones buried in Europe among their comrades where they had died, or to have the remains repatriated to the United States. Somewhat more than one-half of the families availed themselves of this service. However, nearly 31,000 lie in these foreign fields, which are reverently and meticulously maintained by the American Battle Monuments Commission. More than four thousand missing men are also memorialized. Those men who were left behind to gather up and identify the remains of the American dead and to re-inter them in one of the eight new military cemeteries did their job so well that less than 2 percent of the bodies remained unidentified.[28]

Gay Paree

Prior to the Armistice, very few members of the Yankee Division received passes for leave in Paris. The city was full of adventures, all of them fairly expensive, unless the doughboy had the good fortune to get a hot meal or a bed courtesy of the YMCA or other organization. As it happened, Michael O'Connor and Lyman Rollins were sent to Paris on an errand, and they were bound and determined to make the most of the opportunity. Shortly after their arrival, one of the soldiers from the 101st Infantry ran into the pair as they were walking along. Knowing O'Connor to be a soft touch, the doughboy told a convincing story, and the priest broke out his checkbook. Before long, the word was out, and O'Connor had written several more checks. After yet more checks were written, Rollins took a quick peek at the check register, and quietly asked if his companion could spare a little for him also. "How much?" O'Connoer asked, as he signed his name to a blank check. "I'll fill it in," said Rollins, and quickly took the checkbook away. The thrifty New Englander made the check out to "balance," and told O'Connor, "That will stop you!" The latter turned to the small group of disappointed soldiers and said: "He's finished me boys. You'll have to make some of them that got it divide it up with you."[29]

Keeping Occupied

After the Armistice was signed, there was considerable emphasis on keeping the troops occupied until arrangements could be made to transport them home. Accident, disease, and boredom would now be the soldier's principal adversaries. The last was a real concern for the chaplains. With approximately two million men in France, getting them all home would not happen overnight. Idle soldiers, especially those who had served long stretches in France, had lots of pent-up energy. More important, idle soldiers spelled trouble. While the men were happy to be out of harm's way, many enjoying a real bed and bath for the first time in months, the time did weigh heavily. Malcolm Peabody found that the food was adequate, but not so with heat, shelter, and light. The men also felt that General Pershing did not appreciate their efforts. He noted in his diary for December 6: "It seems the powers have forgotten us at times and there is a lot of grousing. Gen.

Pershing's omission of any mention of the Division in his summary of the Army's deeds doesn't help the grousing much either."[30]

Fritz Potter of the 101st Field Artillery told his mother that all was "up in the air" and without any "special duty." He described this period of waiting to go home. "In the meantime we are just soldiering; the same old things we used to do back in training camp," he wrote, "and of course there is nothing we dislike more than that. The drills, the fatigues, the marching, discipline, etc." At times, the lapses of discipline could be breathtaking, as on Sunday morning, November 24, in Esnouveaux, when two drunken members of the 101st Engineers nearly came to blows with the new division commander when they came face-to-face with Maj. Gen. Harry C. Hale. In light of the incident with Gen. Hale, the disciplinary situation was considered so serious that Col. George W. Bunnell assembled the entire regiment for church services, where he told the men what was expected of them, followed by Bishop Brent, who delivered, "a remarkably plain-spoken sermon, during which he showed himself to be very human and very able to reach the hearts and consciences of the soldier."[31]

Of necessity, the role of the chaplain changed, a fact recognized by most of them. "The nature of my work changes in this new situation," wrote Robert Campbell, one of Potter's chaplains, adding that, "Now, more than ever before, I must hold up to the boys the best things in life, trusting that after living like animals in the ground and passing through experiences that would rob them of all that is holy, they may return to the homeland, stronger, nobler, and purer than ever before." On November 24, Malcolm E. Peabody assembled the men of the 102nd Field Artillery for a hillside service. "I spoke on 'cheering up' the line of talk which must improve if the men are to be presentable at home," he wrote in his diary, adding with tongue in cheek, "Now that the mules have gone, the principal source of irritation will have gone!"[32]

It was not simply a question of morals, it was also important to maintain a high state of morale. For starters, a system of leaves was established; enlisted to one area, and officers to another. However, some men simply took matters into their own hands and set off on what was referred to as "French leave." Some simply "extended" their leaves.[33] Although money was in short supply, that did not deter an enterprising doughboy, and there were plenty of them. In either case, the Army called it AWOL (absent without leave) and gave vigilant military policemen the task of finding the scofflaws and returning them to their units for discipline.

Naturally, the AEF turned to the chaplains to help fill the void. Sporting events and competitions (unit vs. unit), as well as entertainments, were arranged and managed by chaplains. Some, like Guthrie Speers, were very creative in their approach. "We worked out a form of soccer that had about a hundred fellas on each team and we had three balls," he recalled. "So everybody would pile up on one ball and you'd see another ball going somewhere else down the field." He added that "it was very exciting and it kept a hundred fellas or two hundred busy for that afternoon." Guthrie found other entertainment like movies, but the enterprising chaplain didn't stop there. "I scoured the country on an old horse that we had inherited from the Germans," he said, "and picked up everything like magazines for the boys to read or chocolate or cigarettes, anything you could find." Chaplains Anderson and Butzer, in cooperation with the YMCA, oversaw sporting events and other entertainment for the men of the 103rd Infantry Regiment.[34]

Likewise, Robert Campbell, now chaplain of the 103rd Machine Gun Battalion, was appointed battalion athletic officer. As such, he arranged and officiated at all the games, which often became a sort of "rough and tumble." "After having fought the Germans, the men are afraid of nothing," he observed. "You may be sure these games are far from being gentle." As part of these duties, Campbell promoted boxing matches, and having seen a few boxing matches in the Arena in Boston, he felt that he had just enough experience to play the announcer and the referee. On occasion, his participation was more than that of a mere observer. He described one such incident:

> We have a husky, enthusiastic officer in the battalion who wanted to beat somebody. He stood before the crowd with gloves on, in the same manner as Goliath of the Philistines stood before the Israelites in days of yore. I was asked to consider the proposition, and coming to the conclusion that boxing was tame compared with firing cannons in a war, I accepted the challenge. As a result, I became the champion by a big margin and [am] now known as "the fighting parson."[35]

The AEF even went so far as to establish a "University" in cooperation with various French educational institutions. These offered the soldier an opportunity to take classes for fun or to improve his chances for employment on his return. On a more basic level, literacy classes were held by chaplains and their assistants or other officers for both native- and foreign-born soldiers. Typical were the schools conducted in the 101st Machine Gun Battalion by Earl Taggart and in the 102nd Machine Gun Battalion by Arthur LeVeer. Chaplain Taggart himself enrolled at the University of Caen, and he left the battalion on March 1.[36]

The war on lice and venereal disease intensified. Pershing and his staff were bound and determined to return every mother's son to her in, as nearly as possible, the "unspoiled" condition in which he had left the United States. Shortly after arriving in France, Pershing had issued several general orders related to the treatment of venereal diseases and the responsibility of commanders at all levels to stamp it out. "The gravest responsibility rests on those to whom the parents of our soldiers have entrusted their sons for battle," he pronounced, "and we fail if we neglect to safeguard them." Any doubts about how venereal disease would be dealt with in the Yankee Division were soon erased when the division surgeon issued Circular Letter No. 101 dated November 26, 1918, which contained the terse message: "Venereals will not go home with this Division."[37]

More Comings and Goings

After the Armistice, the need for experienced chaplains in France and in the Army of Occupation was great, especially at the ports of embarkation and at the various Base Sections. Inevitably, more Yankee Division chaplains were tapped for this job and would not be allowed to return with the division. This was a sore point with Brig. Gen. Charles Cole, commander of the 52nd Infantry Brigade, who had nothing but praise for the Yankee Division chaplains. Cole expressed his feelings in a letter to Senator David Walsh of Massachusetts in January 1919:

> These chaplains, Catholic, Protestant, and Hebrew, have done wonderful work with the men over here. They have been down in the front lines with them; the men have learned to love them and the chaplains love the men in return. The chaplains are a tremendous influence and assistance to the officers in keeping up the morale and discipline of the men, especially now that the war is over, and they should be allowed to return home with their regiments just the same as the other officers who have served over here all this time.[38]

On February 19, John F. Tucker was reassigned to the 102nd Field Artillery, where he would join his friend Malcolm Peabody. As with the 103rd Field Artillery, at first, it would not be "an open arms welcome." Perhaps the men thought that he was going to replace Peabody. The situation could well have been "disagreeable" had the two not been friends. Peabody reasoned that although only one chaplain was normally assigned to the regiment, his friend was there to "look after the RC boys." As was his nature, Tucker worked hard to gain the confidence of the men and went straightaway "through the sick billets getting magazines and literature" to them. For his part, Peabody was confident that he would not be transferred. On a recent visit to Langres, he had "providentially met [Paul] Moody who probably saved my life by promising to send me home with the Division."[39]

The reunion with Peabody would be short-lived, as Tucker was soon reassigned to the 5th Battalion, 20th Forestry Engineers, from March 15 through May 8. He need not have worried about how the soldiers in either artillery regiment felt about him, as was evident from a letter he received shortly after his transfer. The writer told him that his "loss is keenly felt throughout both regiments by all your 'boys.'" The priest went about his new assignment with his usual energy, drawing praise from his commanding officer, who noted his "high sense of duty and the interest he displayed in the welfare of the men." While with the Engineers, he was appointed as the Athletic Supply Officer. He then spent a month at an AEF University and sailed back home, just as he had come, as a casual. Tucker was discharged at Fort Dix, New Jersey, on August 16, 1919.[40]

In early March, while on furlough, Arthur LeVeer was ordered to report to headquarters, Base Section No. 5, at Brest. He did so on March 26, and he was assigned to Fort Fédérés. There, he would be responsible for the "spiritual guidance" of the Catholics, as well visitation at the Army and Navy hospitals, both in the City of Brest. LeVeer received his orders to return home on June 26, and three days later, he boarded the *Leviathan* bound for Hoboken, New Jersey. He was mustered out of service at Camp Dix on July 17, 1919. Albert Butzer was transferred from the 103rd Infantry to the 16th Infantry in the Army of Occupation, and he did not return home until July. On the other hand, Markham W. Stackpole returned to the 102nd Field Artillery in time to sail home with the Yankee Division. Likewise, so did Murray W. Dewart, who returned to the 101st Field Artillery, just as Robert Campbell, who had taken his place, was assigned to the 103rd Machine Gun Battalion on December 6, 1918.[41]

Horrors of the Front Recalled

Gradually, the Yankee Division made its way homeward from its billets near Montigny-le-Roi, first to the Le Mans area, and ultimately to Camp Pontanezan, just outside Brest. The roughly two-day journey to the Embarkation Area took place aboard cold, crowded French box cars. The experience of Fritz Potter of Battery A, 101st Field Artillery was typical. "The trip was uneventful," he told his mother, "and the usual discomforts were enjoyed." He added, for emphasis: "We had thirty-five men in our car, and

"Homeward Bound." *Left to right:* Chaplains Edwards, de Valles, O'Connor, Evans, and Imbrie aboard the *Mt. Vernon*. Reprinted from Sibley, *With the Yankee Division in France*.

at night when we tried to sleep, we laid cross wise in the car, your feet were sticking in the back of the man opposite you and vice versa."[42]

Not so typical was the experience of Chaplain Robert Campbell, which gave proof that the dangers inherent in a soldier's life never really go away. Just when you least expect it, fate steps in to remind us all of that fact. On the evening of Thursday, January 30, 1919, as the men of the 103rd Machine Gun Battalion were issued two days rations and boarded box cars for the first leg of the homeward journey, war must have been the furthest thing from their minds. Despite the cold, and the straw-strewn floor on which they would make their beds, the mood was undoubtedly upbeat. Sometime during the night of January 31, 1919, as the troop train was speeding west toward Le Mans, it happened. Eleven miles southeast of Troyes, near the town of Montiéramey, there was a horrific wreck. The train carrying the sleeping men had crashed into two idle engines on the track ahead. Thankfully unhurt, Chaplain Campbell dressed quickly and went to inspect the situation. He found that two of the train cars had telescoped upon impact. He described the scene: "The horrors of the front were all recalled, it seemed. We lifted out five dead men. Another died soon after. Others were pinned under the wreckage. It was a ghastly sight under the light of a lantern. We sent over twenty men severely injured to the hospital and two of them died the following day." As for the men, he added that, "throughout it all, the same morale which characterized the men on the front was in evidence."[43]

Homeward Bound

Once aboard ship, a chaplain's duties did not cease, as he continued to look out for the welfare of the men. As a case in point, aboard the homebound *America*, "Chaplains O'Connor, Rollins and Mitty worked like beavers throughout the trip." Yet, like all doughboys, the outward euphoria at the prospect of really getting home sometimes masked the inner turmoil for the chaplains as well. Several Yankee Division chaplains traveled together aboard the same ship. For the most part, the mood was decidedly friendly and upbeat. Perhaps, however, it was a display of his natural reserve, or maybe a sense of unease, when Markham Stackpole objected when another chaplain referred to him as "my brother." Malcolm Peabody also noted his own sense of unease in his diary: "My mood of quiet uncommunicativeness is passing gradually into one of enthusiastic vivacity as the day approaches. But neither officers nor men have the foggiest notion of what getting back actually is going to be like."[44]

After their homecoming, the victorious doughboys were feted with parades and welcome home celebrations over the weeks and months that followed. There were also memorial services for those that did not make it home. On Sunday, May 4, 1919, the State Armory in Hartford, Connecticut, was the site for just such a service to honor the men from the 102nd Infantry Regiment who had given their lives. Fittingly, the service was conducted jointly by four chaplains who had served with the regiment in France, namely: Rev. James P. Sherry, Rev. Thomas Guthrie Speers, Rev. Orville H. Petty, and Rev. Burnham North Dell. Dr. Ernest DeFremery Miel, who had served with the Red Cross, addressed the assembly on the subject of "The Glorious Dead."[45]

CHAPTER EIGHT

"Recalled to Life"

BRIEF LIVES WELL-LIVED—LYMAN ROLLINS

As a young man, the mythical Irish hero Cuchulain chose fame and a short life over immortality. Many chaplains chose service and duty, and in the process achieved a measure of fame during and after their shortened lives, at least as long as the memories of those with whom they served. While Chaplains Danker and Mayotte did not return, most chaplains did come home, albeit some, like Lyman Rollins, bore the scars of war. Rollins was discharged at Camp Devens on April 28, 1919, and he returned as the Rector of St. Michael's Episcopal Church in Marblehead, Massachusetts, and later as Pastor of St. Paul's Episcopal Church in White River Junction, Vermont. He was active in various veterans' organizations. However, having been gassed and wounded, the cumulative effects of his service at the front undoubtedly shortened his life, as he continued to experience health problems. As one who had served with him said: "[He was] as truly a casualty of the war as any man shot down in action. For his service, in which he never spared himself when the comfort of others was at stake, he so impaired his health that he was never afterwards able to take an active part in his chosen profession." Rollins never married. He died at his home in Lebanon, New Hampshire, on July 11, 1930, at the age of 49.[1]

Following a funeral service in Lebanon, Rollins was given full military honors in Concord, with burial in Blossom Hill Cemetery. In attendance was his good friend Chaplain Michael J. O'Connor. Despite the ongoing Great Depression, a fund to honor him with a suitable memorial was soon launched, and on Armistice Day, November 11, 1934, a memorial tablet set in a granite boulder was dedicated at his gravesite. The ceremony was attended by General Logan, along with many of his friends, fellow veterans, and civilians. This was a fitting tribute to a man who was proud of his service with the 101st Infantry, of which he frequently said: "I had sooner come home a buck private in the 101st than come home a general."[2]

John B. de Valles

In April 1919, John Baptist de Valles returned with the men of the 104th Infantry on the *Mt. Vernon*, but he did not stay long. The chaplain remained in the service and returned to France, where he was assigned to the Chaplain's Office at the Port of Embarkation at Brest—after all, there were more doughboys to shepherd home, which he did as a shipboard chaplain. He returned to the United States for the final time in October 1919, ill and broken in body. De Valles never actively resumed his pastoral duties at St. John the Baptist Church in New Bedford, Massachusetts. In fact, he did not have long to live. His remaining months were spent in and out of hospitals from Camp Gordon, Georgia, to the Mayo Clinic in Minnesota.[3]

His many friends, including Generals Clarence Ransom Edwards and George H. Shelton, pressed the Army to award him the Distinguished Service Cross and the Medal of Honor. Edwards frequently lauded the courageous priest. On April 21, at the Copley-Plaza in Boston, he told a gathering of the Knights of Columbus: "Typical of these fighting chaplains is this holy man, Fr. de Valles. He literally lived in No Man's Land for four days, and when he could no longer carry the litter to bring in the wounded men, he tied wires to his wrist until they cut deep into the flesh. That was the type of chaplain we had in the 26th Division." At another event, General Edwards again made the case for the awards. He told his audience that he was on his way to visit de Valles in the hospital, calling him "one of the most gallant men I ever saw in the service," and that, "he lived an inspired life." He went on to offer his high praise: "You cannot get anything out of a division of Americans unless they have a soul. A soul will carry on when the body is exhausted, and Fr. de Valles is typical of the soul of my division."[4]

On April 28, a group of veterans of the 104th Infantry wrote to the priest, praising him for his "gallantry and devotion to duty." They went on to offer what amounted to a prayer:

> You were more than a chaplain—you were a true father to the oldest and wisest as well as to the youngest and most foolish. So we receive with much concern the news of your illness and it is our fervent wish that we might return to you a little of the unlimited comfort and compassion you bestowed on us during those dark days when we needed it so badly. Your recovery is prayed for by us all. Would that we might do more than pray.[5]

Members of the Machine Gun Company of the 104th Infantry presented a gold chalice to the priest as he lay in hospital.[6]

The valiant priest died at St. Luke's Hospital in New Bedford on May 12, 1920. The cause of death was stomach cancer. He was ultimately awarded the Distinguished Service Cross, literally on his deathbed, the fact being made known to him only one-half hour before he passed.[7] Secretary of War Newton D. Baker signed the order at 5:00 P.M. on May 12, and it was hand-carried that night to Massachusetts. The citation read:

> For extraordinary heroism near Apremont, Toul sector, France, April 10 to 13, 1918. Chaplain De Valles repeatedly exposed himself to heavy artillery and machine-gun fire in order to assist in the removal of the wounded from exposed points in advance of the lines. He worked long periods of time with stretcher bearers in carrying wounded men to safety. Chaplain De Valles previously rendered gallant service in the Chemin des Dames sector, March 11, 1918, by remaining with a group of wounded during a heavy bombardment.[8]

De Valles was buried with full military honors. Stores closed briefly, and flags flew at half mast on all public buildings in New Bedford. During his funeral service General Edwards pinned the award on the chaplain's breast.[9]

William Farrell

Father "Billy" Farrell returned home with the Yankee Division, and he resumed his pastoral duties at St. Bernard's in West Newton. He also remained active in veterans' affairs, becoming Chaplain of the 101st Infantry of the Massachusetts National Guard. Later, Farrell would serve as a curate at a number of parishes in the Archdiocese of Boston before he was made Pastor of Sacred Heart Church in Groton, Massachusetts, in November 1931. His tenure there was short, as he died at the rectory on February 12, 1933. A Solemn High Mass was celebrated at St. Bernard's Church on February 16, followed by burial at Calvary Cemetery with full military honors.[10]

After Farrell's death, fellow chaplain Markham W. Stackpole paid tribute to "one of his best friends in the army":

> None of the war-time chaplains of the 26th Division was more admired and beloved than Father William J. Farrell. . . . Active and faithful in his various official duties, Father Farrell was notable also for his personal relations with officers and men. He sought them out at the front positions, mingled with them in a friendly way, and in

times of action was at hand to minister to the wounded and dying...
On at least one occasion he went through machine-gun fire to give
the last rites to a dying soldier... Father Farrell suffered in health because of his war experience.... [H]e was one of those men who was
always the same good friend, however seldom one might see him.
None of us who knew him will forget Father Farrell.[11]

Farrell was eulogized in *Yankee Doings* as

a truly humble Christian gentleman... never too poor to give, never
too tired, never too dispirited... a splendid smile the ready laugh,
the spontaneous wit and humor; the common touch... Always "one
of the boys" he scorned the slightest thought of privilege... Jew,
Protestant, Catholic—they were his boys and if one of them needed him, no mud was too deep, no shellfire too heavy to keep him
away.[12]

The City of Newton, Massachusetts, commissioned Edward Brodney to paint a mural memorializing Father Farrell, its "famous son." The large painting depicts Farrell ministering to his men on the battlefield in France. It adorns a wall in City Hall, along with a nearby display dedicated to Farrell and other displays detailing the service and sacrifices of generations of Newton's citizen soldiers.[13]

Lucien Libert

Rev. Lucien Libert returned to the Diocese of Peoria, where, at his request, he was reassigned to the parish in Martinton, Illinois, from which he had departed for France. Although never seriously wounded, the rigors of his front-line duties took a definite toll upon his delicate constitution. Libert contracted pneumonia in November 1919, and while it looked as if he would recover, he took a turn for the worse and died on December 5. He was buried in Clifton, Illinois, following a Solemn High Requiem Mass in both Martinton and Clifton, both of which were well attended by numerous friends, relatives, and clergy.[14]

Murray Wilder Dewart

Murray Wilder Dewart returned home with the 101st Field Artillery and was discharged at Camp Devens on April 29, 1919. He resumed his duties as Rector at the Parish of the Epiphany in Winchester, but not for long.

Rev. Murray W. Dewart. Courtesy of Epiphany Parish, Winchester, MA.

Dewart resigned his pulpit in the spring of 1922 and moved his family to Baltimore, Maryland, where he became Rector of Christ Episcopal Church and entered into the life of the community. Murray brought his usual passion to his job, and he chaired a "small fellowship . . . for study and discussion." A member of that group would later write: "There was a delightful humanness about Dewart. . . . He reveled in the strife of ideas waged in the sincere desire for truth. . . ."[15] Dewart was just as passionate in his hatred of war, even more so since he returned from France, and he spoke out forcefully and frequently against the "insanity and idiocy of modern war." It is somewhat ironic that the chaplain, who had once confided to Mitty that he was "so everlastingly scared to death standing in front of congregations," would become noted for his sermons, and a much sought after public speaker as well. One cannot help but believe that his war-time experience delivering impromptu sermons and conducting short services under less than ideal conditions had forced him to better focus on his message, giving him the confidence to address any audience.

After their rocky start, he had come to know Paul Moody well during his assignment at Langres, but they had drifted apart after the war. After

Moody had become president of Middlebury College in Vermont, the two renewed their friendship at Arlington National Cemetery on May 5, 1926, during the dedication of a memorial to chaplains who had been killed during World War I. Moody extended an invitation to Murray to speak to his students at Middlebury, and he accepted. Later that year, Dewart preached a sermon at Middlebury on the subject of "sportsmanship," which was well received, and he agreed to a return engagement. That was not to be.[16]

At some point after the war, Murray was diagnosed with serious heart disease, something he did not share with many persons outside of his close family circle. He kept up his usual pace, and, once again, the stress and strain of his parochial duties caught up with him; he was granted a leave of absence in the spring of 1927. He and Mitty took the opportunity to sail to California by way of the Panama Canal. Murray returned refreshed and ready to resume his duties. However, his time would be short, as he suffered a massive heart attack on December 4, 1927, at the age of 53. Dewart had delivered his regular Sunday sermon, an "impassioned" homily about the perils of "complacency" for Christians, and he had literally just finished greeting the last of his congregants on the church steps when he was fatally stricken. His teenage son, Kenneth, rushed his father to Union Memorial Hospital, to no avail, as he had died en route. Dewart's funeral took place at Christ Church, crowded nearly to overflowing, on December 7. The service was presided over by Bishop John Gardner Murray, Primate of the Episcopal Church in America and Bishop of Maryland. Burial followed at Greenmount Cemetery.[17]

The following week, the Vestry at Christ Church passed a Resolution praising Dewart and lauding his many fine qualities. Their Resolution reads in part:

> Love was the keynote of his life, love for his God and his fellow men. . . . He had the rare gift of the understanding heart and the high courage that made him live life fully and without thought of self. His absolute sincerity and simplicity made his appeal that of friend and comrade, and won him the confidence and love of all ranks of life among whom he made no discriminations in his ministrations and friendly intimacies. . . . He was a fearless seeker after truth, and nothing but the truth would satisfy him. . . . His sermons were never critical or denunciatory of men, but he could scathe with fiery eloquence principles and practices which conflicted with what he thought was eternally right. His sermons were always directed towards inspiring in his hearers the desire for a better and higher life.[18]

A Memorial Service was also held in Winchester, Massachusetts, at the Parish of the Epiphany on the evening of December 7, 1927. There, many old friends and colleagues offered remembrances of Dewart. One friend, a fellow clergyman, Rev. William S. Packer, praised Dewart for his desire to find the good in everyone and to apply his Christian faith for the benefit of his fellow man. Packer also observed that Dewart's war experiences had profoundly affected him. "It was the World War that really killed him," he wrote. "He went to front line duty when he was far too old to go . . . [and] . . . the horrors of war ate into his soul." Dewart himself had told his congregation as late as November 13, that the war was "the greatest calamity in history," and that "not one in a hundred who fights any war knows what the war is about." Including, he told them, the men in his own regiment. Even he admitted, at the time, that he himself did not have a good answer. A fellow chaplain paid him a high compliment when he declared that Murray, "absolutely transcended denominationalism."[19]

Brig. Gen. John H. Sherburne, who commanded the 101st Field Artillery in France and served with Dewart there and on the Mexican border, told of Dewart's natural leadership and his ability to make friends. Sherburne said: "Away from all whom he loved, under the horrors of the World War, horrors of both sound and sight, Murray was once more an inspiration and a leader." He recalled the chaplain's "tender ministering to the sick and his loyal affection for all the men of the regiment."[20] Another friend and classmate said:

> We all loved Murray for his good fellowship. . . . We loved him also for his zest for the game, for his scorn of shame, for his utter honesty and for his courage to speak the truth at all times . . . [and] he loved to preach . . . and he always threw himself with all the ardor of his soul into whatever message he felt he had to give.[21]

His widow, Mitty, remained in Baltimore until her death in December 1978.[22] Their youngest son, also Murray W. Dewart, would follow his father into the ministry.

Charles E. Hesselgrave

Like Murray Dewart, when Doc Hesselgrave went off to war, he was substantially older than the men that he served. As YMCA Secretary-cum-chaplain, his duties often entailed long hours and placed him in dangerous situations. After he returned to South Manchester in April 1919, he took a short rest before resuming his ministry at the Centre Congregational Church. However, rheumatism and the stress and strain of war finally caught up with him, and he tendered his resignation to the congregation in 1920. Those same forces also took a toll on his marriage, and he and his wife separated and were later divorced. Hesselgrave moved to Seattle, Washington, where he served as a university chaplain and regained some of his health. He left the ministry and became a successful insurance salesman. Following his divorce, he married Anna DeLacey Cary, another YMCA worker with whom he had worked closely in France. Doc Hesselgrave died in Seattle on April 10, 1927, following a brief illness. Upon learning of his death, members of the Chatham, New Jersey, community where he had served as pastor recalled his "friendship, charming personality, and great mental gifts."[23]

Business as Usual

Most of the Yankee Division chaplains returned and took up with their lives where they had left off. Typical was Michael J. O'Connor, who came home with the Yankee Division and was discharged on April 29, 1919. O'Connor also resumed his pastoral duties as an Assistant at St. Peter's Church in Cambridge. Later he was appointed Pastor of St. Bridget's in Framingham, where he would oversee the construction of a new church building in the midst of the Great Depression.

Although still a parish priest, O'Connor would continue his service in the Massachusetts National Guard, where he was designated as Chaplain Emeritus and eventually promoted to the rank of brigadier general. He would also remain active in veterans' organizations, particularly with the Yankee Division Club. Nevertheless, recalling the horrors that he had seen in France, he was adamantly and publically against the country getting involved in another war in Europe. However, after December 1941, once the country was in that struggle, his patriotism waxed strong, particularly when he reflected upon the sacrifices of the young men in uniform. He gave his portable altar, the one that he had used all throughout France, to Fr. James Dunford, a former Curate at St. Bridget's, who was then serving as an Army Chaplain in the Pacific Theater.[24] The altar was used during battles at Guadalcanal, Bougainville, and in the Solomon Islands.

O'Connor would belatedly receive the Purple Heart on June 1, 1932. He died on September 26, 1944, following a brief illness. He was buried in St. Stephen's Cemetery in Framingham.[25]

Osias Boucher

Osias Boucher returned home in March 1919, where he took on various diocesan assignments. Like Fr. O'Connor, he also remained active in the

Massachusetts National Guard. Boucher was appointed as Pastor of Blessed Sacrament Church in Fall River, where he remained until his death on May 13, 1955. He was elevated to Monsignor, and at the time of his death, he held the rank of brigadier general in the Massachusetts National Guard. His funeral was a large affair, with military and church leaders present, along with parishioners and the men with whom he had served in France. To those men, his "beloved comrades," he left a message in his Last Will and Testament. "Carry on, be alert. Have a one right, loving and fearing conscience . . . shun the double conscience," he told them. And, he added, "have a thought for me in your daily prayers." Boucher was buried in Notre Dame Cemetery in Fall River.[26]

ORVILLE ANDERSON PETTY

Orville Anderson Petty returned to the United States on June 6, 1919, and he was discharged four days later. In the interim, he was promoted to the rank of major, and, in addition to the Silver Star, he was awarded both a Croix de Guerre and the Etoile Noire Chevalier by France, as well as the Belgian Order de la Cournonne. Petty resumed his pastoral duties at Pilgrim Congregational Church in New Haven until 1929. Later, he would become the head of the Arnold Physical Culture College, also of New Haven. From 1938 to 1941, he was a lecturer at Yale University in the Department of Race Relations. Petty was very active in community affairs, and he served as president of Grace Hospital, the Connecticut Council of Religious Education, and the New Haven City Missionary Society, maintaining a lifelong interest in the peoples of the Far East. He also authored a number of books on religious subjects and remained active in the Connecticut National Guard. Upon his retirement in 1938, he was promoted to the rank of brigadier general by act of the Connecticut General Assembly. He was awarded an honorary degree from Yale University in 1919. Petty had undergone several operations shortly before he died at his home in New Haven on August 13, 1942.[27]

H. BOYD EDWARDS

H. Boyd Edwards came home with the 101st Engineers and was discharged on April 30, 1919. He returned as Rector to St. Michael's Episcopal Church in Milton, Massachusetts; however, "the war had taken a toll of his strength, and he felt that a long rest was imperative." His resignation as Rector in April 1921 was "reluctantly accepted" by the Vestry. In 1922, Edwards was appointed Dean of Trinity Cathedral in Little Rock, Arkansas, and he served in that capacity until 1926, when he became Rector of the Church of the Ascension in Pittsburgh, Pennsylvania. For the next twenty years Edwards ministered in the "Steel City" until his retirement on September 1, 1946. Announcing his intention to retire, Edwards cited Bishop Lawrence's suggestion that those who reach the age sixty-eight should retire and make way for younger men. During his ministry in Pittsburgh, he was active in Diocesan affairs. Earlier, in 1931, there had been some talk that he was being considered as Bishop of Arkansas.[28] That did not happen.

Following his retirement, Edwards moved to Nashville, North Carolina, where he engaged in missionary work. In 1962, he returned to New Vernon, New Jersey. Dr. Edwards died in Morristown, New Jersey, on November 21, 1970.[29]

Chauncey Allen Adams

For Chauncey Allen Adams, service was in his blood. Upon his return from France, he returned to his pulpit at Danville, Vermont, where he served as pastor until October 1923. He left Danville and, for the next eleven years, was pastor of the Waterbury Congregational Church. In the aftermath of a major flood in November 1927, the church opened its doors to the local Methodist Church until the damage to their house of worship was repaired, and it provided meals for those who had been rendered homeless. He was also active in a variety of organizations and causes from religious education to the Anti-Saloon League, as well as the Vermont Bible Society and the Masons. Adams was also Editor of *Congregational Vermont* from 1934–1936. He was undoubtedly proud when he received an Honorary Doctor of Divinity from Middlebury College on June 12, 1933. The degree was conferred upon him by a fellow Yankee Division chaplain, Paul Dwight Moody, then president of the college. When Adams left Waterbury to take an active role in the Vermont Conference of Congregational Churches, the *Waterbury (VT) Record* proclaimed, in a front page article, that, "the community is a better place to live by having Dr. Adams a resident." It went on to state: "He has been a real citizen, has taken a prominent part in everything that was for the betterment of the people of Waterbury."[30]

From his election in May 1934 until his retirement in June 1946, Adams served as Secretary for the Vermont Conference of Congregational Churches. In that capacity, he traveled the length and breadth of the state, "often at great personal inconvenience," to address the needs of the denomination. He was lauded as a "wise counselor and trusted friend." All the while, Adams maintained his connection with soldiers. Throughout the postwar

Chauncey Allen Adams, DD.
Courtesy of Pilgrim
Place Archives.

years, Adams remained involved in military matters as well. In 1922, he succeeded Paul D. Moody as chaplain to the 172nd Infantry of the Vermont National Guard until 1939, and he later served in that same capacity in the Vermont State Guard from 1943 to 1948.

His wife, Marion, died in 1946, and he later moved to Claremont, California, where he became a resident of Pilgrim House, a "senior community" for retired clergy or those who had worked with charitable organizations. Chauncey Allen Adams died there on September 8, 1959.[31]

Robert Campbell, Jr.

Robert Campbell, Jr., returned to the Congregational Church in Warren, Massachusetts, and picked up where he had left off. On June 29, 1920, he married Marjorie Perkins of Warren, and in December of that year, he resigned as minister. Thereafter, he served as pastor at a succession of Congregational churches throughout the area, including Troy, New York, and Swampscott, Worcester, Salem, Hamilton, and Woburn, Massachusetts. After his retirement, the couple moved to Marblehead, Massachusetts, where Marjorie died on December 13, 1963. Though retired, Robert continued to serve as a guest minister at various area churches. Campbell died of a heart attack on August 31, 1969, while preaching at the First Congregational Church in Chelsea, Massachusetts. He and Marjorie are buried in Waterside Cemetery in Marblehead.[32]

George S. L. Connor

Shortly after his discharge on April 28, 1919, Chaplain Connor was assigned to St. Joseph's Church in Pittsfield, Massachusetts, where he served as curate until 1925. Thereafter, he was assigned as Rector at St. Michael's Cathedral in Springfield, where he became known as "a man of action, energy, and courage," as well as an "inspiring and competent organizer and leader." He held the position of Rector until August 1937, when he was appointed as the Pastor of Holy Name Church in Chicopee. He would hold this assignment for the balance of his ministry. Meanwhile, he was appointed Vicar General of the Diocese of Springfield on September 8, 1950, and on November 15 of that same year, he was elevated to Monsignor.[33] In 1951, the rank of Prothonotary Apostolic Prelate was conferred on him by the Vatican, and as a result, he was able to offer Pontifical Masses. Connor was responsible for the construction of a new social center in Springfield, and he was, as well, a driving force behind the establishment of two area parishes.

Connor was active in other church and community affairs, including a nearly lifelong association with Holy Cross College. So much so, that to all of his friends he was known as "Mr. Holy Cross" or simply "Cross." From 1954 to 1957, he served on the Associate Board of Trustees, and in the latter year, he was honored when his beloved alma mater inducted him into the Holy Cross College Athletic Hall of Fame. Connor was also active in the Knights of Columbus, where he served as chaplain to the local Assembly. In 1936, Connor was one of three persons to receive the Pynchon Medal by the Springfield Advertising Club for distinguished service. During the Second World War, he was one of eight Vicar Delegates chosen by Cardinal Spellman to assist with the Military Ordinariate, which was responsible for the work of military chaplains, as well as the welfare of Catholics serving in the military.[34]

On June 26, 1962, the longtime pastor was taken suddenly ill and died while on a vacation with several other priests at Wareham, Massachusetts. Only the year before, he had celebrated the 50th anniversary of his ordination. He was buried in St. Michael's Cemetery following a Requiem Mass.[35]

Charles K. Imbrie

Following his discharge on April 8, 1919, Charles K. Imbrie returned to his ministry, but not at Lancaster. Rather, he accepted the call at the First Presbyterian Church in the village of Penn Yan, in the Finger Lakes Region of New York. He served there until January 28, 1927, when he was installed as the pastor of the First Presbyterian Church at Newburgh, New York. His service there and his subsequent steps are hard to follow, until late in his career when he surfaced at Montauk, New York. He was installed as Pastor of the Montauk Community Church on October 2, 1947. His stay was short, but Imbrie was obviously pleased with his ministry there, and the congregation responded in kind. Accordingly, the Elders were "shocked and saddened" when, on June 1, 1949, Dr. Imbrie announced his intention to retire sometime that Fall. On October 19, on the eve of his departure, the church members held a covered dish testimonial dinner and presented him with a gift of money. The church hall was crowded with nearly 125 friends and well-wishers, when E. V. Conway rose to present the purse to the Imbries. Mid-way through his remarks, the speaker collapsed and died, adding an obviously jarring note to what should have been an otherwise memorable evening for the couple.[36]

In the meantime, Imbrie thought enough of the small church that he took real pains to create a job description for potential successors. He went on at length about the obvious attributes of the church building and the manse, the "healthy climate" and the "natural beauty" of the surroundings, as well as a description of the Montauk community itself, with its mix of fishermen, businessmen, and the seasonal folk. Perhaps in a nod to the ecumenical spirit with which many returning chaplains were imbued, Imbrie mentioned the long distance to the nearest Protestant church, and the "friendly relations" with the nearby Catholic church, a mission like Montauk Community. However, in colorful language, he strongly suggested just who should apply, or rather, who should not:

> Not a young man, because Montauk offers limited opportunities for expansion that the ambitions of youth usually seek. At the same time, Montauk deserves more than a 'springboard' for some larger church. It is a field that responds better to experience than to experiment. Nor is the church seeking a man moribund in body or mind, but in middle or later life, perhaps some pastor of a larger parish who has become a bit "weary in well doing" and upon whose shoulders "the grasshopper has begun to be a burden," but one who could renew his youth through the exercise of his accumulated store of wisdom among some of the choicest folk in New York State.[37]

He and his wife retired to Penney Farms, Florida, where he died at his home on January 26, 1958.[38]

Arthur J. LeVeer

After a month's rest following his return from France, Arthur LeVeer reported to his former parish, Our Lady of *Victoires* in St. Johnsbury, Vermont, but almost immediately was assigned as Pastor at Randolph, where he served from September 1919 to August 1920.[39] The duties there included mission churches in Bethel, Rochester, and South Royalton. This was followed by St. Norbert's in Hardwick, where he was Pastor for the next twenty-six years. His assignment there also included St. Michael's Mission in Greensboro Bend. Known as an "energetic administrator," he embarked upon an ambitious building program that included a new rectory and an enlargement of the church. His final assignment was Pastor at Holy Angels Church in St. Albans. While there, he built a new school and made major improvements to the church.

Throughout the period following his return from overseas, Fr. LeVeer was active in the American Legion and the Knights of Columbus. Arthur LeVeer retired as an active priest on February 4, 1963. He died at St. Alban's Hospital on September 2, 1964, following a long illness, and he was buried at Mt. Calvary Cemetery.[40]

Thomas F. Temple

Although assigned briefly to the 101st Infantry regiment, Thomas Temple did not return with the Yankee Division. Like many of his colleagues, he was held in France a little longer to assist with other units. In his case, he served as chaplain to the 1st Air Depot, and he returned with them in mid-July. He was discharged at Camp Dix, New Jersey, on July 21, 1919. Temple went on to serve at various parishes throughout the Archdiocese of New York. From 1919 to 1937, he was Parochial Vicar at St. John's Church on Kingsbridge Avenue in the Bronx. Thereafter, he served as Pastor, first at St. Mary's Church in Katonah, New York, from 1937 to 1944, and for the balance of his ministry as Pastor at St. Francis de Sales Church in Manhattan. While there, he was elevated to Monsignor, and in 1947, he was appointed Papal Chamberlain (April) and then Domestic Prelate (November). Msgr. Temple died on October 27, 1955, at St. Elizabeth's Hospital in Manhattan after a short illness.[41]

Difficult Days

Although he lived a long life, Fr. George F. Jonaitis was severely limited by his wound. Upon his discharge on March 1, 1919, with the rank of

Rev. George F. Jonaitis. Courtesy of the Archdiocese of Omaha.

major, he was granted a leave of absence and embarked on a six-month lecture tour. Thereafter, Jonaitis organized St. Peter's Church in Detroit, Michigan, and he served as Pastor from September 3, 1919 until January 1, 1927. Granted another leave of absence, he traveled throughout Europe for the next ten months, until November 4, 1927. When he returned, he was assigned as Pastor of St. Peter's Church in Stanton, Nebraska, where he served until April 15, 1931. The priest was active in veterans' affairs, both nationally and in Nebraska, as a member of Disabled American Veterans, the American Legion, and the Veterans of Foreign Wars. His next assignment was as Pastor of St. Francis Borgia Church in Blair, Nebraska. This was during the depths of the Great Depression, and the assignment ultimately proved to be too much both physically and fiscally.[42]

Unable to use his right hand, Jonaitis learned to write with his left. In the meantime, he underwent numerous surgeries on his right forearm in an effort to regain function in that hand, and at times simply to save the arm. Complicating matters was the painful arthritis he had developed in his left arm. In mid-July 1934, he took sick leave to travel to the VA Hospital in Hines, Illinois, for an operation, and he was still a patient there on September 18. The first operation was not successful, and he would need a second.

However, as a priest, the worst effect was that each of those conditions impacted his ability to celebrate Mass with both hands, as required. Jonaitis was ultimately able to obtain a Papal dispensation in 1948.[43]

During his recuperation at Hines, Jonaitis had heard of troubles back home in Blair. He wrote to Bishop Rummel, requesting an extension of his leave of absence and for help with his parish:

> I have received letters from the people and the Priest at Blair to the effect that they want to close the Parish House for the winter, because the situation there is grave. The knowledge of this fact worries me very much and it is breaking my heart. I have worked so hard for many years during the depression and now the people at Blair seem unwilling to support their Parish.... I cannot handle the situation at Blair from here now that my life is in jeopardy, so I am asking Your Excellency to please take up this matter at once and see what can be done until I am able to return to Blair.[44]

Bishop Rummel replied with good wishes to the priest and his upcoming operation, and he addressed his concerns: "The situation in Blair is also a source of anxiety to me as well as yourself, however, I will send someone there shortly who will make every effort to restore order and peace among the seemingly distracted parishioners."[45]

After his release from Hines in April 1934, Fr. Jonaitis spent a total of approximately six of the next fourteen months in Blair, the rest in hospitals and clinics. He was off to Hot Springs, Arkansas, in May 1936, where he stayed with an old Army buddy. There the priest consulted a Dr. Leonard R. Ellis and seemed to derive some relief for his arthritis in the hot baths. While in Arkansas, he began to experience the first of his money troubles. He asked the Bishop for help: "Now your Excellency, I suppose you understand that my financial troubles have begun as I have been paying all my hospital bills and doctors and private nurses since I became ill and the fountain is exhausted. So I am writing you this letter and asking you if it will be possible to help me out financially for the present time."[46]

In December 1936, Jonaitis traveled to Tucson, Arizona, where he became a patient at St. Mary's Hospital and Sanatorium, run by the Sisters of St. Joseph, and where he also received treatment at the Wyatt Clinic. His financial troubles persisted. He was not receiving a salary as Pastor at Blair, and more importantly, he had received word that his prior plea for diocesan assistance had been rejected. On the exterior, he must have maintained a positive attitude, because Dr. Thompson at the Wyatt Clinic found him to be "a very interesting and entertaining person, as well as a very cooperative patient." There is, however, in his correspondence with Omaha, a profound sense of desperation and a feeling of disappointment that he had been abandoned by his ecclesiastical superiors. He was accumulating bills, and he wanted to avoid going to the VA hospital in Tucson. He wrote to the bishop to renew his plea, and the uncharacteristically uncharitable and pessimistic tone of his words was interesting, especially coming from the man who had shared all the privations of the battlefield with his "boys," and demonstrated the deep level of his frustration:

> I feel that having so faithfully served the . . . diocese of Omaha as I have for twenty-seven years, I merited at least a decision from the proper authority. . . . Unfortunately for me, my poor health has placed me under heavy expenditures during the past three years, so much so that I have now exhausted all my funds. . . . I am again asking the diocese to come to my help. In the event that this fails me, I will, by the end of the year, be forced to go to the Veterans Hospital in Tucson. I am loathe to do this and I hope I can avoid it for the reason that, there, I will have no privacy whatever and will be thrown among all kinds of human riff-raff and companionship distinctly foreign to my clerical dignity.[47]

There is no clear evidence that the diocese reconsidered the request, but, after all, it was in the midst of the Great Depression. George Jonaitis was physically unable to fulfill his responsibilities as Pastor at St. Francis Borgia, and he resigned effective October 30, 1937. As further evidence that Jonaitis's money troubles persisted, the Omaha doctor who had treated him off and on for ten years wrote to the bishop on his behalf, asking for "a fair remuneration" for his patient.[48] There is no record of a reply.

Jonaitis moved to the Southwest, serving both in Vail, Arizona, from 1942 to 1948, and in Tucson. He appears to have adjusted well to his new circumstances, and the change of venue gave a boost to his spirits. He made many friends by force of his personality. On Sunday, April 23, 1950, a number of the priest's many friends—including the governor of Arizona, the mayor of Tucson, and the Lithuanian consul from Los Angeles—joined him to celebrate both his fortieth year as a priest and his seventieth birthday. The day began when he celebrated Mass at Saints

Peter & Paul Church, followed by a reception at his home, and a dinner at the Hungarian Village. In recognition for Jonaitis's having settled the meatpackers' strike at Omaha in 1915, Edward Cudahy supplied all the meat for the feast.[49]

Father Jonaitis returned to Omaha in 1962, and he took up residence at St. Vincent's Home for the Aged, where he died on December 26, 1963, at the age of 83. Following a Pontifical Mass at St. Cecelia's Cathedral, he was buried at Calvary Cemetery with full military honors.[50]

Allen Evans, Jr.

Allen Evans, Jr., who had served as chaplain to the 104th Infantry Regiment, was discharged at Camp Taylor, Kentucky, on April 19, 1919. He returned to his ministry, first as Senior Curate at St. James Episcopal Church in Philadelphia until 1921, when he was elected Rector of the Church of the Ascension in Morton, Delaware County, Pennsylvania. Later, he succeeded Murray Dewart as Rector at the Parish of the Epiphany in Winchester, Massachusetts, on January 21, 1923. While at Epiphany, Evans oversaw a major addition to the parish house and a general increase in communicants, as well as the formation of several new groups.[51]

In one of his last sermons at Winchester, Evans called for Christian unity, especially in light of a worldwide conference scheduled to take place in Switzerland later in the year. He pointed to what he found to be the "increasing spirit of good will and fellowship" and a lessening of "prejudice" among the various Christian denominations. He went on to say:

> In approaching the problem of Christian reunion, we must admit frankly and in a sympathetic spirit that other churches have tenets or beliefs that are at variance. . . . No one church possesses all the truth. There are obvious evidences of the Holy Spirit in all of them. The members of any one church are not the only ones who will be saved. . . . Each church has its possible contribution to the whole.

The Rector called for unity of "spirit" and "co-operation in charity, reasonableness, and fellowship in the discipleship of Christ."[52]

A week later, in early April, Evans resigned as Rector of Epiphany to accept the same position at Trinity Church in Hewlett, Long Island, where he would serve for the next decade. In 1937, he became Dean of the Philadelphia Divinity School (now the Episcopal Divinity School in Cambridge, MA), an Episcopal seminary, acting in that capacity for another ten years. Evans became Rector of St. Peter's Church by vote of the Vestry in September 1947. It was at this point, toward the end of his career, that he faced his biggest challenges, with declining membership and a fall off of Sunday attendance, and worse, "constant warfare with the Vestry," which "took a toll on his health." Not surprisingly, he resigned his position in 1954 and retired to his home in Haverford.[53]

Allen Evans, Jr., died at Bryn Mawr Hospital on December 16, 1960.[54]

James Peter Sherry

James Peter Sherry returned to Boston, Massachusetts, aboard the *Agamemnon* on April 8, 1919, and he was discharged three weeks later. He resumed his duties at St. Thomas Church in Jamaica Plain in May. For the next seven years, he served there and at St. Anthony's in Cohasset and St. James in Arlington. However, for the balance of his life, he was plagued by health issues. Sherry took a long leave of absence in the fall of 1926, and he returned to his duties in 1932 and served several other parishes over the course of the next decade. In June 1942, he entered the Veterans' Hospital in Roxbury, later transferring to Cushing V.A. Hospital in Framingham, where he died on July 4, 1947.[55]

Michael Nivard

Michael Nivard returned to the United States on April 6, 1919, and was discharged three weeks later. At some point, Nivard left the Missionaries of the Sacred Heart and became a diocesan priest in the Upper Peninsula of Michigan. He served briefly at St. Joseph's Church in Lake Linden, and for many years at Dollar Bay; however, serious illness forced him to take long medical leaves and eventually led to his retirement. He was a well-known and beloved resident of "Copper Country." Nivard died June 9, 1950. No doubt his battlefield experiences helped him through his last illness, as his obituary read that he "served his parishes to the best of his ability in spite of a chronic and fatal illness."[56]

Roads Not Taken

For several Yankee Division chaplains, the active or full-time ministry was not their primary occupation. For some, this was so prior to the war, and for others, it was a gradual transition. Burnham North Dell returned to Boston, but not to Emmanuel Church, at least not for long. Perhaps it was his experiences as a chaplain in France, but his life's path diverged from the ministry. Dell was discharged on April 24, 1919. He would assist at the wedding of a friend that May, and shortly thereafter enrolled at Harvard, where he obtained a Master of Arts degree in 1921. He still played competitive tennis. In 1923, he was the only winner for the Boston team in play for the Church Cup, which the New York team would win, defeating one from Philadelphia 6–3. After that, it was back to Princeton, where he earned his Ph.D. in 1933, and where he would remain for the balance of his career, as both a teacher and an administrator.[57]

Dell took time out during the Second World War to re-enlist in the Army. He was commissioned as a major and assigned to a special section that educated selected German prisoners of war to prepare them as administrators and civil servants in a democratic postwar Germany. At the war's end, he left the Army with the rank of Colonel, but he did not return to Princeton. Rather, he and Margaret retired to Nantucket, where he took up painting, and where the couple became active in the St. Paul's Episcopal Church, as well as numerous other civic activities on the island. In November 1948, he addressed a forum sponsored by St. Paul's Church on the topic of civil rights for African-Americans and other minorities. Dell died at New England Deaconess Hospital in Boston, on September 14, 1963. His funeral and burial were on Nantucket.[58]

Dell was eulogized by a friend as one who brought to the task at hand:

> qualities of friendliness, graciousness, gentlemanliness and understanding of others that so endeared him to his neighbors and associates.... [He] was a minister, a teacher and an administrator, but most of all he was the kind of man upon whom other men could rely, and an ever-responsive guide, philosopher and friend for the thousands of persons who will retain, throughout their lifetime, fond memories of him.[59]

Dr. Worcester of Emmanuel Church was right on the mark nearly fifty years before, when he referred to the "sweetness" of this young clergyman's disposition.

John Harvey Creighton

John Harvey Creighton came home from France and took up where he left off. He moved his family to Roanoke, Virginia, serving there as YMCA Secretary. In 1921, he moved yet again, this time to Mobile, Alabama, working in the same capacity. Creighton was active in community and church affairs. He served on the Library Board and the Juvenile Court Commission, was a member of the Rotary Club, and president of the Round Table

Club. In addition, he served as secretary of the Mobile Ministers Association and a Steward of the St. Francis Street Methodist Church, where he was in charge of Sunday school. Creighton died at his home on January 18, 1933, as a result of a stroke he had suffered two days before. The funeral took place from his home the next day, and he was buried at Pine Crest Cemetery.[60]

Earl R. Taggart

Earl Taggart also returned to a full-time job as an auditor at the Treasury Department.[61] From 1920 to 1921, he served as an Assistant Pastor for the National City Christian Church, and later, he served part-time as a pastor at a number of churches affiliated with the Disciples of Christ in the Washington, D.C., area. Earl was also an Elder in the National City Christian Church, president of the Christian Endeavor Union of Washington, and a Mason.

However, it was in 1921 that he began his employment with the Government Accounting Office, where he would serve one time as Chief of Personnel, and another as Chief of the Civil Division. At various times, his job required overseas audits in Europe and the Panama Canal Zone. In 1932, he reorganized the accounting system of the Haitian government at its request. He retired from government service in 1953 as a GAO Investigator. In retirement, he volunteered his time as a fiscal officer at CARE, the international relief organization.

Earl's wife, Julia Broderick, died in 1955. He died after a short illness on December 22, 1961, and both of them are buried in Arlington National Cemetery.[62]

Paul Dwight Moody

Major Paul Dwight Moody returned from France on June 30, 1919, and he was discharged at Camp Dix, New Jersey, three days later. He returned to St. Johnsbury, where he served as assistant at the South Church for the summer. That fall, he answered the call at the Madison Avenue Presbyterian Church, where he served as Assistant Minister for nearly two years. Perhaps it was the administrative skills that he developed or honed while serving in the AEF Chief Chaplain's Office, more recently as the Chief Chaplain himself, as he chose a decidedly different life path. It was at this time that he was offered the Presidency of Middlebury College in Vermont. He was elected to that position on August 19, 1921, and he would serve in that capacity until his retirement in 1942.[63]

President Moody and faculty of the Breadloaf School of English at the dedication of the Davison Library, July 21, 1930. *Left to right:* Vernon C. Harrington, Charles Baker Wright, Robert M. Gay, Paul D. Moody, Robert Frost, and Edward Day Collins. Courtesy of the Special Collections and Archives, Middlebury College.

Moody thrived in his new position. He was a frequent lecturer and oversaw the growth of Middlebury College. In 1923, during the presidency of Calvin Coolidge, when plans were made for a national Christmas tree in Washington, D.C., it was Dr. Moody that donated the first tree.[64] In July 1927, he preached a sermon at the Madison Avenue Presbyterian Church, and the topic was service. No doubt harking back to his days as a chaplain, he told the congregation:

> The measure of a man is not in the number of his servants, but in the number of people whom he serves. . . . I feel that the greatest of those who constructed our bridges and opened up the wilderness of the West did it, not for self gain, but that it might benefit those who followed them. . . . the soldier, sailor, fireman, policeman, telephone girl, all who remain at their post when danger threatens, have the reward of service.[65]

After he left Middlebury, Moody returned briefly to the pulpit, serving as Associate Minister at the First Presbyterian Church in New York City until 1946. He and his wife, Charlotte, retired to their home in Shrewsbury, Vermont, where he died of heart failure on August 18, 1947. He was buried in Northfield Center, Massachusetts.[66]

Israel Bettan

Israel Bettan returned to his congregation in Charleston, West Virginia, serving until 1922, when he left to assume a teaching position at Hebrew Union College in Cincinnati, Ohio, where he remained for the next thirty-five years.[67] He was a popular professor, active in civic affairs, lectured frequently, and wrote prolifically on scholarly subjects. It was in Cincinnati that he met Ida Goldstein, whom he married in 1927. They were the parents of one child, a daughter named Anita Esther.

Bettan was an outspoken advocate of Jewish unity and for the rights of minorities. At their convention in Atlantic City, New Jersey, on June 28, 1956, the Central Conference of American Rabbis unanimously elected him president of that body. At that same convention, in addition to a demand that the Soviet government grant more freedom for Jews to practice their religion, it was proposed that "a religious summit conference of Catholic, Protestant and Jewish groups" be formed "to work out a modus operandi to guide clergymen and laymen" concerning segregation.[68]

The rabbi was re-elected in June of the following year at a conference of Reform rabbis in Miami Beach, Florida. There he spoke about a subject that had been near to his heart for nearly four decades. During the First World War, he experienced firsthand what cooperation can accomplish when he and two other clergymen, a Catholic and a Protestant, shared the same stage as they crisscrossed West Virginia during a bond drive. Likewise, he experienced firsthand the opposite effect, when a lack of cooperation within the Jewish Community, among other things, delayed the appointment of a sufficient number of Jewish chaplains in the AEF until late in the war. These basic lessons were so well absorbed by the young man and ingrained in his thinking that he would return to them throughout his career. In his address to that gathering of 400 rabbis, he observed, "the American Jewish community, although united by a common history and living tradition, is far from presenting a harmonious whole." For the past decade, he added, every effort at cooperation had been thwarted by "ideological differences." He urged all Jews to, at the very least, explore those important areas where there is no disagreement "without forcing surrender of principles." He also challenged the faithful to not simply go to synagogue, but to embrace the "newer social legislation" and not to resist "attempts to right the wrong inflicted on minority groups."[69]

It was undoubtedly Rabbi Bettan's last major public speech, as he died suddenly at his home in Cincinnati six weeks later on August 5, 1957, just prior to his planned retirement.[70] Shortly after his death, a column appeared in a local newspaper that quoted a longtime colleague of Bettan's, who praised his many attributes, including his "wonderful sense of humor, his kindly and gentle manner, his unusual ability as a master of ceremonies, his Biblical scholarship, his understanding of the fine art of preaching, and his outstanding abilities as a teacher." The columnist himself phrased it more succinctly. "Cincinnati and the Jewish community at large this week lost a master of the fine art of preaching."[71]

Markham Winslow Stackpole

Markham Winslow Stackpole came home with the 102nd Field Artillery on April 10, 1919, and he was discharged at Camp Devens on April 29. While in France awaiting transport home, he received a promotion to the rank of captain, and, in addition, in 1919, he was decorated by the French Army with the Croix de Guerre and Bronze Star. The citation read: "He contributed to maintain a high morale among the troops that he accompanied." Stackpole returned to Phillips Andover and resumed his prior duties until 1922, when he resigned to engage in a year-long course of self-study. In 1923, he joined the faculty at Milton Academy, where he taught English and served as School Minister.[72]

While at Milton, he authored a book honoring the war service of former students and faculty, particularly those who had died, entitled: *World War Memoirs of Milton Academy, 1914–1919*. Interestingly, he makes very little mention of his own service.[73] In an article written shortly before publication of the book, Stackpole explained at length the intended purpose:

> My object in writing the memoirs and compiling the records has been in part the preservation . . . of significant biographical information. It has been my purpose, also, to contribute toward a present and future understanding of the World War, . . . particularly in its effect upon the men and women connected with Milton Academy. I have sought to describe some of the individual experiences which warfare involves, to point out the qualities of character and comradeship which it reveals, and to show its irreparable cost in human lives. It has not been my desire to stimulate a desire for military adventure and glory or to place military duties, virtues, and achievements above those of peace times. The spirit and the sacrifices which war duty involves have always seemed to call for special recognition, but other notable examples of good citizenship should also be kept constantly before the School. I share the earnest hope that our present and future citizens may be free to devote themselves to the duties and virtues of peace.[74]

Stackpole was also active in his community, serving as a member of the Warrant Committee, and he led the Milton Hospital Fund Drive. He was also chaplain of the local American Legion post. In 1943, Colgate University honored him with an award for distinguished service.[75] Upon his retirement from Milton Academy in 1945, Cyril H. Jones, a former headmaster, lauded Mark, his friend and colleague:

> For all that Markham Stackpole has given to Milton we can never be sufficiently grateful. He came to us with an energy and zeal which to some suggested a character from the Old Testament—a man firm in his beliefs, ever consciously seeking the right, complete in his integrity, and yet possessed of a deep love of humanity which never counted the cost of any kindly, thoughtful deed.[76]

Markham Winslow Stackpole died at Milton Hospital on March 17, 1948, following a brief illness.[77]

Notable Achievers

After his return from Europe, Albert Butzer received his discharge on July 30, 1919. He commenced graduate studies at the Union Theological Seminary in New York, where he distinguished himself by winning the Cuyler Preaching Fellowship. Following graduation, he wed Katherine M. Coe of Middlefield, Connecticut, in a ceremony at the First Presbyterian Church in New York City. One of his ushers was Major Charles Ray Cabot of Boston, who had commanded the 3rd Battalion, 103rd Infantry Regiment throughout the war. As Regimental Historian, Cabot told that regiment's story in a book published the previous year. Officiating at the wedding was fellow Yankee Division chaplain, T. Guthrie Speers.[78]

Shortly thereafter, Butzer was called to be the Pastor of the West Side Presbyterian Church in Ridgewood, New Jersey, on January 16, 1921. The newly organized congregation had only been in existence since 1912. He came highly recommended by Union Theological Seminary, which described him as "a man of sterling character, of magnetic personality, of deep religious experience and of unusual ability as a speaker." If any of the parishioners harbored any lingering doubts about the ability of their youthful minister, they were immediately dispelled after he preached his first sermon on January 30. Thus began a vibrant, eleven-year relationship, which saw not only the building of a new church and the retirement of the mortgage, but also a substantial growth in the congregation.[79]

If Ridgewood, New Jersey, was a good place for a young minister to blossom, in his next assignment, Albert Butzer burst into full bloom. Following his resignation from West Side Presbyterian in July 1932, he was called to be Pastor of Westminster Presbyterian Church, an urban ministry in the heart of Buffalo, New York. Butzer would spend the balance of his long career there. He quickly became a part of the community. One of his proudest accomplishments was the church's support for Westminster Community House, which was, in his words, "a center of religious tolerance, and racial integration" that addressed juvenile delinquency among the underprivileged African-American population of the neighborhood.[80]

In the early days of the Second World War, Butzer preached a message of faith and optimism, calling the former "the one quality needed more than any other in the trying months and years ahead." He told the young to "plan careers and marriages" in spite of the war. "The future is what we make it," he said, "and it is wrong to take what the future hands out to us just as though we were helpless victims of it." Later in the war, he reminded his congregation that it was not enough to simply pray for an end to the conflict, but also to remember God's "great causes on earth," and to "earnestly pray for a world of justice and righteousness and good-will," in addition to peace.[81]

Albert Butzer didn't simply talk about social action or community service, he believed in it wholeheartedly and, what's more, he lived it. In addition to a popular long-running Sunday radio program reaching a large audience in both Canada and the United States, he served on numerous boards and commissions, both religious and secular. He preached, lectured, wrote, and taught, and he received recognition in the form of several honorary degrees. But the hallmark of his long career was his unwavering work toward a greater "understanding between Catholics, Protestants, and Jews" as he worked with numerous clergymen from all three faiths. On January 9, 1959, he was asked to preach at the National Presbyterian Church in Washington, D.C., at a service attended by President Eisenhower and his ten-year-old grandson, David.[82]

In January 1962, Dr. Butzer announced that he would retire in September, after thirty years at Westminster. He had accomplished much—capital improvements and a tremendous growth in membership. Butzer would not be idle, he announced, hoping to continue as a guest preacher, and perhaps to teach the Bible.[83] In his Farewell Sermon to his congregation, he harked back to his time as an Army chaplain, in particular to the letters he wrote home to his family, as well as to grieving parents:

> I began my ministry at the Front in the First World War in France with 1,200 battle-tested American doughboys as my first parish....

I was rather amazed at myself, that I could have written such letters from rat-infested dugouts, and cootie-permeated clothing, with shells screeching overhead, and mud and blood all around me. There was no self-pity in those letters, but a lot of high-hearted hope in a warless world—and an almost fierce faith in the future, for a just and durable peace.[84]

Albert Butzer died at Buffalo General Hospital on November 28, 1962, following a short illness. At that time, he and his wife were residents of Ridgeway, Ontario, Canada. His memorial service was an outpouring of ecumenical spirit, and he was justly lauded for his outstanding character and a long life of service. Rev. Dr. Ralph W. Loew of Holy Trinity Lutheran Church wrote how Dr. Butzer "loved mankind," and that "long before so many others had caught the spirit of ecumenical understanding, he was a pioneer." Very Rev. Harold B. Robinson, Dean and Rector of St. Paul's Cathedral wrote: "The City of Buffalo has lost a dear friend. . . . He was one of those rare men whose heart was open to all who needed him. He loved and loved deeply. He shall be missed but not forgotten for his good works will live for many generations." Dr. Martin Goldberg, Rabbi of Temple Beth Zion wrote that "we of the Jewish community are poorer in the loss of this great leader and humanitarian."[85]

John Joseph Mitty

John Joseph Mitty returned to Camp Devens, Massachusetts, with the 101st Infantry. He had the dubious distinction of being thrown from his horse during the victory parade in Boston on April 25, 1918. As he was passing the Lenox Hotel, the horse apparently became spooked by all the commotion and threw the chaplain, who broke his ankle in the fall. In the meantime, he had already caught the eye of Archbishop Patrick Hayes of New York. Hayes immediately appointed Mitty to be Pastor of Sacred Heart Church in Highland Falls, and there he developed a lifelong friendship with General Douglas MacArthur, then Superintendent of the United States Military Academy at West Point, which was adjacent. A year earlier, upon the death of Msgr. Cornelius O'Keefe, Pastor of Sacred Heart, the Archbishop named Fr. John Langdon as Pastor of Most Holy Trinity Catholic Chapel at West Point. In that capacity he ministered to the needs of the Catholic cadets, since there were no Catholic military chaplains assigned there at that time. Following three years at Highland Falls, Mitty served the Archdiocese in a number of capacities, and he came to be known as a "no-nonsense," "can do" administrator. It was also during this period that he returned to

Archbishop John J. Mitty. Courtesy of the Archives, Archdiocese of New York.

France in 1925 to revisit the scenes of his time with the Yankee Division in the Meuse-Argonne, where, in his words, he "did his little bit," as well as a trip to the large American cemetery nearby at Romagne. In a letter to Archbishop Hayes, he wrote, "I have enjoyed this part of the trip most of all—it brings back so many memories and makes me thankful to God for the many blessings he gave me here and since."[86]

Thus, when it was learned that the Diocese of Salt Lake City was in dire fiscal straits, his well-deserved reputation propelled him into the bishopric there following the death of Bishop Joseph Glass. His mentor, now Cardinal Hayes, presided at the ceremony there on September 8, 1926. Not only did Mitty place the diocese on sound fiscal footing, despite his somewhat distant, formal manner, but he was supportive of the diocesan priests. Eventually, in 1932, he was appointed Coadjutor of the San Francisco Diocese, with then-Bishop Edward A. Hanna, who was in failing health. At Hanna's retirement three years later, Mitty was consecrated as Archbishop of the Diocese of San Francisco. During his long service there, the Archdiocese witnessed an enormous growth in physical plant to meet the growing population. Moreover, under his watch, more than eight hundred priests were ordained. His last years were spent in near monastic isolation at his residence at St. Patrick's Seminary, where he died on October 15, 1961.[87]

HARRISON RAY ANDERSON

Harrison Ray Anderson returned to Ellsworth, Kansas, and his pastorate at the First Presbyterian Church. Ray had been recommended for the Distinguished Service Cross, and twice cited for battlefield bravery, yet he received no medals—the end of the war, Army red tape, and the death of Col. Arnold in an accident on January 25, no doubt the reasons. In late summer 1921, the Andersons moved to Wichita, Kansas, where Ray served as pastor at the First Presbyterian Church until September 1928. While there, the church membership nearly doubled, educational and outreach programs were enhanced, and Anderson played a pivotal role in strengthening cooperation among all of the Presbyterian churches in the city. He also faced issues like Prohibition and the Ku Klux Klan.[88]

In 1928, Anderson succeeded his beloved mentor or "dominie," John Timothy Stone, as pastor at the Fourth Presbyterian Church of Chicago. For the next thirty-three years, he not only strengthened the local church itself, but he also used his pastorate as a platform from which he launched his lifelong effort to reunify the Presbyterian Church in the United States and to secure world peace. He also had a strong sense of right and fair play, and the courage to act, all of which were severely tested shortly after Pearl Harbor. At that time, a group of Japanese-Americans had formed a nondenominational congregation in Chicago, but because of the strict restrictions on their right to gather, they had no place to hold religious services. Anderson, supported by most of his church members, offered the use of the smaller chapel at Fourth Presbyterian on Sunday afternoons. When things became tense, both within and without his flock, Ray himself would "stand guard" outside the chapel to ensure peaceful worship. As the Japanese-American congregation grew, it began to use the larger chapel, and in 1947, it was "accepted as a member of the Chicago presbytery" as the Church of Christ (Japanese). Its members acquired their own church building in 1953.[89]

It certainly was a proud moment for the former chaplain and his congregation when they, amidst all the hysteria, took action to ensure the rights of these American citizens to assemble and to worship. It was several years before Justice Robert Jackson's vigorous dissent in the *Korematsu* case, where he declared that it was a "fundamental assumption" of our democracy that "guilt was personal and not inherited," and at least a generation before steps were taken to right the grievous wrong done to a segment of our citizenry.[90] Ray could have taken the easy way out, but just as so many years ago in France, when he had told his father about his choice to become a frontline chaplain, he did not.

Throughout his pastorate at Fourth Presbyterian, Anderson immersed himself in the work of the Presbyterian Church, serving on many boards and assuming various leadership roles, both locally and nationally. Ray served as an alternate delegate to the first conference of the World Council of Churches in Amsterdam in 1948. He was a frequent speaker and conducted many seminars across the country. On May 25, 1951, he was elected Moderator of the Presbyterian Church in the United States, the highest office in that denomination, at their General Assembly in Cincinnati, Ohio, and the following year, at the invitation of Dwight Eisenhower, he gave an invocation at the Republican National Convention.[91]

As Moderator, Anderson traveled extensively, everywhere preaching unity. On a trip to Europe, he purchased two Celtic crosses (he would later obtain a third), and then laid them both on the pulpit at St. Giles Church in Edinburgh and later at St. Peter's Cathedral in Geneva. Upon his return, he gave one each to the Moderators of the two branches of the Presbyterian Church, to be passed on to their successors and, hopefully, to be united one day. It was his fondest hope, and in his farewell address, when he stepped down as Moderator, he expressed his hope that it would be accomplished within his lifetime. Anderson would not live to see that day, however, it was short in coming, when the Presbyterian Church became one again in 1983.[92]

He and Margaret Ann were the parents of three children. Upon his retirement in 1961, Ray moved to Santa Barbara, California, where he died on October 18, 1979. He is buried in Junction City, Kansas.[93]

Malcolm Endicott Peabody

It would take two more generations of soldiers for talk of Post Traumatic Stress Disorder (PTSD) to become commonplace. However, during the First Word War, only the most severe or obvious cases were diagnosed with neurasthenia, colloquially referred to as "shell shock." No doubt, countless doughboys suffered from some form of stress related to the war, but without benefit of a clear explanation, they continued to suffer the effects long after they came home. Years later, as Malcolm Peabody wrote out the story of his life, he described his homecoming:

> Mary and my parents were there on the dock, together with little Marietta, over a year old, and was I glad to see them? Interestingly enough, my heart did not accelerate one beat even when I saw them down there on the dock, for I had been so torn to pieces emotionally for two years that I had no further capacity for feeling. The family

thought that this was odd, and I confess that I acted oddly for almost two years to come.

He offered a simple explanation: "War is a terrible experience, but the pressures under which you live have got to be experienced to be understood."[94] In time, Peabody was able to move on.

Upon his discharge at Camp Devens on April 29, 1919, Malcolm Endicott Peabody returned to his family in Lawrence, Massachusetts, and his ministry at Grace Episcopal Church, where he would become Rector. In 1925, he and the family moved to Philadelphia, Pennsylvania, where, for the next thirteen years, he served as Rector of St. Paul's Episcopal Church in the Chestnut Hill Section. Peabody became Bishop of the Diocese of Central New York in 1938, then for the region in 1942, and finally Bishop of Syracuse until his retirement in 1960. At that time, the Peabodys returned to Cambridge, Massachusetts. For the next five years, he served various area parishes from Concord and Salem to Brookline. Peabody died in Boston on June 20, 1974.[95]

John Francis Tucker

Fr. Tucker returned to teaching at the Salesianum High School in Wilmington, Delaware; however, he was destined for other things. In 1922, he was appointed as the first American Provincial of the Oblates in the United States, and two years later, given his fluency in Italian, he was named Pastor of the newly formed St. Anthony's Church, which served Wilmington's large Italian community. At first, services were held in a small wooden structure, but this was soon replaced with a large basilica. These two large responsibilities he took on with vigor, particularly, spreading the reach of the Oblates throughout the Northeast from Detroit to Philadelphia. In 1949, he was called to Rome to serve on the Oblates General Council. However, within a short time, he was asked by the Pope to serve as the private chaplain to Prince Ranier of Monaco. Along with that post came the pastorate of St. Charles Church in Monte Carlo. As a result of this assignment, he was instrumental in introducing Grace Kelly to the prince, and thereafter he became a trusted friend and confidant to both of them and their families.[96]

Throughout his long career, he was known for his magnetic personality and persuasive skills as an orator. Upon his retirement from active ministry, Francis Tucker returned to his alma mater, Salesianum High School, the place where he began his remarkable life's journey. He resided there in the faculty residence until November 1, 1972, when he died following a stroke at the age of 83. He was buried in Wilmington after a Requiem Mass at St. Anthony's Church.[97]

Thomas Guthrie Speers and the Leap of Faith

Guthrie Speers came home with the Yankee Division; however, it was an uneasy transition to civilian life. He returned to New York City shortly after the memorial service in Hartford on May 4, 1919. On the surface, things appeared fine, but his experiences during the war no doubt had left him physically and emotionally exhausted, along with a nagging inner turmoil —should he continue his ministry or take another path? Recognizing a young man at the crossroads, the older and wiser co-rectors with whom he was associated at the First Presbyterian Church, Drs. Alexander and Fosdick, convinced their young colleague to don his uniform once again and take the time to visit, unannounced, some of the bereaved families, those who had lost sons. The war had a long reach, from the battlefields of France to the heartland of America. It would be a journey to help heal those families, and, in turn, to renew and to heal himself.[98] So, not quite knowing what to expect, he set off to do just that.

Gathering up his lists of the dead soldiers from the 102nd Infantry Regiment, as well as assorted letters to him from their families, he prepared a rough itinerary. Most of the young men on his lists had been replacements: National Army men, draftees from the Midwest, who had been assigned to the 102nd Infantry, only to die a short time later in the raid at Marchéville, or charging a machine gun in the Bois d'Ormont. Beginning in Chicago on May 20, he traveled through downstate Illinois, then on to Wisconsin, Minnesota, Nebraska, and finally through the middle of Iowa headed east, reaching the river towns along the Mississippi by early June. He traveled by train and the Interurban to reach the larger cities and towns, and once there, by automobile. However, many of the families lived outside of the towns on nearly impassable unpaved roads and lanes. Here he would resort to horse and buggy.[99] He found the countryside lush and green, and the people friendly and forthcoming. At each stop, he sought to bring closure to most of those families, and hopefully, for himself as well.

Guthrie's first stop was Chicago, Illinois, where he met with Mary Burke, to talk about her son, Christopher. Mary, a good Catholic, born in Limerick, Ireland, told of her son's previous job as a street car conductor, describing him as a "nice, quiet little fellow" and "the dear lover." Speers prayed with her just before he left, and afterwards she assured him, "I'll not worry anymore." The woman must have assumed that he was a priest, as at the door she told him, with tears in her eyes, "Aw, Father, but you're the peacemaker for mothers' hearts." The chaplain prayed silently to himself: "God grant me to be that."[100]

For the most part, the families expressed, first their surprise, and then their gratitude, for the fact that someone from their son's regiment actually took the time to visit. He found in households where the mother had yet to accept the fact that her son was never coming home, that his sad task was made more difficult. One mother in Davenport, Iowa, told Speers that before he left for France, her son had said: "Don't worry, I'll be back, mother." In her skewed logic, she knew that therefore, "he must come home." She even had his best suit cleaned and pressed, and she had laid it out in his room in anticipation of that day. Guthrie's "heart went out to her." Even when those women knew in their hearts the sad truth, they questioned the fairness of it all. In Marshalltown, Iowa, another woman, who, in Speers's words, was "a dear motherly person," lamented bitterly: "Why should a good, home-loving boy be killed, when other worthless boys come back?" Edward Gaudur's mother was very embittered toward the Germans, while Charles Rieker's sister complained to the chaplain that her brother's "life was wasted."[101]

The days could be long, tiring, and no doubt emotionally draining. May 26 began in Brownville, Nebraska, a small town on the Missouri River. There, that morning, Corp. Gale Miller's little sister met him at the station and took him to the family home. Her brother had been killed by a shell burst on October 26 just north of Verdun. When the visit was over, Mr. Miller drove Speers to the McMann home, also in Brownville. All the way over, the two traveled in silence, but as they parted in front of the McManns', Mr. Miller, in a voice quaking with emotion, tearfully told the chaplain: "You know, I can't talk about this." Guthrie choked back his own tears as they said good-bye.[102]

The McMann home was "a terribly untidy house," with eleven lively children running all over, the youngest named Woodrow Pershing, and a distinct contrast with the previous visit. Mrs. McMann told Speers that the neighbors had been gossiping about some new purchases the family had made, like her new hat, as being possible only with the proceeds from their son Arthur's life insurance. The chaplain must have shaken his head at the thought, as he later wrote that "some people can be pretty low." Guthrie left the home with a sense that he had not helped the family, especially when he watched Mr. McMann abruptly rise to go outside "to plant corn," saying as he strode through the door: "You stay and visit with the women folks as long as you've a mind to."[103]

Then it was on to Crab Orchard, forty-four miles away, for his visit with the parents of George Little of Company B, killed at Marchéville. By then it was raining, and the home was more than two miles outside of town. The chaplain's Ford "skidded most of the way there." Once settled in the parlor, the couple was warm and welcoming, and each of them told boyhood stories about their son. The chaplain wrote that Mr. Little "had the biggest heart of all," and that he "would choke up every now and then, but would go on so bravely." Guthrie called this "one of the finest visits so far, but so hard," and he found it "awfully hard to go away and leave them alone." However, he had two more visits to make that day, in Beatrice, Nebraska, another twenty-two miles away.[104]

He arrived in Beatrice later that afternoon, following what he described as a "wild, rough ride." He met first with the family of Fred Thober, including his older brother John, another YD man, who had been wounded during a raid on St. Hilaire. The family expressed their gratitude for the visit. After he left, he ran into a number of men from the regiment. They held a small reunion, and Speers was given a tour of the town. He described it as a "community of retired farmers," with paved streets and a very good hotel.[105] At 8:00 P.M. that evening, Speers met with the parents of Arthur Bittings, also killed during the Marchéville raid. He described the mother as "pale and worn," and the father, sitting on the couch, rocking silently back and forth. Both parents were obviously still distraught. Later that same evening, the chaplain accompanied the family to a memorial service at the local Lutheran church, where a new minister, who had not taken the time to find out anything special about the young man, read from a text written out by Mr. Bittings himself. The family was so put off, Speers wrote, that "they are off the Lutheran Church for life."[106] No doubt Guthrie took this lesson to heart.

On June 1, in Perry, Iowa, the chaplain met with the parents of Venner Tighe. He was their only son and was also killed during the Marchéville raid. They had worked all their lives for Venner, and they were now very well-to-do. Now, Mr. Tighe told Speers: "If he had only come back. We had everything for him. And now there [is] no one left for us to work for." The chaplain noted that, "all the wealth in the world isn't much good after all."[107] The same could be said for the parents of James H. Collins, also an only son. They had a 400 acre farm in Alden, Iowa, to turn over to him, and were now at a loss. Nevertheless, they were so grateful to the chaplain for the visit that they even offered to pay him.[108]

The chaplain entered into the spirit of the enterprise, and found that he liked exploring his new surroundings and getting to know the local people. After his visit with the father of Alfred Hedum on May 28, in Soldier, Iowa, Guthrie returned to his hotel, where he sat around the lobby a good part of the afternoon talking with the local farmers about crops and hogs, as well as the general prosperity of the region. He found the conversation "mighty interesting."[109] Several days later, found Guthrie in Hiteman, a small coal mining camp, a short trolley ride from Albia in south central Iowa. During a visit to the Anderson home, Speers enjoyed lunch and an early supper with the family and their neighbors.

He was especially taken with Mr. Anderson, who had turned to farming after forty-three years in the coal mines. Anderson, a self-described Socialist, offered Guthrie some sound advice: "Speers, if I know you right, I think you will be in the great fight. Don't let any financial temptations lead you astray. You may be in a place sometime where you need help. Promise me that you will let me know." Later on, as Guthrie left the family, Mr. Anderson accompanied him on the train as far as Ottumwa, and the pair continued their conversation. Anderson asked the chaplain if he could pay his expenses. Guthrie declined, saying, "I couldn't be happy at home until I had seen you." Anderson looked at the young man and said: "You couldn't be happy while I should suffer! Speers, the time will come when this nation can't be happy while any other nation suffers." Guthrie later wrote that Anderson was a "remarkable man; a prophet," and he "gave me a wonderful charge for the fight of life."

While in Hiteman, Speers became acquainted with Mr. and Mrs. Yaningham, whom he had met in the general store. Yaningham was also a coal miner with twenty-three years experience, and also an ardent Socialist and a union man to boot. Yaningham gave Guthrie a tour of the No. 11 Mine of the Smokey Valley Coal Company. Down they went, 154 feet to the bottom of the shaft, in order to view a four-to-five-foot seam of coal lying beneath more than 100 feet of slate and gravel. Guthrie thought Yaningham was joking when he told him that the low tunnel was a "nice high mine," but his guide assured him that there were other mines only twenty inches high. He was shown the "room" where Yaningham worked, and the underground stable for the mules, some of which had spent twenty-five years below the earth. The man was proud of his job and of the union, and the "wonderful things" it had done for miners, from higher wages to the systemization of their work. After the visit with Yaningham, Guthrie wrote: "Socialism has one good thing to its credit. It has made people begin to think about economics and politics and think in world terms."[110]

Speers's trip proved invaluable for his development, and its lessons echoed throughout his subsequent career. Once back in New York, Guthrie applied himself to his ministry with a new sense of purpose. On February 18, 1920, he was elected Associate Pastor of the First Presbyterian Church at Fifth Avenue and Eleventh Street in Manhattan and installed in a ceremony held on April 18. The church had only recently merged with two others, and the young minister would play an important role in its growth.[111]

While he was still in the seminary, the emphasis of Guthrie's studies began to change with the introduction of the "Social Gospel," which involved "the application of Christ's principles to the social and economic areas." Speers found a focus for his ministry in these tenets, and thus by following Christ's example to "love thy neighbor," his approach to Christianity was more interactive and less reflective. In November 1926, in the midst of a prolonged strike of workers in the paper box industry, he and several other New York Area ministers offered their services to mediate an end to the dispute. "In the field of industry, international relations and the treatment of criminals we are . . . old fashioned," he told his congregation, "Jesus has discovered the only satisfactory law for life, and wherever men have followed it they have found it leading them to happiness and courage and power."[112]

In October 1928, after nearly a decade as associate pastor, Guthrie left the First Presbyterian Church to become pastor of Brown Memorial Presbyterian Church in Baltimore, Maryland. He would remain there until his retirement thirty years later. In his farewell sermon, he expressed his heartfelt view that doing was more important than preaching, although he also enjoyed a reputation as a fine speaker. "The minister's task is not to commend Christian views to the minds of men but to show Jesus to the eyes of men," he said. "Christianity is a revelation not an argument. . . . You cannot argue a man into the church," he added for emphasis.[113]

If Speers left for France a self-described "quasi-pacifist," he came home more committed than ever to the idea that war was "a wicked thing, and that we ought to do everything in our power to get rid of war from this earth." With Guthrie it wasn't just words. "I worked very hard on that when I got back from France," he would later recount, and "[I] went around talking about peace and the League of Nations in Baltimore, Maryland, and over on the Eastern Shore." The minister decried the trend of placing profit above all else, especially when it touched upon war. When a motion picture was released depicting the death of Edith Cavell, a courageous British nurse, shot by a German firing squad in occupied Belgium in 1915, his criticism was blunt. "When a moving picture company can revive past hatreds and exploit them as in the picture of Edith Cavell," he told his congregation one Sunday, "that is putting money above everything fine in life."[114]

At a symposium in Philadelphia in February 1931, Speers joined other Presbyterian ministers who had either been chaplains or combatants in World War I. The purpose of the gathering was to "ascertain the sober judgment" of the group, and at the conclusion, it was agreed "never again to participate in war or approve of war." Asked to comment, Speers observed that "the conqueror and conquered both lose in any war and that all war does is to sow the dragon's teeth of hatred leading to further wars."[115]

Once in Baltimore, Guthrie continued to speak out on social issues. He served as Chairman of the Committee on Social and Industrial Relations of the Board of National Missions of the Presbyterian Church. After a two-day meeting in New York in April 1936, the board adopted a report prepared by his committee condemning child labor as exploitive. It stated in part: "The use of children as wealth producers should be condemned for folly and injustice, and in the future the demand of industry not be allowed to prevent any child from securing the full opportunities of education as a human being and as a citizen."[116]

He was also a zealous advocate for the rights of minorities and the disadvantaged. In June 1940, at a meeting at the University of Virginia sponsored by the National Conference of Protestants, Catholics and Jews and the University's Institute of Public Affairs, he called for unity among the faithful of all three and urged them to rally around the issue of minority rights, especially in light of current events in Europe. He believed that religion could make a "tremendous contribution." He told the audience that the solution to the problem was "to be found in preserving and expanding our democratic liberties." Speers went on to say: "Religion can make us fit for freedom by insisting steadily that since God is the Father of us all, therefore liberty is not a privilege of some but the right of all ... [and] ... we cannot keep liberty for ourselves unless we uphold it for all."[117]

Dr. Speers applied his beliefs to his own daily life and work, and so it should come as no surprise that during his ministry at Brown Memorial, he "ended racial segregation within the church and abolished the system of pew rentals." He also reached out to the local Jewish community and, from time to time, swapped pulpits. The minister continued to call for a "personally possessed religion," not a formulaic practice, but rather a daily individual battle against "fear, suspicion, despair and cynical doubt." He referred to the latter as the "demons of today."[118]

Guthrie retired as pastor at Brown Memorial in 1957, after nearly thirty years. Thereafter, he served as a minister at the Interdenominational Chapel by the Sea in Captiva, Florida, a chaplain at the Darrow School in New Lebanon, New York, and for five years adjunct Professor of Religion and chaplain at Goucher College in Baltimore. He died at Greater Baltimore Medical Center at the age of 93 on May 9, 1984. At that time, he was a resident of Broadmead in Cockeysville, Maryland. Idleness did not suit him, and while there, in supposed retirement, he taught a regular Bible class.[119]

In the days following his death, many who knew him paid tribute to his life and character. One wrote:

> He preached and lived the social gospel, working to break down the barriers that separate mankind. He built bridges of understanding between races, between religions, and between labor and management. He sought justice for the oppressed, help for the poor, and peace. . . . He loved people, and they loved him. His warmth, deep faith, humility, sense of humor, understanding, and good nature carried a message even more meaningful than his eloquent sermons.[120]

Another praised him for his modesty and his commitment to social issues. He described Speers as "a man of simple faith and profound intellect, a man without bitterness or cynicism who read the scriptures as a Word which God was speaking across the centuries to him and his people in this time." Perhaps a more fitting tribute for the former chaplain, for any chaplain for that matter, were the simple words that he had read more than sixty years before, written by Harry W. Congdon of Company C, 102nd Infantry, to his mother shortly before his own death: "Chaplain Speers is the father to all the boys and their friend."[121]

Afterword

Birth of the Chaplain Corps

It could be truly said that the modern U.S. Army Chaplain Corps emerged from the American experience of the First World War—trained by Major Pruden and led by Bishop Brent and the GHQ Staff Chaplains Office. In fact, General Pershing's appointment of Bishop Brent to be the senior chaplain in the AEF proved to be a pivotal decision in that evolutionary process. For years, denominational rivalries had impeded just such an essential step. The United States Army was now poised to form the Chaplain Corps with a working model in place, based upon wartime experience, with a body of trained men to carry it forward. Congress took the final step with the Defense Act of June 4, 1920, and the creation of a Chief of Chaplains who would hold the rank of full colonel. The first Chief of Chaplains was Rev. John T. Axton.[1]

Brent came home, his work with the AEF done. He assumed his duties as Bishop of the Episcopal Diocese of Western New York, but he did not abandon his place upon the world stage. In 1921, he lectured at Aberdeen, Edinburgh, and Glasgow universities in Scotland, and two years later, President Warren G. Harding appointed him to the Advisory Committee on Narcotics of the League of Nations. Brent also believed strongly that Christian unity was essential, and he was instrumental in the formation of the World Conference on Faith and Order. He was elected president of that body at the initial conference held in Lausanne, Switzerland, in 1927. The bishop died there on March 27, 1929, and he was buried in the Bois de Vaux Cemetery.[2]

Brent and Pruden would wind up on opposite sides of a bitter insignia of rank controversy. A minister first and last, Brent grasped the significance of the issue, but he was never comfortable in military garb, and he recommended to Pershing that insignia of rank not be worn by chaplains. Pershing agreed and recommended that the War Department issue such an order, which it did in March 1918. Pruden felt strongly that in an army where rank equated with status and power, the visible insignia of rank gave the chaplains a firm place in the military hierarchy, the ability to assert their authority, and to command respect. Pruden urged his students

Chaplain Aldred A. Pruden. Courtesy of the U.S. Army Chaplain Corps Museum, Fort Jackson, SC.

to write their congressmen and others to protest the order, and for that he was relieved of command of the school. Though he would lose the first round, Pruden's views ultimately prevailed. In 1926, the Army changed its policy. Following his relief, Aldred A. Pruden was transferred to other duties, and he was later promoted to lieutenant colonel on June 4, 1920. Pruden retired from active duty in 1922 and died twenty years later. He is buried in Arlington National Cemetery.[3]

Tested in the Fire

The story of the Yankee Division chaplains, or for that matter, all Army chaplains, did not end with the Armistice. Like Meshach, Shadrach, and Abednego,[4] the faith and the courage of these men had been put to the test in the furnace of war. Every doughboy, including the chaplain, was affected in some fashion by his experiences during the war. For some, their wounds, both psychological and physical, would take a long time to heal, if ever. Others went right back to their day-to-day lives with an underlying sense of pride, while for others, the war was a motivator, driving them to achieve greater material or professional success in life. The chaplains were no exception, and their postwar experiences mirrored those of their comrades in arms. In fact, it could be argued that for some of these extraordinary men, their wartime experiences enhanced their continued service to their fellow men, not only as clergymen, but also as citizens—the social gospel writ large.

Most of the returning doughboys were proud of their service, and they participated in various veterans associations. The men of the 26th Division even formed their own organization, one that exists to this day. Some continued their service in the National Guard. Chaplains Petty, O'Connor, and Boucher also remained active within the National Guard throughout their postwar lives, each ultimately achieving the rank of brigadier general.

The Army chaplains were ordinary men, who, like the soldiers they served, were called upon to do some extraordinary things. They were trained to minister to the spiritual needs of their congregations in peacetime. For the younger chaplains like Al Butzer, their service was often looked upon as their "first parish." For many chaplains, it was the performance of the sometimes heroic, but more often, the ordinary, mundane duties in concert with the front-line soldiers, that shared experience, which had the most impact. Like Fr. de Valles, in the face of danger, they dug deep within themselves and found the courage to overcome their fears. It was their duty. Many were much older men, though some were not much older than the men they served with. In either case, almost all referred to the soldiers as "boys."

Were the Yankee Division chaplains braver than those of other divisions? It is hard to say given the relatively scant amount of information written about chaplains in general, but probably not. However, one thing that can be said with reasonable certainty is that more of them were exposed to the extreme adversity of battle and its aftermath than were the majority of chaplains in the other divisions in the AEF, given the length of time the 26th Division spent in France, and, in particular, its time in the front line.

The Army chaplains were an inspiration to all the men that they served, in the true spirit of the social gospel many had studied in divinity school. As a result, they earned the love and respect of the common soldier. Many got "their blood up" in the midst of a fight, and had no hesitation to serve a machine gun, drive an ambulance, or pull the lanyard on an artillery piece. For senior commanders like General Pershing, chaplains also became instruments to implement the AEF policy of purity, which was certainly successful, as the AEF had the lowest rate of venereal disease of all the Allies, by far. More important, building upon the experiences of the AEF chaplains, new Army chaplains soon became an integral part of the military, no longer asked to perform their duties ad hoc or on the whim of their commanding officer. After the insignia of rank controversy was resolved, the position of chaplain finally achieved the respect that it rightfully deserved within the military establishment, something that the Yankee Division chaplains had already earned from the men with whom they had served so faithfully.

APPENDIX

Yankee Division Chaplains

Chaplains Who Served with the Division in France[1]

Adams, Chauncey Allen
   Religious Affiliation: Protestant (Congregational)
   Rank: American Field Service (AFS); Chaplain (1st Lt.)
   Unit: 101st Ammunition Train
   Born: November 15, 1879, Eaton, Quebec, Canada
   Died: September 8, 1959, Claremont, CA
   Residence at time of service: Danville, VT

Anderson, Harrison Ray
   Religious Affiliation: Protestant (Presbyterian)
   Rank: Chaplain (1st Lt.)
   Unit: 512th Eng. Service Bn.; 103rd Infantry Regiment
   Born: January 24, 1893, Manhattan, KS
   Died: October 18, 1979, Santa Barbara, CA
   Residence at time of service: Ellsworth, KS
   Awards: two Citations in General Orders; recommended for DSC

Bettan, Israel
   Religious Affiliation: Jewish
   Rank: Chaplain (1st Lt.)
   Unit: 26th Division Headquarters
   Born: January 16, 1889, Kovno, Lithuania
   Died: August 5, 1957, Cincinnati, OH
   Residence at time of service: Charleston, WV

Boucher, Osias
   Religious Affiliation: Catholic

Rank: Chaplain, Knights of Columbus (K of C)
Unit: 101st Infantry Regiment
Born: August 17, 1880, St. Madeleine, Quebec, Canada
Died: May 13, 1955, Fall River, MA
Residence at time of service: New Bedford, MA
Awards: *Croix de Guerre*, Legion of Honor (France)

Butzer, Albert George, Sr.
Religious Affiliation: Protestant (Presbyterian)
Rank: Chaplain (1st Lt.)
Unit: 103rd Infantry Regiment
Born: July 19, 1893, Buffalo, NY
Died: November 28, 1967, Buffalo, NY
Residence at time of service: Buffalo, NY

Campbell, Robert, Jr.
Religious Affiliation: Protestant (Congregational)
Rank: YMCA; Chaplain (1st Lt.)
Unit: 101st Field Artillery Regiment; 103rd Machine Gun Battalion
Born: November 22, 1887, Boston, MA
Died: August 31, 1969, Chelsea, MA
Residence at time of service: Warren, MA

Connor, George S. L.
Religious Affiliation: Catholic
Rank: Chaplain (Captain)
Unit: 101st Infantry Regiment (Headquarters Train and Military Police Company)
Born: September 2, 1885, Holyoke, MA
Died: June 6, 1962, Wareham, MA
Residence at time of service: Springfield, MA
Awards: *Croix de Guerre* with Silver Star

Creighton, John Harvey
Religious Affiliation: Protestant
Rank: Chaplain, Young Men's Christian Association (YMCA)
Unit: 101st Field Signal Battalion; 102nd Infantry Regiment
Born: August 23, 1869, Alexandria, VA
Died: January 18, 1933, Mobile, AL
Residence at time of service: Philadelphia, PA

Danker, Walton Stoutenburgh
Religious Affiliation: Protestant (Episcopalian)
Rank: Chaplain (Captain)
Unit: 104th Infantry Regiment

Born: January 26, 1874, Little Falls, NY
Died: June 18, 1918, Royaumeix, France
Residence at time of service: Worcester, MA
Awards: Silver Star, *Croix de Guerre* with star

Dell, Burnham North
Religious Affiliation: Protestant (Episcopalian)
Rank: Chaplain (1st Lt.)
Unit: 101st Infantry Regiment; 102nd Infantry Regiment
Born: July 7, 1889, Jacksonville, FL
Died: September 14, 1963, Boston, MA
Residence at time of service: Boston, MA

De Valles, John Baptist
Religious Affiliation: Catholic
Rank: K of C; Chaplain (1st Lt.)
Unit: 104th Infantry Regiment
Born: August 29, 1879, St. Michael, Azores
Died: May 12, 1920, New Bedford, MA
Residence at time of service: New Bedford, MA
Awards: Distinguished Service Cross; *Croix de Guerre*

Dewart, Murray Wilder
Religious Affiliation: Protestant (Episcopalian)
Rank: Chaplain (1st Lt.)
Unit: 101st Field Artillery Regiment
Born: February 14, 1874, Chardon, OH
Died: December 4, 1927, Baltimore, MD
Residence at time of service: Winchester, MA

Edwards, Henry Boyd
Religious Affiliation: Protestant (Episcopalian)
Rank: Chaplain (1st Lt.)
Unit: 101st Engineer Regiment
Born: February 27, 1884, East Orange, NJ
Died: November 21, 1970, Morristown, NJ
Residence at time of service: Milton, MA

Evans, Allen, Jr.
Religious Affiliation: Protestant (Episcopalian)
Rank: Chaplain (1st Lt.)
Unit: 104th Infantry Regiment
Born: March 28, 1891, Haverford, PA
Died: December 17, 1960, Bryn Mawr, PA
Residence at time of service: Haverford, PA

Farrell, William J.
  Religious Affiliation: Catholic
  Rank: K of C; Chaplain (1st Lt.)
  Unit: 103rd Field Artillery; 104th Infantry Regiment
  Born: December 24, 1877, Boston, MA
  Died: February 13, 1933, Groton, MA
  Residence at time of service: Newton, MA
  Awards: Distinguished Service Cross; Silver Star; *Croix de Guerre* with star

Hesselgrave, Charles Everett[2]
  Religious Affiliation: Protestant (Congregational)
  Rank: YMCA
  Unit: 101st Machine Gun Battalion
  Born: October 12, 1868, New York State
  Died: April 10, 1927, Seattle, WA
  Residence at time of Service: South Manchester, CT

Imbrie, Charles K.
  Religious Affiliation: Protestant (Presbyterian)
  Rank: Chaplain (1st Lt.)
  Unit: 104th Infantry Regiment
  Born: December 10, 1881, Tokyo, Japan
  Died: June 26, 1958, Penney Farms, FL
  Residence at time of service: Lancaster, NY

Jonaitis, George F.
  Religious Affiliation: Catholic
  Rank: Chaplain (1st Lt.)'
  Unit: 102nd Infantry Regiment; 313th Infantry Regiment (79th Division)
  Born: April 23, 1880, Kursenai, Lithuania
  Died: December 26, 1963, Omaha, NE
  Residence at time of service: Omaha, NE

LeVeer, Arthur Joseph
  Religious Affiliation: Catholic
  Rank: Chaplain (1st Lt.)
  Unit: 102nd Machine Gun Battalion
  Born: February 3, 1886, Bloomfield, VT
  Died: September 2, 1964, St. Albans, VT
  Residence at time of service: St. Johnsbury, VT

Libert, Lucien Gaspard
  Religious Affiliation: Catholic
  Rank: Chaplain, K of C

Unit: 101st Engineer Regiment
Born: July 31, 1872, St. George, IL
Died: December 5, 1919, Martinton, IL
Residence at time of service: Martinton, IL

Mayotte, Anselm Joseph
Religious Affiliation: Catholic
Rank: Chaplain (1st Lt.)
Unit: 102nd Infantry Regiment; 12th Field Artillery Regiment (2nd Div.)
Born: December 11, 1888, St. Dominique, Quebec, Canada
Died: December 5, 1918, Echternacht, Luxemburg
Residence at time of service: Putnam, CT
Award: Silver Star

Mitty, John Joseph
Religious Affiliation: Catholic
Rank: Chaplain (1st Lt.)
Unit: 49th Infantry Regiment; 101st Infantry Regiment
Born: January 20, 1884, New York, NY
Died: October 15, 1961, Menlo Park, CA
Residence at time of service: New York, NY

Moody, Paul Dwight
Religious Affiliation: Protestant (Congregational)
Rank: Chaplain (Major)
Unit: 103rd Infantry Regiment; GHQ Chaplains' Office
Born: April 11, 1879, Baltimore, MD
Died: August 18, 1947, Shrewsbury, VT
Residence at time of service: St. Johnsbury, VT

Nivard, Michael
Religious Affiliation: Catholic (K of C)
Rank: K of C; Chaplain (1st Lt.)
Unit: 103rd Infantry Regiment
Born: September 28, 1873, Hoorn, Netherlands
Died: June 9, 1950, Houghton, MI
Residence at time of service: Sparta, WI

O'Connor, Michael J.
Religious Affiliation: Catholic
Rank: Chaplain (Captain)
Unit: 101st Infantry Regiment; Senior Chaplain, 26th Division Headquarters
Born: July 12, 1869, Ireland
Died: September 26, 1944, Framingham, MA

Residence at time of service: Roxbury, MA
Award: Purple Heart

Peabody, Malcolm Endicott
Religious Affiliation: Protestant (Episcopalian)
Rank: Chaplain (1st Lt.)
Unit: 102nd Field Artillery Regiment
Born: June 12, 1888, Danvers, MA
Died: June 20, 1974, Boston, MA
Residence at time of service: Lawrence, MA

Petty, Orville Anderson
Religious Affiliation: Protestant (Congregational)
Rank: Chaplain (Major)
Unit: 102nd Infantry Regiment
Born: February 20, 1874, Cadiz, OH
Died: August 12, 1942, New Haven, CT
Residence at time of service: New Haven, CT
Awards: Silver Star; *Croix de Guerre* (France); *Chevalier de l'Ordre de l'Etoile Noire* (France); *Chevalier de la Caronne* (Belgium).

Riseman, Benjamin
Religious Affiliation: Jewish
Rank: Acting Rabbi, Jewish Welfare Board
Unit: 26th Division Headquarters
Born: About 1868, Russia
Died: Not known.
Residence at time of service: Boston, MA

Rollins, Lyman
Religious Affiliation: Protestant (Episcopalian)
Rank: Chaplain (1st Lt.)
Unit: 101st Infantry Regiment; 3rd Army
Born: April 21, 1881, Concord, NH
Died: July 11, 1930, Lebanon, NH
Residence at time of service: Marblehead, MA
Award: *Croix de Guerre*

Sherry, James Peter
Religious Affiliation: Catholic
Rank: Chaplain (1st Lt.)
Unit: 303rd Stevedore Regiment; 102nd Infantry Regiment
Born: July 28, 1886, Peabody, MA
Died: July 4, 1957, Framingham, MA

Residence at time of service: Jamaica Plain, MA
Award: Citation in General Orders

Speers, Thomas Guthrie
Religious Affiliation: Protestant (Presbyterian)
Rank: Chaplain (1st Lt.)
Unit: 102nd Infantry Regiment
Born: August 27, 1890, Atlantic Highlands, NJ
Died: May 9, 1984, Baltimore, MD
Residence at time of service: New York, NY
Awards: Distinguished Service Cross; *Croix de Guerre* with Palm

Stackpole, Markham Winslow
Religious Affiliation: Protestant (Congregational)
Rank: Chaplain (Captain)
Unit: 102nd Field Artillery Regiment
Born: June 5, 1873, Westboro, MA
Died: March 17, 1948, Milton, MA
Residence at time of service: Andover, MA
Awards: *Croix de Guerre* with star

Taggart, Earl R.
Religious Affiliation: Protestant (Disciples of Christ)
Rank: Chaplain (Captain)
Unit: 101st Machine Gun Battalion
Born: July 6, 1888, Bethany, MO
Died: December 22, 1961, Arlington, VA
Residence at time of service: Washington, D.C.

Temple, Thomas F.
Religious Affiliation: Catholic
Rank: Chaplain (1st Lt.)
Unit: 101st Train HQ and MP; 101st Infantry Regiment; 1st Air Depot
Born: August 26, 1890, Shannon Harbor, County Offaly, Ireland
Died: October 27, 1955, New York, NY
Residence at time of service: New York, NY

Tucker, John Francis
Religious Affiliation: Catholic
Rank: Chaplain (1st Lt.)
Unit: 103rd Field Artillery Regiment; 102nd Field Artillery Regiment; Forestry Engineers
Born: January 8, 1889, Wilmington, DE

Died: November 1, 1972, Wilmington, DE
Residence at time of service: Wilmington, DE

Chaplains Who Did Not Serve with the Division in France

Cochrane, James Edward
 Religious Affiliation: Protestant (Baptist)
 Rank: Chaplain (Captain)
 Unit: 2nd Maine Infantry Regiment; 57th Pioneer Infantry Regiment
 Born: July 4, 1854, Monmouth, ME
 Died: Not known
 Residence at time of service: Hallowell, ME
Page, Herman Riddle
 Religious Affiliation: Protestant (Episcopalian)
 Rank: Chaplain
 Unit: Massachusetts Field Signal Battalion
 Born: May 3, 1892, Coeur D'Alene, WA
 Died: November 10, 1977, Menominee, MI
 Residence at time of service: Boston, MA
Starr, Harris Elwood
 Religious Affiliation: Protestant (Congregational)
 Rank: YMCA; Chaplain (1st Lt.)
 Unit: 2nd Connecticut Infantry Regiment; 154th Depot Brigade
 Born: May 7, 1875, Phoenix, RI
 Died: Not known
 Residence at time of service: New Haven, CT

Notes

Preface

1. Edward M. Coffman, *The War to End All Wars* (Madison: University of Wisconsin Press, 1986), 79–80; James T. Duane, *Dear Old "K"* (Boston: Thomas Todd, 1922), 78; Bert Ford, *The Fighting Yankees Overseas* (Boston: McPhail, 1919), 182.

2. Coffman, *The War to End All Wars*, 79. Some chaplains were required to "demonstrate proficiency" with the pistol. Chaplain Ray Anderson carried a pistol, which is among his family's mementos from his service, including a German helmet, a bayonet, and his mess kit. Harrison Ray Anderson, Jr., to author, March 3, 2012, HRA.

3. Frederick Palmer, *Newton D. Baker: America at War*, vol. 1 (New York: Dodd, Mead, 1931), 321. Earl F. Stover, *Up from Handymen: The United States Army Chaplaincy, 1865-1920* (Honolulu: University Press of the Pacific, 2004), 192.

4. Robert Graves, *Good-bye to All That* (New York: Anchor, 1985), 189–90. The chaplains Alexander D. Goode (Jewish), George L. Fox (Methodist), Clark V. Poling (Dutch Reform), and John P. Washington (Catholic) gave their lives on February 3, 1943, off the coast of Newfoundland. Available at http://www.fourchaplains.org/story.html.

5. Frank P. Sibley, *With the Yankee Division in France* (Boston: Little, Brown, 1919), 170–71.

Chapter One: "Sky Pilots"

1. Paul Lockhart, *The Whites of Their Eyes: Bunker Hill, the First American Army, and the Emergence of George Washington* (New York: Harper Collins, 2011), 88 and 183; Richard M. Ketchum, *Decisive Day: The Battle for Bunker Hill*, 86.

2. Quote available at http://www.beliefnet.com.

3. Jack McCallum, *Leonard Wood: Rough Rider, Surgeon, Architect of American Imperialism* (New York: New York University Press, 2006), 239–41; Edward M. Coffman, *The Regulars: The American Army 1898-1941* (Boston: Harvard University Press, 2007), 142–43 and 160; Stover, *Up from Handymen*, 144–45.

4. Coffman, *The Regulars*, 117–18.

5. Palmer, *Newton D. Baker*, vol. 1, 321. Stover, *Up from Handymen*, 147–154, 155–56, and 206–8. Eventually, since military chaplains were scattered over a wide area, the Vatican created, in essence, a military diocese for them known as the Military Vicariate. Headquartered in New York, the offices would be known as the Military Ordinariate. A bishop was appointed as an Ordinary for that diocese. Archdiocese for the Military Services, U.S.A., *Priests' Manual, Appendix* (Washington, D.C.: Archdiocese for the Military Services, U.S.A., 2009), 4; Roy J. Honeywell, *Chaplains of the United States Army* (Washington, D.C.: GPO, 1958), 225.

6. Stover, *Up from Handymen*, 208; Honeywell, *Chaplains*, 174–76; Brent, Final Report of Senior Chaplain, General Headquarters, April 26, 1919, *United States Army in the World War, 1917–1919*, vol. 15 (Washington, D.C.: GPO, 1948), 419, 420; John J. Pershing, *My Experiences in the First World War* (New York: Da Capo, 1995), 284; Stover, *Up from Handymen*, 188–89.

7. Library of Congress, Biographical Note, Charles Henry Brent Papers, available at http://www.loc.gov/rr/mss/text/brent.html; *New York Times*, May 7, 1908, 7; James Kiefer, "Charles Henry Brent, Missionary Bishop, 27 March 1929," *Biographical Sketches of Memorable Christians of the Past*, available at http://justus.anglican.org/resources/bio/116.html. Pierpont L. Stackpole diary, September 9, 1918, GCML.

8. Richard M. Budd, *Serving Two Masters: The Development of American Military Chaplaincy, 1860–1920* (Lincoln: University of Nebraska Press, 2002), 31–36. In a case of history repeating itself, Budd points out that the shortage of chaplains in World War I mirrored a similar shortage during the early days of the Civil War, and that one of the reasons that the YMCA started the Christian Commission was "the insufficient numbers of military chaplains." Stover, *Up from Handymen*, 212. Budd, *Serving Two Masters*, 138.

9. Brent, Final Report, vol. 15, 420–22, AWW; Stover, *Up from Handymen*, 122. Yale University, *Obituary Record of Graduates of Yale University Deceased During the Year 1947–1948*, 45, no.1 (1 January 1949): 63–64; 1910 U.S. Census, New York, Suffolk County, Town of Islip (Series T624, Roll 1082, Page 4); *Vermont Roster 1917–1919*, Adjutant General, State of Vermont, Vermont Office of Veterans Affairs, 902.

10. Paul D. Moody, "Practical Work for the Soldiers," *The Missionary Review of the World* 40, no. 7 (July 1917): 529–30.

11. Biographical Information, A. A. Pruden Papers, 1898–1931 (#04997-z), University of North Carolina, available at http://www.lib.unc.edu/mss/inv/p/Pruden,A.A.html.

12. Honeywell, *Chaplains of the United States Army*, 174–76; Budd, *Serving Two Masters*, 146–47. Stover, *Up from Handymen*, 215–17; Honeywell, *Chaplains of the United States Army*, 174–76.

13. "Chaplain School History," U.S. Army Chaplaincy Museum, available at http://www.usachcs.army.mil/corps_museum.html. Stover, *Up from Handymen*, 217; Budd, *Serving Two Masters*, 147–48.

14. Palmer, *Newton D. Baker*, vol. 1, 321–22. Archdiocese for the Military Services, U.S.A., 4.

15. Stover, *Up from Handymen*, 150, 188–89, and 211. 1910 U.S. Census, Massachusetts, Suffolk County, City of Boston (Series T624, Roll 616, Page 209). Sarah Diamant, Special Collections, The Ratner Center, Jewish Theological Seminary, to Author, February 9, 2012.

16. Honeywell, *Chaplains of the United States Army*, 178–79. Palmer, *Newton D. Baker*, vol. 1, 323–24. Stover, *Up from Handymen*, 203–6; James P. Nickols, "Religious Pluralism: A Challenge to the Chaplain Corps," *Military Chaplains' Review* 15, no. 4 (Fall 1986): 89–90; Honeywell, *Chaplains of the United States Army*, 179.

17. Michael E. Shay, *Revered Commander, Maligned General: The Life of Clarence Ransom Edwards, 1859–1931* (Columbia: University of Missouri Press, 2011).

18. *Framingham Evening News*, August 21, 1917, 1; Carl O. Harding diary, August 21, 1917, MANG; Harry A. Benwell, *History of the Yankee Division* (Boston: Cornhill, 1919), 16.

19. Mark E. Grotelueschen, *Doctrine under Trial: American Artillery Employment in World War I* (Westport, CT: Greenwood Press, 2001), 150.

20. *Boston Globe*, September 10, 1917, 7; *New York Times*, August 26, 1917. In fact, the September 12, 1917, referendum failed forty thousand to twenty thousand on an all-male vote, and it wasn't until late 1919—when a special session of the Maine Legislature ratified the federal amendment, and a later state referendum, which followed quickly thereafter—that women's suffrage was finally approved in Maine. "Debates Over Suffrage," *Maine History Online*, available at http://www.mainememory.net/sitebuilder/site/170/slideshow/202/display?format=list&slid... Accessed 6/30/2013.

21. *Maine Roster, 1917–1919*, 377, Veterans' Affairs, State of Maine; William Morrell Emery, *The History of Sanford Maine, 1661–1900* (Salem, MA: Salem Press, 1901), 426.

22. *Harvard College, Class of 1913, Secretary's Third Report, June 1920* (Norwood, MA: Plimpton, 1920), 293–95.

23. Secretary of the State, Connecticut, *Register and Manual 1918* (Hartford: State of Connecticut, 1918), 299; Daniel W. Strickland, *Connecticut Fights: The Story of the 102nd Regiment* (New Haven, CT: Quinnipiack Press, 1930), 63. Frederick Sumner Mead, *Harvard's Military Record in the World War*, 898–99; Connecticut, *Register and Manual 1918*, 299; Adjutant General, State of Connecticut, *Service Records Connecticut Men and Women in the Armed Forces of the United States during World War 1917–1920* (Hartford: Office of the Adjutant General, 1920), 2032.

24. In order to efficiently manage the enormous American effort, France (and a portion of southern England) was administratively divided into three sections: Advance (i.e., closest to the front line), Intermediate, and Base. The last was subdivided into eight Base Sections. Service Record, Form No. 84b-1, A.G.O., MANG; *The Phillips Bulletin*, 2, no. 2 (January, 1908): 1; Everett Schermerhorn Stackpole, *History and Genealogy of the Stackpole Family* (Lewiston, ME: Press of Journal Company, 1899), 163.

25. Leon F. Denis, "The Cruise of the *Montpelier*," *Yankee Doings* 8, no. 7 (July/August 1927): 9–10, CSL.

26. Ford, *Fighting Yankees Overseas*, 184. *Holy Cross Service Record, War of 1917* (Worcester, MA: Holy Cross College, 1920), 70; 1920 U.S. Census, Massachusetts, Middlesex County, City of Cambridge (Series T625, Roll 708, Page 209). Military Record, Form 1m-1'30, No. 7616, MANG; *Saint Bridget's Church, 75th Anniversary, 1878–1953*, ADB; *Holy Cross College, Service Record*, 70.

27. Ford, *Fighting Yankees Overseas*, 184. John Leo Connolly to mother, May 12, 1918, MANG.

28. *The Pilot*, September 27, 1917, 1; Duane, *Dear Old "K,"* 5–6; *Framingham News*, September 27, 1944, 7.

29. Service Record and Form No. 84b-7, A.G.O., MANG; *Worcester Telegram*, June 24, 1918, 1; *Hartford Courant*, June 24, 1918, 12; *Brattleboro Daily Reformer*, June 24, 1918.

30. Service Record, Form No. 84b-1, A.G.O., MANG. 1900 U.S. Census, Minnesota, Hennepin County, Minneapolis (Series T623, Roll 766, Page 149). *Boston Globe*, December 4, 1927; "The Rev. Murray Wilder Dewart," *The Maryland Churchman* (n.d.), Scrapbook, Parish of the Epiphany, Winchester, MA.

31. John H. Sherburne, *Boston Globe*, December 8, 1927, Scrapbook, Parish of the Epiphany, Winchester, MA. Russell Gordon Carter, *The 101st Field Artillery*

A.E.F., 1917–1919 (Boston: Houghton, Mifflin, 1940), 24. Murray W. Dewart to Submit ("Mitty") Dewart, September 25, 1917, MWD; Carter, *101st Field Artillery*, 25–26. Dewart referred to him as a member of the crew, who turned the lights on at "exactly" 10:00 P.M. three nights in a row. This was no doubt a shipboard rumor, which grew with each telling.

32. Service Record, Form No. 84b-1, A.G.O., MANG; Bradford Updike Eddy, "According to This Beginning: A Brief Account of the Development of the Parish of the Epiphany at Winchester, Massachusetts 1882–1954," *An Anthology of Epiphany History 1888–1988* (Winchester, MA: n.p., 1954), 47–48; John Nesmith Greely and Dwight E. Aultman, eds., *The Field Artillery Journal* 6 (1916): 101. Robert E. Goodwin, "Murray Dewart, Army Chaplain," *The Maryland Churchman* (n.d.), Scrapbook, Parish of the Epiphany, Winchester, MA.

33. *Holyoke Daily Transcript*, March 5, 1918. Service Record, Form No. 84b-1, A.G.O.; *New York Times*, June 28, 1962, 31; Archives, Diocese of Springfield, Springfield, MA; Charles S. Zack, *Holyoke in the Great War* (Holyoke, MA: Transcript Publishing, 1919), 80; *Holyoke Daily Transcript-Telegram*, June 26, 1962, 1; *Holy Cross College Service Record*, 87.

34. Service Record, Form No. 84d-8, A.G.O., MANG; Biographical data and assignments, Archives, Diocese of Fall River; Connell Albertine, *The Yankee Doughboy* (Boston: Branden Press, 1968), 104. D. W. Meinig, *A Geographical Perspective on 500 Years of History, Volume 3, Transcontinental America, 1850–1915* (New Haven: Yale University Press, 1998), 279. Biographical data and assignments, Archives, Diocese of Fall River; Albertine, *The Yankee Doughboy*, 104.

35. John Baptist de Valles to D. F. Feehan, February 5, 1918, Archives, Diocese of Fall River.

36. Sibley, *With the Yankee Division*, 120. Stillman F. Westbrook, *Those Eighteen Months, October 9, 1917–April 8, 1919* (Hartford, CT: Case, Lockwood, 1934), 103. Albertine, *The Yankee Doughboy*, 105 and 118. Service Record, Form No. 84d-8, A.G.O., MANG.

37. *New York Times*, June 9, 1899; "Ruth Hesselgrave, Biographical History," Ruth Hesselgrave Papers, 1835–1984, Stewart–Smith Research Center, Henry Sheldon Museum of Vermont History, available at http://henrysheldonmuseum.org/research/Finding_Aids/hesselgraveFA.html. *Hartford Times*, April 16, 1927. 1910 U.S. Census, New Jersey, Morris County, Chatham Borough (Series T624, Roll 902, Page 98). Charles E. Hesselgrave, *The 101st Machine Gun Battalion as Seen from the Y. M. C. A.* (typescript, n.d.), 1–3, Connecticut Historical Society; *Hartford Times*, April 16, 1927.

38. 1920 U.S. Census, Connecticut, Hartford County, City of Bristol (Series T625, Roll 180, Page 125). 1920 U.S. Census, Connecticut, New Haven County, City of New Haven (Series T625, Roll 180, Page 125); Everett G. Hill, *A Modern History of New Haven and Eastern New Haven County*, vol. 1 (New York: Clarke Publishing, 1918), 113 and 120–21; "History, New Haven Center Church on-the-Green," http://www.newhavencenterchurch.org/history.html. 1920 U.S. Census, Connecticut, New Haven County, City of New Haven (Series T625, Roll 191, Page 160); *Bridgeport Standard Telegram*, February 17, 1919, 11; Elliott Barske, "Our History," available at http://www.uccredeemer.org.

39. Service Record, Form No. 84d-1, A.G.O., MANG; 1910 U.S. Census, Massachusetts, Middlesex County, Everett (Series T624, Roll 598, Page 93); *Boston Globe*, September 1, 1969, 62.

40. 1870 U.S. Census, Virginia, Alexandria (Series M563, Roll 1632, Page 147);

1910 U.S. Census, Pennsylvania, Philadelphia City (Series T624, Roll 1396, Page 170); *Mobile Register,* January 19, 1933; Robert John McCarthy, ed., *A History of Troop A Cavalry, Connecticut National Guard and Its Service in the Great War as Co. D, 102nd Machine Gun Battalion* (Westville, CT: Tuttle, Morehouse, 1919), 69.

41. James Cardinal Gibbons to Thomas Woodrow Wilson, April 18, 1917. Quoted in a pastoral letter dated September 26, 1919, available at http://www.ewtn.com/library/bishops/PL1919.htm. David Goldstein and Martha Moore Avery, *Campaigning for Christ* (Boston: Pilot Publishing, 1924), 440.

42. Ronald Schaffer, *America in the Great War: The Rise of the War Welfare State* (New York: Oxford University Press, 1991), 13–15 and 28–29; Edward Robb Ellis, *Echoes of Distant Thunder: Life in the United States, 1914–1918* (New York: Kodansha, 1996), 190–91 and 434–39.

43. *Omaha World Herald, Morning Edition,* December 27, 1963, 36; Strickland, *Connecticut Fights,* 324 and 332; Records and Archives of the Archdiocese of Omaha.

44. Certificate of Identity No. 5362, War Department, IBP Box 6.13; "Biographical Sketch," *A Finding Aid to the Israel Bettan Papers,* American Jewish Archives, Hebrew Union College, available at http://americanjewisharchives.org/aja/FindingAids/Bettan.htm.

45. David M. Kennedy, *Over Here: The First World War and American Society* (New York: Oxford University Press, 1982), 61. Israel Bettan, "Four Minute Talk," IBP 1.42.

46. "Real Citizenship," *The American Israelite,* November/December 1917, IPB 1.42.

47. Israel Bettan, "Bond Rally Speech," IBP 1.42.

48. "Patriotism's Pentecost," *Huntington Herald-Dispatch,* April 24, 1918, IBP 1.42.

49. *Roster of Company H, Sixth Training Regiment, Federal Training Camp, Plattsburg, N.Y., Wed. 12th July–Tues. 8th Aug., 1916,* 8, IBP 6.11. Extract, Order No. 231, Par. 86, War Department, Washington, D.C., October 2, 1918; Telegram, Harris, Acting Adjutant General to Israel Bettan, October 3, 1918; Special Orders No. 317, Par. 155, G. H. Q., American Expeditionary Forces, November 13, 1918, IBP 6.13.

50. Malcolm Endicott Peabody, Chapter 8, Autobiography, 1970, MPP 15.1; Scrapbook, MPP 28.FB.1v; *New York Times,* June 21, 1974, 40.

51. Peabody, Chapter 8, Autobiography, 1970, MPP 15.1. Harvey Cushing, *From a Surgeon's Journal* (Boston: Little, Brown, 1936), 158–59.

52. Malcolm Endicott Peabody to New England Division, American Red Cross, undated letter reprinted in unnamed newspaper, Scrapbook, MPP 28.FB.1v.

53. Malcolm Endicott Peabody to *Harvard Alumni Bulletin,* undated letter reprinted in unnamed newspaper, Scrapbook, MPP 28.FB.1v. Malcolm Endicott Peabody, Chapter 8, Autobiography, 1970, MPP 15.1. Malcolm Endicott Peabody, "Base Hospital Work," MPP 14.13.

54. Philip S. Wainwright, ed., *History of the 101st Machine Gun Battalion* (Hartford, CT: 101st Machine Gun Battalion Association, 1922), 317; Karin Peterson, "What Happened in May Long Ago?" *Voice of Trinity* 10, vol. 4 (April 22, 2010): 5. Wainwright, *101st Machine Gun Battalion,* 244.

55. Arlen J. Hansen, *Gentlemen Volunteers: The Story of American Ambulance Drivers in the Great War, August 1914—September 1918* (New York: Arcade, 1994), 39–55; Duane, *Dear Old "K,"* 3.

56. *Vermont Roster 1917–1919*, Summary Service Record, VTVA; 1920 U.S. Census, Vermont, Caledonia County, Town of Danville (Series T625, Roll 1871, Page 44); Files and Records of the Waterbury Congregational Church, Waterbury, VT; John E. Nutting, *Becoming the United Church of Christ in Vermont, 1795–1995* (Burlington, VT: n.p., 2000), 37; *Burlington Free Press*, September 12, 1959, 2; *Book of Remembrance*, vol. 6, 15, Archives, Pilgrim Place, Claremont, CA.

57. Marilee Munger Scroggs, *A Light in the City: The Fourth Presbyterian Church of Chicago* (Chicago: Fourth Presbyterian Church, 1990), 121. Anderson Family Papers, Kansas Historical Society; *Topeka Journal*, February 25, 1925.

58. Harrison Ray Anderson, Compilation of Notes and Writings, HRA; Scroggs, *A Light in the City*, 99. Harrison Ray Anderson to mother, April 1, 1918, HRA.

59. Anderson, Compilation of Notes and Writings, HRA; Scroggs, *A Light in the City*, 99.

60. Service Record, Form No. 84d–1, A.G.O., MANG; *Daily Record*, November 24, 1970, 2; 1910 U.S. Census, New York, County of New York, Manhattan (Series T624, Roll 1035, Page 70); "The Rev. H. Boyd Edwards, D. D.," *The Church News* (September, 1945): 13, Archives, Church of the Ascension.

61. Porter B. Chase diary, January 9, 1918, MANG. Carroll Swan, *My Company* (Boston: Houghton Mifflin, 1918), 45.

62. Hugh Young, *A Surgeon's Autobiography* (New York: Harcourt, 1940), 332. Stover, *Up from Handymen*, 200–203. Chase diary, January 21, 1918, MANG.

63. Clarence R. Edwards, Memorandum of the News, January 2, 1918, CRE 14.6. Clarence R. Edwards, Memorandum of the News, January 15, 1918, CRE 14.6.

64. Michael J. O'Connor to Editor, January 2, 1918, *The Pilot*, February 9, 1918, 1. Murray W. Dewart to Submit Dewart, January 23 and 28, 1918, MWD; Duane, *Dear Old "K,"* 21 and 78. Henry G. Fay to Editor, October 28, 1918, *The Pilot*, December 1, 1918.

Chapter Two: Early Days

1. Emerson G. Taylor, *New England in France, 1917–1919: A History of the Twenty-Sixth Division U.S.A.* (Boston: Houghton, Mifflin, 1920), 34–36. James H. Fifield, *The Regiment: A History of the 104th U.S. Infantry, A.E.F. 1917-1919* (Springfield, MA: Springfield Union, 1946), 39–44.

2. Carter, *The 101st Field Artillery*, 29–31. Michael E. Shay, *The Yankee Division in the First World War: In the Highest Tradition* (College Station: Texas A & M University Press, 2008), 38–39.

3. Murray W. Dewart to Submit Dewart, October 13, 1917, MWD. Shay, *The Yankee Division*, 38–39. Taylor, *New England in France*, 33.

4. Dewart to Submit Dewart, October 31, 1917, MWD.

5. Rush truck: A one-half-ton truck manufactured by the Rush Motor Truck Company of Philadelphia, PA. Dewart, "My Temperamental Truck," MWD. Dewart to Submit Dewart, October 31, 1917, MWD; Shay, *The Yankee Division*, 40–41. The "Toonerville Trolley" was a popular comic strip of the same name created by Fontaine Fox (1884–1964); *History of Battery B, One Hundred Third Field Artillery, Twenty-Sixth Division, April, 1917 to April, 1919* (Providence, RI: E. L. Freeman, 1922), 32. Passengers often had to jump off and push the train up steep inclines. Dewart to Submit Dewart, October 14, 1917, MWD.

6. Dewart to Submit Dewart, January 14, 1918, MWD. Dewart to Submit Dewart, January 19, 1918, MWD. Dewart to Submit Dewart, November 4, 1917, MWD.

7. Dewart to Submit Dewart, January 1, 1918, MWD. Dewart to Submit Dewart, October 27, 1917, MWD. Dewart to Submit Dewart, November 18, 1917, MWD.

8. Duane, *Dear Old "K,"* 12–13. Dewart to Submit Dewart, November 4, 1917, MWD. Charles M. Streeter to mother, November 4, 1917, MANG. *History of the 101st Engineers, American Expeditionary Forces, 1917-1918-1919* (Cambridge, MA: University Press, 1926), 56.

9. Edward D. Sirois, William McGinnis, and John Hogan, eds., *Smashing through the "World War" with Fighting Battery C, 102nd F. A. "Yankee Division," 1917-1918-1919* (Salem, MA: Meek Press, 1919), 27; Duane, *Dear Old "K,"* 22–23. Taylor, *New England in France*, 41. Arthur C. Havlin, *The History of Company A, 102 Machine Gun Battalion, Twenty-Sixth Division, A.E.F.* (Boston: Harry C. Rodd, 1928), 35.

10. Michael J. O'Connor to editor, January 2, 1918, *The Pilot*, February 9, 1918, 1.

11. Strickland, *Connecticut Fights*, 74, 76.

12. "Forty and eights": Reference to the capacity of the French box cars marked on the outside, "Hommes 40/Chevaux 8," used to transport troops and horses. Carter, *101st Field Artillery*, 29, 48.

13. Karlton K. Priest, letter, February 2, 1918, MANG; Taylor, *New England in France*, 66. Craig R. Whitney, "Etched in Stone: Words from Great War's Dead," *New York Times*, November 8, 1998. Dewart to Submit Dewart, February 14, 1918, MWD. John J. Dalton to sister, *The Pilot*, April 27, 1918, 1; Duane, *Dear Old "K,"* 30.

14. Sibley, *With the Yankee Division in France*, 78.

15. Hesselgrave, *The 101st Machine Gun Battalion*, 5, CHS. John F. Herbert, Jr., to Mr. and Mrs. Gravel, *The Pilot*, April 27, 1918, 2.

16. Lyman Rollins to Lewis T. Thorburn, Archives, St. Michael's Church, Marblehead, MA; Duane, *Dear Old "K,"* 30.

17. Service Record, Form No. 84b–9, A.G.O., MANG; "1909 Brochure on Ordination of Lyman Rollins at Curtis Memorial Church, Concord, New Hampshire," available at http://heirloomsreunited.blogspot.com; *Concord Daily Monitor*, July 12, 1930, 1.

18. Carter, *The 101st Field Artillery*, 49.

19. Robert E. Goodwin, "Murray Dewart, Army Chaplain," *The Maryland Churchman*, Archives, Epiphany Parish, Winchester, MA.

20. Dewart to Submit Dewart, February 16, 1918, MWD. Dewart to Submit Dewart, February 28 and March 2, 1918, MWD. Dewart to Submit Dewart, March 10, 1918, MWD.

21. Dewart to Submit Dewart, [undated letter, most likely February 1918], MWD. Dewart to Submit Dewart, March 15, 1918, MWD.

22. Military Record, Form No. 1m(b)-7-45-16634, MANG. Ford, *Fighting Yankees*, 184; *The Stars & Stripes*, Friday, March 15, 1918, 1–2.

23. Osias Boucher to D. F. Feehan, November 21, 1917, Archives, Diocese of Fall River.

24. Boucher to D. F. Feehan, February 22, 1918, Archives, Diocese of Fall River.

25. Carter, *The 101st Field Artillery*, 63. W. F. Kernan and Henry T. Samson, eds., *History of the 103rd Field Artillery (Twenty-Sixth Division, A.E.F.) World War 1917–1919* (Providence, RI: Remington Printing, n.d.), 29. Carter, *The 101st Field Artillery*, 63–64.

26. Sibley, *With the Yankee Division*, 81–83. Sibley seems to have mistakenly switched the leaders of both groups, and I have made the correction. Taylor, *New England in France*, 78–79.

27. Sibley, *With the Yankee Division*, 81–83; Taylor, *New England in France*, 78–79.

28. Sibley, *With the Yankee Division*, 93; *Stars & Stripes*, March 15, 1918, 1–2; Duane, *Dear Old "K,"* 22–23.

29. Boucher to D. F. Feehan, March 17, 1918, Archives, Diocese of Fall River. Fr. Boucher's humility was on display when, sometime after the ceremony, correspondent Frank Sibley asked the priest about the award, in particular, "his bringing in wounded under fire." Boucher matter-of-factly responded: "Oh, we always did that." Sibley, *With the Yankee Division*, 93.

30. Thomas A. Leahy, Letter, April 14, 1918, MANG.

31. Robert Campbell, Jr., to Marjorie Tucker, March 3, 1918, KJB.

32. Swan, *My Company*, 37–38 and 117–18. Arthur J. Winslow, Letter, April 7, 1918, *New London Day*, May 11, 1918, NLPL; Albert M. Heilman, Jr., to Miss James, March 7, 1918, MHI. A. L. Packard to Henry S. Packard, July 26, 1918, MANG. James Harrison Dankert, Letter, May 6, 1918, MANG.

33. Charles M. Streeter to mother, September 24, 1918, MANG. See also, George C. Marshall, *Memoirs of My Services in the World War, 1917–1918* (Boston: Houghton Mifflin, 1976), 20–21. Marshall wrote that early, much publicized efforts of the YMCA were made in Paris for the benefit of headquarters troops and did not reach the foot soldier in the field until much later. This generated lasting bad feelings for some soldiers.

34. Everett Taylor to mother, December 15, 1918, MHI. Frederick Wells Potter to mother, September 8, 1918, MHS. David Goldstein and Martha Moore Avery, *Campaigning for Christ* (Boston: Pilot Publishing, 1924), 440.

35. James Y. Rodger, Letter, *Lowell Courier-Citizen*, December 28, 1918.

36. Thomas Stephen Duggan, *The Catholic Church in Connecticut* (New York: States History, 1930), 186.

37. Diocesan Archives, Archdiocese of Hartford; 1900 U.S. Census, Massachusetts, Worcester County, Webster, Southbridge, and Quinebaug (CT) Village (Series T623, Roll 691, Page 174). *Windham County Observer*, January 22, 1919, 1.

38. Adjutant General, State of Connecticut, *Service Record*, 2607. This record is incorrect, in that it indicates that he was assigned to the 103rd Infantry Regiment, when, in fact, he was actually initially assigned to the 102nd Infantry Regiment. Mayotte to John J. Nilan, undated letter, Diocesan Archives, Archdiocese of Hartford. Sibley, *With the Yankee Division*, 46. Mayotte to John J. Nilan, May 3, 1918, Diocesan Archives, Archdiocese of Hartford. *Danbury Evening News*, February 18, 1918. Mayotte to John J. Nilan, May 3, 1918, Diocesan Archives, Archdiocese of Hartford.

39. Fifield, *The Regiment*, 88–89. Fifield writes that the bomber was returning from its mission, but he also says that there were two intact bombs on her undercarriage when it crashed. Accordingly, I have assumed that it was on its way to Paris. Chase diary, March 16, 1918, MANG; *History of the 101st Engineers*, 102.

40. John B. de Valles, Memorandum, March 18, 1918, Archives, Diocese of Fall River.

41. Boucher to D. F. Feehan, March 17, 1918, Archives, Diocese of Fall River.

42. Dewart to Submit Dewart, March 14, 1918, MWD.

43. Dewart to Submit Dewart, January 28, 1918, MWD. Dewart to Submit Dewart, [undated letter, most likely February 1918], MWD. Goodwin, "Murray Dewart, Army Chaplain," *The Maryland Churchman*, Archives, Epiphany Parish, Winchester, MA.

44. De Valles, Memorandum, March 18, 1918, Archives, Diocese of Fall River.
45. Harry G. Wright, *With Co. L, 104th U.S. Infantry, 52nd Brigade, 26th Division 1917-1918-1919* (Typescript, n.p.), MHI.
46. Taylor, *New England in France*, 80-82 and 84.

Chapter Three: Toul Sector

1. Taylor, *New England in France*, 85-87.
2. John Keegan, *The First World War* (New York: Knopf, 1999), 396-405.
3. Dewart to Submit Dewart, March 26, 1918, MWD.
4. Coffman, *The War to End All Wars*, 156-59.
5. Dewart, "My Temperamental Truck" (undated, unpublished typescript) 6-7; Dewart to Submit Dewart, Good Friday, 1918 (March 29), MWD. Horatio Rogers, *World War I through My Sights* (San Rafael, CA: Presidio, 1976), 85-94.
6. Dewart to Submit Dewart, March 26, 1918, MWD.
7. Duane, *Dear Old "K,"* 12-13. During the first three years of the war, 25,000 Catholic priests served in the French Army, 7,000 of whom died in service.
8. Ford, *Fighting Yankees*, 187; Carter, *The 101st Field Artillery*, 78.
9. John H. Sherburne, *Boston Globe*, December 8, 1927.
10. Fifield, *The Regiment*, 101. Albertine, *The Yankee Doughboy*, 109-10.
11. Duane, *Dear Old "K,"* 56; Sibley, *With the Yankee Division*, 111; Taylor, *New England in France*, 101-3 and 106. R. S. Porter, *History, 101st Sanitary Train, 26th Division, A.E.F.* (typescript, March 20, 1919), 621, MANG.
12. Taylor, *New England in France*, 139. Duane, *Dear Old "K,"* 61.
13. Taylor, *New England in France*, 111-15. Fox Connor, Memorandum for Chief of Staff, April 16, 1918, vol. 3, 611-12, AWW.
14. *Daily Hampshire Gazette*, April 30, 1918; Sibley, *With the Yankee Division*, 121. Service Record, Form No. 84b-9, A.G.O., MANG.
15. Albertine, *The Yankee Doughboy*, 122; Michael E. Shay, *A Grateful Heart: The History of a World War I Field Hospital* (Westport, CT: Greenwood, 2002), 60.
16. Fifield, *The Regiment*, 117-18 and 138; Porter, *History, 101st Sanitary Train*, 621, MANG; Albertine, *The Yankee Doughboy*, 123; Sibley, *With the Yankee Division*, 120-21 and 130; Shay, *A Grateful Heart*, 59-60. During its stay in the Toul Sector, the 104th Field Hospital acted as the sorting station for the western zone, operating first at Aulnois-sous-Vertuzy, then Vignot, and finally to Abbe-de-Rangeval.
17. Service Record, Form No. 84d-8, A.G.O., MANG; *Boston Globe*, April 19, 1918. Goldstein and Avery, *Campaigning for Christ*, 441. *Boston Globe*, April 19, 1918. Albertine, *The Yankee Doughboy*, 125.
18. Ford, *Fighting Yankees*, 185.
19. Fifield, *The Regiment*, 139-40; Albertine, *Yankee Doughboy*, 126.
20. Taylor, *New England in France*, 115-16; Fifield, *The Regiment*, 142-44; Albertine, *Yankee Doughboy*, 127; Sibley, *With the Yankee Division*, 161-62.
21. Taylor, *New England in France*, 117-22.
22. Sibley, *With the Yankee Division*, 143 and 148. *New York Times*, April 26, 1918.
23. Shay, *The Yankee Division*, 78-89. Duane, *Dear Old "K,"* 59.
24. Service Record, Form No. 84b-9, A.G.O., MANG; *The Pilot*, February 18, 1933; Charles F. Donovan, *Boston College's Boston Priests* (Chestnut Hill, MA: Boston College, 1993), available at http://escholarship.bc.edu/donovan/18. Frank L. Houlihan to mother, July 11, 1918, *Natick Bulletin*, August 30, 1918. Kernan and

Samson, *History of the 103rd Field Artillery*, 39–40; Ford, *Fighting Yankees*, 186–87; Service Record, Form No. 84b–9 A.G.O. (lists his wound as "moderate to severe"), MANG; *History of Battery B, One Hundred Third Field Artillery, Twenty-sixth Division, April, 1917 to April, 1919* (Providence, RI: E. L. Freeman, 1922), 55–56.

25. Kenneth N. Burnham to mother, May 17, 1918, MANG. Houlihan to mother, July 11, 1918, *Natick Bulletin*, August 30, 1918, 1. Service Record, Form No. 84b–9 A.G.O., MANG.

26. 1880 U.S. Census, Ohio, Harrison County, Short Creek Township (Series T9, Roll 1031, Page 490). *New York Times*, August 14, 1942. 1920 U.S. Census, Connecticut, New Haven County, City of New Haven (Series T625, Roll 191, Page 4); Adjutant General, Connecticut, *Service Records*, 1967; Everett G. Hill, *A Modern History of New Haven and Eastern New Haven County* (New York: Clarke, 1918), 118. Strickland, *Connecticut Fights*, 60.

27. Strickland, *Connecticut Fights*, 144 and 152–53; Military Times Hall of Valor, available at: http://militarytimes.com/citations-medals-awards/recipient.php?recipientid=82944.

28. Mayotte to John J. Nilan, June 2, 1918, Diocesan Archives, Archdiocese of Hartford. Adjutant General, Connecticut, *Service Records*, 2607.

29. Taylor, *New England in France*, 147–48. Duane, *Dear Old "K,"* 63–65. Shay, *The Yankee Division*, 90. Carter, *The 101st Field Artillery*, 104.

30. Taylor, *New England in France*, 148–50; Duane, *Dear Old "K,"* 75. Carter, *The 101st Field Artillery*, 104–5.

31. Service Record, Form No. 84b–9 A.G.O., MANG. Duane, *Dear Old "K,"* 75.

32. Service Record, Form No. 84b–9, A.G.O., MANG.; Sibley, *With the Yankee Division*, 171. Rollins's Service Card shows a break in his overseas service between June 20 and July 12, 1918, along with a reference to Camp Taylor, Kentucky. That facility did not open until the spring of 1918 and was closed in early 1919, and at both times Rollins was definitely in France with the division.

33. Sibley, *With the Yankee Division*, 121. Donald Dinsmore to mother, February 1918, MHI.

34. Henry Lamb to mother, June 18, 1918, MANG. Lamb was killed in action on November 10, 1918, one day before the Armistice.

35. Sibley, *With the Yankee Division*, 190–91; Taylor, *New England in France*, 153.

36. Willard R. Smith diary, June 16, 1918, excerpted in *Worcester Sunday Telegram*, November 10, 1968, 18–19. Stover, *Up from Handymen*, 252; *Brattleboro Daily Reformer*, June 24, 1918; *Hartford Courant*, June 24, 1918, 12.

37. Sibley, *With the Yankee Division*, 190; Taylor, *New England in France*, 153; *Framingham News*, September 27, 1944, 1; Benwell, *History of the Yankee Division*, 84.

38. Fifield, *The Regiment*, 172–74, 176–77. Smith diary, June 20, 1918, excerpted in *Worcester Sunday Telegram*, November 10, 1968, 18–19. Westbrook, *Those Eighteen Months*, 120.

39. Boucher to D. F. Feehan, June 24, 1918, Archives, Diocese of Fall River.

Chapter Four: Aisne-Marne

1. Coffman, *The War to End All Wars*, 212–22.

2. Taylor, *New England in France*, 158–61. Donald S. Chase, Company D, 103rd Infantry, 26th Division, *Questionnaire*, MHI. Hesselgrave, *The 101st Machine Gun Battalion*; *Hartford Times*, April 16, 1927. Chase diary, July 3, 1918, MANG.

3. Mayotte to John J. Nilan, July 1, 1918, Diocesan Archives, Archdiocese of Hartford.
4. Anderson to mother, August 24, 1918, HRA. Anderson to mother, July 11, 1918, HRA.
5. Anderson to father, June 29, 1918, HRA.
6. Shay, *A Grateful Heart*, 78. Robert Asprey, *At Belleau Wood* (Denton: University of North Texas Press, 1996), 343–44.
7. Harrison Ray Anderson, Personal Reminiscences on His Service as a Chaplain, HRA. Anderson to mother, July 11, 1918, HRA.
8. Service Summary Card, Form No. 84d–1 A.G.O. and Veteran's Compensation Application, Commonwealth of Pennsylvania, Bureau of Archives and History; Albertine, *Yankee Doughboy*, 162; "Rectors at St. Peter's," *History*, St. Peter's Church, available at http://stpetershistory.org/stpetershistoryrectorsc.html; Scrapbook, Parish of the Epiphany, Winchester, MA.
9. Pierpont L. Stackpole diary, July 6, 1918, GCML. Swan, *My Company*, 170–75. *History of the 101st Engineers*, 190; Sibley, *With the Yankee Division*, 198.
10. Asprey, *At Belleau Wood*, 343–44. Duane, *Dear Old "K,"* 92–95. Graves, *Good-bye to All That*, 163. Denis Winter, *Death's Men* (London: Penguin, 1979), 207–8.
11. Corporal Buswell died in captivity on July 31, 1918, from wounds received during the attack on July 18. Service Record, Form No. 724–7 A.G.O. (November 22, 1919), MANG. Elmer N. Buswell diary, July 6, 1918, MANG.
12. Shay, *The Yankee Division*, 106. Swan, *My Company*, 174–75.
13. Laurence Stallings, *The Doughboys: The Story of the AEF, 1917–1918* (New York: Harper, 1963), 125–35. Duane, *Dear Old "K,"* 98.
14. Kernan and Samson, *History of the 103rd Field Artillery*, 65; *History of the One Hundred Second Field Artillery, July, 1917–April, 1919* (Boston: n.p., 1927), 72–74. Shay, *A Grateful Heart*, 78. Sirois, McGinnis, and Hogan, *Smashing through the "World War,"* 73 and 126–27.
15. Shay, *The Yankee Division*, 128–29. Stanhope Bayne-Jones to Marian Jones, July 28, 1918, NLM. Horace P. Hobbs diary, August 23, 1918, MHI.
16. Grotelueschen, *The AEF Way of War*, 43–45. David Trask, *The AEF and Coalition Warmaking, 1917–1918* (Lawrence: University Press of Kansas, 1993), 140–41.
17. Mark E. Grotelueschen, *Doctrine under Fire: American Artillery Employment in World War I* (Westport, CT: Greenwood, 2001), 18. Hunter Liggett, *A.E.F.: Ten Years Ago in France* (Cranbury, NJ: Scholar's Bookshelf, 2005), 250. Grotelueschen, *The AEF Way of War*, 266–68; Grotelueschen, *The AEF Way of War*, 354–55.
18. Frederick W. Potter to mother, August 8, 1918, MHS.
19. Taylor, *New England in France*, 140–43. Potter to mother, August 8, 1918, MHS.
20. Dewart, "My Temperamental Truck," 12–13, MWD.
21. Shay, *The Yankee Division*, 124; Albertine, *The Yankee Doughboy*, 123.
22. Anderson to John Timothy Stone ("My Dear Dominie"), *The Fourth Church Monthly Magazine* (October 1918): 272, Archives, Fourth Presbyterian Church.
23. Taylor, *New England in France*, 204–5; American Battle Monuments Commission, *26th Division: Summary of Operations in the World War* (Washington, D.C.: GPO, 1944), 20; *History of the 101st Engineers*, 220. Carter, *The 101st Field Artillery A.E.F.*, 182.

24. "Black care rarely sits behind a rider whose pace is fast enough." Theodore Roosevelt. Undoubtedly, Roosevelt harkened back to his school days and translations of the poet Horace: ". . . black Sorrow sits behind the horseman as he rides his horse," Horace, *Odes*, iii.1, "Ostentation" (translated by David Ferry). Paul Dwight Moody, "Murray Dewart: A Knightly Man of God," *The Churchman* (n.d.), MWD.

25. *Clifton Advocate*, December 12, 1919; Norma Meier, *Pioneer Profiles*, vol. 1 (Clifton, IL: n.p., 2009), 143–46; *Ordination Register*, Office of Archives of the Catholic Diocese of Peoria. Martinton is now in the Joliet Diocese. Joseph J. Thompson, *A History of the Knights of Columbus in Illinois* (Chicago: Universal Press, 1921), 840; *Ordination Register*, Office of Archives of the Catholic Diocese of Peoria; Record of Soldier in World War, Iroquois County (IL) Genealogical Society.

26. Service Record, Form No. 84d–1 A.G.O., MANG; *Inquirer and Mirror*, September 19, 1963; *New York Times*, June 4, 1916.

27. *The Year Book of Emmanuel Parish Boston (1917)*, 3, 29, and 43, Archives, Emmanuel Church. Service Record, Form No. 84d–1 A.G.O., MANG.

28. Anderson to mother, August 2, 1918, HRA. ABMC, *26th Division*, 21.

29. Charles R. Cabot, *History of the 103rd U.S. Infantry, 1917–1919* (n.p.: 103rd U.S. Infantry, 1919), 21.

30. Douglas V. Johnson, II, and Rolf L. Hillman, Jr., *Soissons 1918* (College Station: Texas A & M University Press, 1999), 58–62.

31. Mayotte to John J. Nilan, September 16, 1918, *Catholic Transcript*, October 17, 1918, Diocesan Archives, Archdiocese of Hartford.

32. Campbell to "Dear Friends," June 12, 1918, KJB. Campbell to "Dear Friends," August 12, 1918, KJB.

33. Service Record, Form No. 84d-1, A.G.O., MANG. Campbell to "Dear Friends," August 12, 1918, KJB.

34. Boucher to D. F. Feehan, August 18, 1918, Archives, Diocese of Fall River.

35. Anderson to John Timothy Stone ("Dear Dominie"), "Letters from Men in Uniform," *Fourth Church Magazine* (November 1918): 310; Anderson to Mother, July 4, 1918, HRA.

36. Albert G. Butzer, Sr., *Autobiographical Sketch*, courtesy of Albert G. Butzer, III. Anderson to father, September 21, 1918, HRA.

37. Service Record, Form No. 84d–1 A.G.O., Wisconsin Department of Veterans Affairs; *Daily Mining Gazette*, June 10, 1950, 10; *125th Anniversary History, St. Anthony's* (Cazenovia, WI: n.p., 1982), 17, Archives, Diocese of La Crosse; 1920 U.S. Census, Wisconsin, Monroe County, City of Sparta (Series T625, Roll 2007, Page 221); 1910 U.S. Census, Wisconsin, Richland County, Village of Cazenovia (Series T624, Roll 1732, Page 278).

38. Service Record, Form 84d–1 A.G.O.; *Penn Yan Democrat*, August 15, 1919, 1; 1910 U.S. Census, Pennsylvania, Dauphin County, Harrisburg (Series T624, Roll 1336, Page 142); *New York Times*, June 27, 1958, 25.

39. Lancaster (NY) Presbyterian Church, Session Minutes, June 19, 1916, Archives, Lancaster Presbyterian Church. Session Minutes, December 14, 1917, Archives, Lancaster Presbyterian Church. Session Minutes, May 29, 1918, Archives, Lancaster Presbyterian Church. Fifield, *The Regiment*, 264.

40. Assignment Record, ADB; *The Pilot*, July 10, 1947. Service Record, Form No. 84d–1 A.G.O., MANG.

41. 1910 U.S. Census, New Jersey, Essex County, Montclair Township (Series T624, Roll 883, Page 192). *Evening Sun*, May 11, 1984, C4; *New York Times*, Febru-

ary 28, 1920; Irving Pollitt, *Memento*, Brown Memorial Park Avenue Presbyterian Church, 146–47; T. Guthrie Speers, Interview, October 6, 1978, TGS.

42. *New York Times*, February 28, 1929. Speers, Interview, October 6, 1978, TGS. Service Record, Form No. 43c, A.G.O., New Jersey State Archives; Strickland, *Connecticut Fights*, 333.

43. For administrative purposes, the Services of Supply ("SOS") divided the area of AEF operations into different zones, or Base Sections, one in England (Base Section No. 3) and the rest in France. William E. Haseltine, *The Services of Supply of the American Expeditionary Force: A Statistical Summary* (Washington, D.C.: GPO, 1919).

44. Charles H. Brent to Clarence Edwards, August 23, 1918, CRE 14.18.

45. Sibley, *With the Yankee Division*, 171. Lyman Rollins to Clarence R. Edwards, September 5, 1918, CRE 14.19.

Chapter Five: St. Mihiel and Troyon

1. Shay, *The Yankee Division*, 148–49. Dale E. Wilson, *Treat 'em Rough!: The Birth of American Armor, 1917–1920* (Novato, CA: Presidio, 1989), 100 and 106–7.

2. Coffman, *The War to End All Wars*, 277. Westbrook, *Those Eighteen Months*, 159–60. Campbell to "Dear Friends," September 15, 1918, KJB.

3. Mayotte to John J. Nilan, September 16, 1918, *Catholic Transcript*, October 17, 1918, Diocesan Archives, Archdiocese of Hartford.

4. Coffman, *The War to End All Wars*, 278–79. Mayotte to John J. Nilan, September 16, 1918, *Catholic Transcript*, October 17, 1918, Diocesan Archives, Archdiocese of Hartford.

5. ABMC, *26th Division*, 48.

6. Campbell to "Dear Friends," September 15, 1918, KJB.

7. Cabot, *History of the 103rd Infantry*, 22–23. Anderson to father, September 21, 1918, HRA.

8. Shay, *The Yankee Division*, 163–67; Cabot, *History of the 103rd Infantry*, 22–23; Sirois, McGinnis, and Hogan, *Smashing through the "World War,"* 104–5. Anderson to father, September 21, 1918, HRA. Anderson to father, September 30, 1918, HRA.

9. Fifield, *The Regiment*, 278. Albertine, *The Yankee Doughboy*, 186–87. Fifield, *The Regiment*, 278–79; Albertine, *The Yankee Doughboy*, 192.

10. Horace P. Hobbs to Edna Hobbs, September 13, 1918, MHI.

11. Shay, *The Yankee Division*, 163–67.

12. Benwell, *History of the Yankee Division*, 166. General Orders No. 88, 26th Division, AEF, cited in Strickland, *Connecticut Fights*, 240–41; Service Record, Form No. 84d-1 A.G.O., MANG.

13. Anderson to John Timothy Stone, "Letters from Men in Uniform," *Fourth Church Magazine* (November 1918): 310–11. Anderson to father, September 21, 1918, HRA.

14. Hesselgrave, *The 101st Machine Gun Battalion*, 23–24, CHS.

15. Taylor, *New England in France*, 233–35.

16. Ibid., 235–36. *History of the 101st United States Engineers*, 262; Arthur C. Havlin, *The History of Company A, 102nd Machine Gun Battalion, Twenty-Sixth Division, A.E.F.* (Boston: Harry C. Rodd, 1928), 142.

17. Cabot, *History of the 103rd U.S. Infantry*, 24–25. Strickland, *Connecticut Fights*, 242–48; *History of the 101st United States Engineers*, 258–64.

18. Havlin, *The History of Company A*, 145–47.
19. Speers, Interview, October 6, 1978, TGS. Shay, *The Yankee Division*, 170.
20. Speers, Interview, October 6, 1978, TGS.
21. Service Record, Form No. 43c, A.G.O., New Jersey State Archives; Strickland, *Connecticut Fights*, 245; Citation available at www.militarytimes.com/citations-medals-awards. Thomas Guthrie Speers, Chaplain's Notes, Thomas F. Sullivan (9/26/18), TGS.
22. 1900 U.S. Census, Vermont, Essex County, Town of Bloomfield (Series T623, Roll 1691, Page 165); Clergy Biographical Data, Archives, Diocese of Burlington.
23. Adjutant General of Vermont, *Vermont Roster 1917–1919*, Vermont Office of Veterans' Affairs; A. J. LeVeer, Statement of Military Career, November 7, 1921, Archives, Diocese of Burlington.
24. *Washington Star*, December 24, 1962; *Washington Post*, December 24, 1961. Wainwright, ed., *History of the 101st Machine Gun Battalion*, 122 and 177; 1910 U.S. Census, District of Columbia, Series (T624, Roll 150, Page 58). Hesselgrave, *The 101st Machine Gun Battalion*, 24–25, CHS.
25. Honeywell, *Chaplains*, 181.

CHAPTER SIX: VERDUN

1. Taylor, *New England in France*, 244. Havlin, *History of Company A*, 154–55. Arthur J. LeVeer, Statement of Military Career, Archives, Diocese of Burlington. The 104th Ambulance Company initially established a dressing station in tents at Samogneux. Heavy shellfire forced its closure, and the company went into reserve. Its place was taken by the 102nd Ambulance Company, which established the station in dugouts 5 km to the rear. Shay, *A Grateful Heart*, 116.
2. Campbell to "Dear Friends," October 20, 1918, KJB.
3. Alistair Horne, *The Price of Glory: Verdun, 1916* (New York: Penguin, 1993), 327-28. Shay, *The Yankee Division*, 175.
4. Stanhope Bayne-Jones to Edith Bayne Denegre ("Tante E"), July 15, 1918; Stanhope Bayne-Jones to George Denegre ("Uncle George"), October 15, 1918, NLM. Potter to mother, October 20, 1918, MHS.
5. Edward G. Lengel, *To Conquer Hell: The Meuse-Argonne, 1918* (New York: Henry Holt, 2008), 256, 275–78, and 283–85.
6. Chase diary, October 19, 1918, MANG.
7. Campbell to "Dear Friends," October 27, 1918, KJB.
8. Anderson to father, October 23, 1918, HRA.
9. Lengel, *To Conquer Hell*, 362; Westbrook, *Those Eighteen Months*, 210–11. Albertine, *The Yankee Doughboy*, 210.
10. Speers, Interview, October 6, 1978, TGSIII.
11. Service Record, Form No. 84b–9 A.G.O., MANG; Fifield, *The Regiment*, 285; Albertine, *The Yankee Doughboy*, 239. Albertine states that Fr. Farrell joined the battalion as chaplain on the march to the rest area. Perhaps there was some overlap, but his orders clearly list October 13, 1918, as the day he joined the 104th Infantry. He described Farrell as "a very nice man, but a different type from Chaplain de Valles." The roster of officers in the 103rd Field Artillery for October 10, 1918, lists 1st Lt. John F. Tucker as Regimental Chaplain, so there must have been a short transition period for Fr. Farrell to pass the reins. Kernan and Samson, *History of the 103rd Field Artillery*, 119. Malcolm E. Peabody diary, December 9, 1918,

MPP 14.8. John A. Naulty, "Very Reverend J. Francis Tucker, O.S.F.S: A Biographical Sketch in Commemoration of his Golden Jubilee of Ordination" (1962): 6; Certificate of Identity, Form No. 633–1–A.G.O., and Extract of Order No. 215, War Department, September 13, 1918, Archives, Oblates of St. Francis de Sales; Delaware War History Record, Delaware Public Archives. Peabody diary, December 9, 1918, MPP 14.8.

12. Laurence Stallings, *The Doughboys: The Story of the AEF, 1917–1918* (New York: Harper Row, 1963), 375–77. Jack Barry to John Francis Tucker, June 10, 1919, Archives, Oblates of St. Francis de Sales. Ben Lerry to John Francis Tucker, November 16, 1921, Archives, Oblates of St. Francis de Sales. Christopher Michael Conlon to John Francis Tucker, January 16, 1956, Archives, Oblates of St. Francis de Sales.

13. Service Record, Form No. 84b–9 A.G.O., MANG. Lyman Rollins to Horace P. Hobbs, February 20, 1919, Hobbs Papers, MHI.

14. Shay, *The Yankee Division*, 187–94. Albertine, *The Yankee Doughboy*, 219.

15. Wainwright, ed., *History of the 101st Machine Gun Battalion*, 127 and 167. *Ohio State University Monthly* 10, no. 7 (April 1919): 15.

16. Carter, *The 101st Field Artillery*, 231.

17. Campbell to "Dear Friends," October 27, 1918, KJB.

18. Anderson to John Timothy Stone, *Fourth Church Magazine* (February 1919): 419, Archives, Fourth Presbyterian Church; Anderson to father, November 4, 1918, and November 6, 1918, HRA. The hospital was most likely the 101st Field Hospital, which was stationed at Vacherauville and had the Mobile De-Gassing Unit attached. Shay, *A Grateful Heart*, 116.

19. Speers, Chaplain's Notes, Stanley Bejeko (10/26/18) and Jesse Hardwick (10/29/18), TGS.

20. Steven M. Avela, "John J. Mitty, Archbishop of San Francisco, 1935–1961," in *Catholic San Francisco: Sesquicentennial Essays*, ed. Jeffrey M. Burns (Menlo Park, CA: Archives of the Archdiocese of San Francisco, 2005), 47–49.

21. John J. Mitty to Eugene P. Clark, November 22, 1918, "The Knights of Columbus War Service," *Catholic Educational Review* 17 (January–May 1919): 116; "Reverend John J. Mitty, D. D.," *Yankee Doings* 7, no. 7 (July–August 1926): 24; Service Record, Archives, Archdiocese of San Francisco; Avela, "John J. Mitty," 49.

22. Frederick Sumner Mead, ed., *Harvard's Military Record in the World War* (Cambridge, MA: Harvard University Press, 1921), 895. Service Record, Form No. 84d–1 A.G.O., MANG.

23. Malcolm E. Peabody, Chapter 8, "Lawrence and the War," *Malcolm Peabody Autobiography* (Cambridge, MA: n.p., 1970), 5, MPP.

24. Sibley, *With the Yankee Division*, 307–8.

25. C. H. Brent to Clarence Edwards, October 21, 1918, CRE 14.23.

26. Michael E. Shay, *Revered Commander, Maligned General: The Life of Clarence Ransom Edwards, 1859–1931* (Columbia: University of Missouri Press, 2011), 167–69, 175, and 213–15.

27. LeVeer, Statement of Military Career, Archives, Diocese of Burlington. Coffman, *The War to End All Wars*, 84.

28. Horace P. Hobbs, Memorandum re Inspector's Report on Morale, November 6, 1918, *History, 51st Infantry Brigade, 26th Division*, Appendix H, Hugh A. Drum Papers, MHI; W. S. Grant, Memorandum for Chief of Staff, Headquarters First Army, American Expeditionary Forces, Office of the Chief of Staff, November 5, 1918, Hobbs papers, MHI.

29. Lengel, *To Conquer Hell*, 82.

30. Strickland, *Connecticut Fights*, 291; Records and Archives of the Archdiocese of Omaha; Sara Mullin Baldwin and Robert Morton Baldwin, eds., *Nebraskana* (Hebron, NE: Baldwin, 1932), 625.

31. *Holyoke Daily Transcript-Daily Telegram*, June 26, 1962, 1. Service Record, Form No. 84d-1 A.G.O., NY State Archives; Archives, Archdiocese of New York; *New York Times*, October 29, 1955, 19.

32. Anderson to father, November 12, 1918, HRA.

33. In the 104th Infantry Regiment two men died of wounds on November 9, 1918: one on November 10, and two more on November 11. Albert G. Love, ed., *The Medical Department of the United States Army in the World War*, vol. 15, part 2 (Washington, D.C.: GPO, 1925), 1092–93. Cpl. Henry L. Lamb, Company A, 104th Infantry, was the sole man killed in action on November 10 in that regiment; he had earlier offered a firsthand account of the death of Chaplain Danker in the Toul sector. Service Record Form No. 724-6, A.G.O., MANG. Service Record, Form No. 84b-9 A.G.O., MANG.

34. Wainwright, ed., *History of the 101st Machine Gun Battalion*, 132.

35. ABMC, *26th Division: Summary of Operations in the World War* (Washington, D.C.: GPO, 1944), 57. Westbrook, *Those Eighteen Months*, 216. Evans had two brothers: John L. Evans, a lawyer aged 39, and Rowland, aged 28. I have assumed the younger brother was in the service. 1910 U.S. Census, Pennsylvania, Montgomery County, Lower Merion Township (Series T624, Roll 1378, Page 189). The 1910 U.S. Census, Pennsylvania, Montgomery County, Lower Merion Township (Series T624, Roll 1378, Page 189) lists the children of Allen Evans, Sr., as John L. (31), Margaret E. (28), Rowland (20), and Allen, Jr. (19).

36. Albertine, *The Yankee Doughboy*, 228–29. Campbell to "Dear Friends," November 18, 1918, KJB.

37. Albertine, *The Yankee Doughboy*, 233–35.

38. Albert G. Butzer, Sr., to "My Dear Folks," November 11, 1918. Courtesy of Albert G. Butzer, III.

39. Anderson to John Timothy Stone, *The Fourth Church Magazine* (February 1919): 419–20, FPCA.

40. ABMC, *26th Division*, 63.

41. Campbell to "Dear Friends," October 20, 1918, KJB.

42. Peabody, *Autobiography*, MPP 15.1. Anderson to father, November 6, 1918, HRA. Westbrook, *Those Eighteen Months*, 228–29.

Chapter Seven: Going Home

1. Anderson to father, November 12, 1918, HRA.

2. Hobbs to Edna Hobbs, November 15, 1918, MHI. Carter, *The 101st Field Artillery*, 259.

3. Mrs. Mortimer E. Brislot to Thomas Guthrie Speers, December 18, 1918, TGS. Brislot to Thomas Guthrie Speers, February 3, 1919, TGS.

4. Carter, *The 101st Field Artillery*, 260–61. Paul Dwight Moody, "Murray Dewart: A Knightly Man of God," *The Churchman* (nd.), MWD. Anderson to father, November 27, 1918, HRA.

5. Chase diary, December 25, 1918, MANG. *History of the 101st United States Engineers*, 304. Benwell, *History of the Yankee Division*, 218–21.

6. LeVeer, Statement of Military Career, Archives, Diocese of Burlington.

7. Peabody, diary, November 22, 1918, MPP 14.8. Peabody, diary, November 21, 1918, MPP 14.8.

8. Young, *A Surgeon's Autobiography*, 378. Peabody, *Autobiography*, MPP 15.1.

9. *Catholic Transcript*, January 23, 1919, 1, Archives, Archdiocese of Hartford; another account states that the chaplain "fell from his horse and contracted pneumonia," *Windham County Observer*, January 22, 1919, 1. Douglas Wahl to Bishop of Hartford, December 28, 1918, *Catholic Transcript*, January 30, 1919, Archives, Archdiocese of Hartford.

10. *Catholic Transcript*, January 23, 1919, 4, Archives, Archdiocese of Hartford.

11. *Adjutant General, Connecticut*, 2607.

12. Extract, Special Orders No. 317, November 13, 1918, American Expeditionary Forces, IBP 6.

13. Henry Englander to Israel Bettan, April 19, 1919, IBP 5.3.

14. Englander to Israel Bettan, April 19, 1919, IBP 5.3. Known as the "Fighting Rabbi," Elkan Voorsanger enlisted as a private in the Army at the start of World War I, and he was sent to France with the first contingent of the AEF. He rose through the ranks and eventually became the chaplain of the 77th Division, a National Army division, which drew from an eclectic mix of ethnic New Yorkers. After the Armistice, he stayed on in Europe to head the Jewish Welfare Board. *New York Times*, October 12, 1919. Elkan Voorsanger to Israel Bettan, March 2, 1919, IBP 6.10. "Program for Cooperation between Jewish Chaplains and the Jewish Welfare Board in the A.E.F.," IBP 6.13. Englander to Israel Bettan, April 19, 1919, IBP 5.3.

15. Telegram, Division Adjutant to Israel Bettan, March 12, 1919, IBP 6.13. Reference to Par. 124, Special Orders #58. Bettan, Officer's Record Book, IBP 6.13.

16. Extract, Special Orders No. 191, July 10, 1919, IBP 6.13.

17. The title for this section comes from Archibald Bulloch Roosevelt to Theodore Roosevelt, Jr., January 6, 1919, quoted in Edward J. Renehan, Jr., *The Lion's Pride: Theodore Roosevelt and His Family in Peace and War* (New York: Oxford University Press, 1998), 222. Edmund Morris, *Colonel Roosevelt* (New York: Random House, 2011), 553.

18. Frederick A. Pottle, *Stretchers: The Story of a Hospital Unit on the Western Front* (New Haven: Yale University Press, 1929), 329. Chase diary, February 9, 1919, MANG. Erwin Funk to John Francis Tucker, January 9, 1956, Archives, Oblates of St. Francis de Sales. Quoting from his letter to the *Rogers* (Arkansas) *Democrat*; *Evening Bulletin*, November 4, 1972 ("gravel-voiced priest").

19. Budd, *Serving Two Masters*, 156.

20. Albertine, *The Yankee Doughboy*, 104–5. Campbell to "Dear Friends," October 27, 1918, KJB. Campbell to "Dear Friends," January 11, 1919, KJB.

21. Anderson to father, January 11, 1919, HRA.

22. Houlihan to mother, January 7, 1919, *Natick Bulletin*, February 7, 1919, 1. His companions were more than likely Pfc. John H. Kelly and Pfc. John B. LaChapelle, both members of Battery F, as was Cpl. Houlihan. Carter, *The 101st Field Artillery*, 293–94.

23. Ford, *Fighting Yankees*, 89.

24. O'Connor to Editor, *The Pilot*, October 26, 1918. Everett E. Taylor to mother, March 16, 1919, MHI.

25. Campbell to "Dear Friends," November 18, 1918, KJB.

26. Stover, *Up from Handymen*, 195. Budd, *Serving Two Masters*, 69. Meirion Harries and Susie Harries, *The Last Days of Innocence: America at War, 1917–1918* (New York: Random House, 1997), 451–52; even temporary burials were conducted with as much reverence as the situation would allow, with a chaplain and a

marker with the doughboy's identity disc attached. Albertine, *The Yankee Doughboy*, 161.

27. Ezra Hoop to Speers, December 29, 1918, TGS. Mary Kalbaza to Thomas Speers, December 20, 1918, TGS. Speers, Chaplain's Notes, May 24, 1919, TGS. Speers, Chaplain's Notes, May 26, 1919, TGS.

28. Martin Gilbert, *The First World War* (New York: Henry Holt, 1994), 515. ABMC, *American Memorials and Overseas Military Cemeteries* (Washington, D.C., 1994), 2; *Stars & Stripes*, Friday, February 28, 1919, 1–2. ABMC, *Flanders Field American Cemetery and Memorial* (Washington, D.C., 1944), 20 (30,921 graves and 4,452 memorials to the missing). Harries and Harries, *The Last Days of Innocence*, 451-52.

29. *Framingham News*, September 27, 1944, 7.

30. Peabody diary, December 6, 1918, Scrap Book, MPP 28.FB1v.

31. Potter to mother, December 4, 1919, MHS. Chase diary, November 24, 1918, MANG; *History of the 101st United States Engineers*, 301–2.

32. Campbell to "Dear Friends," November 18, 1918, KJB. Peabody diary, November 24, 1918, MPP 14.8.

33. Horatio Rogers, *World War I through My Sights* (San Rafael, CA: Presidio, 1976), 242–51.

34. Speers, Interview, October 6, 1978, TGSIII. Cabot, *History of the 103rd U.S. Infantry*, 31.

35. Campbell to "Dear Friends," January 11, 1919, KJB.

36. Wainwright, ed., *History of the 101st Machine Gun Battalion*, 139. LeVeer, Statement of Military Career, Archives, Diocese of Burlington. Wainwright, ed., *History of the 101st Machine Gun Battalion*, 141 and 177; *Washington Star*, December 24, 1961.

37. Young, *A Surgeon's Autobiography*, 332. Shay, *A Grateful Heart*, 184.

38. Stover, *Up from Handymen*, 198. Charles H. Cole to David I. Walsh, January 19, 1919, David I. Walsh Papers, Archives and Special Collections, College of the Holy Cross.

39. John Francis Tucker, Delaware War History Record, Delaware Public Archives, RG 1800.50. Peabody diary, December 25, 1918, through February 9, 1919, and February 21, 1919, MPP 14.8. Peabody diary, December 25, 1918, through February 9, 1919, MPP 14.8.

40. Tucker, Delaware War History Record, RG 1800.50; Extract, Battalion Special Order No. 334, Headquarters, 5th Battalion, 20th Engineers, March 31, 1919, Archives, Oblates of St. Francis de Sales. John E. Corcoran to John Francis Tucker, March 20, 1919, Archives, Oblates of St. Francis de Sales. Tucker, Officer's Record Book, Archives, Oblates of St. Francis de Sales. Memorandum, Headquarters, 5th Battalion, 20th Engineers, Archives, Oblates of St. Francis de Sales. Tucker, Delaware War History Record, RG 1800.50.

41. LeVeer, Statement of Military Career, Archives, Diocese of Burlington. Butzer, Service Record, Form No. 84d–1 A.G.O., New York State Archives. Campbell, Service Record, Form 84d–1 A.G.O., MANG.

42. Potter to mother, January 28, 1919, MHS.

43. Campbell to "Dear Friends," February 20, 1919, KJB; Shay, *A Grateful Heart*, 143.

44. Ford, *The Fighting Yankees*, 245. Peabody diary, April 3, 1919, MPP 14.8. Peabody diary, April 5, 1919, MPP 14.8.

45. *Hartford Courant*, May 2, 1919, 10.

Chapter Eight: "Recalled to Life"

1. Augusta Gregory, *Cuchulain of Muirthemne* (Gerrads Cross, Bucks: Colin Smythe, 1984), 28. Service Record, Form No. 84b-8 A.G.O., MANG; *New York Times*, May 16, 1920.

2. Service Record, Form No. 84b-9 A.G.O., MANG; 1920 U.S. Census, Massachusetts, Essex County, Marblehead (Series T625, Roll 691, Page 92); "Taps," *Yankee Doings* 11, no. 10 (November 1930): 23; "Memorial Dedicated to Chaplain Lyman Rollins," *Yankee Doings* 15, no. 9 (November 1934): 7. "Memorial Dedicated to Chaplain Lyman Rollins," *Yankee Doings* 15, no. 9 (November 1934): 7. *Concord Daily Monitor*, July 12, 1930, 5.

3. Service Record, Form No. 84d-8 A.G.O, MANG; Albertine, *The Yankee Doughboy*, 303. *New Bedford Standard*, January 18, 1920.

4. *New Bedford Standard*, May 10, 1920.

5. Ibid.

6. *New Bedford Standard*, April 8, 1920.

7. Service Record, Form No. 84d-8 A.G.O., MANG. Albertine, *The Yankee Doughboy*, 303.

8. Service Record, Form No. 84d-8 A.G.O., MANG. De Valles was previously awarded the Silver Star for these actions, and upon the award of the DSC, the Silver Star was rescinded by GHQ AEF pursuant to Citation Orders No. 9, August 1, 1920. Available at http://www.militarytimes.com/citations-medals-awards/citation.php?citation=48036.

9. *New Bedford Standard*, May 14, 1920; Biographical Information, Archives, Diocese of Fall River. *New York Times*, May 16, 1920. Per the chaplain's wish, the decoration was removed and given to his sister and only living relative, Mary Hill, so that she might donate it to a council of the Knights of Columbus. *New Bedford Standard*, May 14, 1920.

10. *New York Times*, February 14, 1933, 18; *Newtown Graphic*, February 17, 1933, 1; *The Pilot*, February 18, 1933, 1.

11. Markham W. Stackpole, "Chaplain Farrell," *Yankee Doings* 14, no. 3 (March 1933): 5.

12. "Reverend William J. Farrell," *Yankee Doings* 14, no. 3 (March 1933): 4.

13. Edward Brodney (1910-2002). Douglas Martin, "Edward Brodney, 92, Who Painted War Scenes," *New York Times*, August 19, 2002.

14. Illinois State Archives, Statewide Death Index, available at http://www.ilsos/isavital/idphDeath Search.do; Joseph J. Thompson, *A History of the Knights of Columbus in Illinois* (Chicago: Universal Press, 1921), 840; *Clifton Advocate*, December 12, 1919, 1; *Ordination Register*, Office of Archives of the Catholic Diocese of Peoria.

15. Romilly F. Humphries, "Murray Wilder Dewart" (undated typescript), MWD.

16. Moody, "Murray Dewart: A Knightly Man of God," MWD.

17. *Boston Globe*, December 4 and 5, 1927; *New York Times*, December 5, 1927, 23; Health Department, Bureau of Vital Statistics, City of Baltimore, Death Record Index 1875-1972, Maryland State Archives, #MSACE42; as to the topic of his final sermon, Murray Dewart to author, October 29, 2012. *Baltimore Sun*, December 7, 1927; "Rev. M. W. Dewart Laid at Rest in Baltimore," Baltimore, December 7, 1927, unspecified source, Archives, Parish of the Epiphany, Winchester, MA.

18. Vestry, Christ Church, "Resolution," December 12, 1927, *The Maryland Churchman*, Archives, Epiphany Parish, Winchester, MA.

19. William S. Packer, Tribute to Murray W. Dewart, December 7, 1927, Archives, Epiphany Parish, Winchester, MA. Moody, "Murray Dewart: A Knightly Man of God," MWD.

20. John H. Sherburne, *Boston Globe*, December 8, 1927.

21. Smith Owen Dexter, ibid.

22. 1930 U.S. Census, Maryland, Baltimore (Series T626, Roll 869, Page 169).

23. *Hartford Times*, April 16, 1927. Undated, unidentified news clipping, Ruth Hesselgrave Papers 12.8, Stewart-Smith Research Center, Henry Sheldon Museum of Vermont History.

24. The Massachusetts Militia, of which O'Connor was a member prior to the formation of the Yankee Division, equipped their five chaplains with various items for use in France, including a vehicle and a portable altar. Dewart, "My Temperamental Truck," 1, MWD.

25. *The Pilot*, September 30, 1944, 1; *Framingham News*, September 27, 1944, 1; *Framingham News*, September 29, 1944, 1; Military Record, Form 1m-1'30, No. 7616, MANG; *Yankee Doings* 15, no. 10 (November 1944): 10.

26. "Monsignor Osias Boucher," *Yankee Doings* 25, no. 107 (May–June 1955): 14; Military Record, Form 1m(b)-7-45-16634, MANG.

27. Adjutant General, Connecticut, 1967; 1920 U.S. Census, Connecticut, New Haven County, City of New Haven (Series T625, Roll 191, Page 4). *New York Times*, August 14, 1942, 17.

28. Service Record, Form No. 84b-1 A.G.O., MANG. *The Story of St. Michael's Parish of Milton, Massachusetts* (Milton, MA: n.p., 1945), 11. "The Rev. H. Boyd Edwards, D. D.," *The Church News* (December 1945): 13. *Pittsburgh Press*, June 7, 1931.

29. *Daily Record*, November 24, 1970, 2; "The Rev. H. Boyd Edwards, D. D.," 13, Archives, Church of the Ascension, Pittsburgh, PA.

30. *Burlington Free Press*, September 12, 1959, 2; undated newspaper article from files and records of the Waterbury Congregational Church, Waterbury, VT. *New York Times*, June 13, 1933, 13. *Waterbury Record*, May 9, 1934, 1; "History of Waterbury Congregational Church," available at http://waterburyucc.org.

31. *Burlington Free Press*, September 12, 1959; *Book of Remembrance*, vol. 6, p. 15, Archives, Pilgrim Place, Claremont, CA; undated newspaper article from files and records of the Waterbury Congregational Church, Waterbury, VT.

32. 1920 U.S. Census, Massachusetts, Worcester County, Town of Warren (Series T625, Roll 748, Page 248). Kenneth J. Buck, Introduction to "Letters from Rev. Robert Campbell, 1918–1919." *Boston Globe*, September 1, 1969; Records, Marblehead Cemetery Department.

33. Assignments and Necrology, Archives, Diocese of Springfield; "A Century of Catholicism in Western Massachusetts," *The Catholic Mirror* (1931).

34. *New York Times*, June 28, 1962, 31; *Holyoke Daily Transcript-Daily Telegram*, June 26, 1962, 1.

35. *New York Times*, June 28, 1962, 31; Assignments and Necrology, Archives, Diocese of Springfield.

36. 1920 U.S. Census, New York, Yates County, Penn Yan Village (Series T625, Roll 1281, Page 209); *Penn Yan Democrat*, August 15, 1919, 1; "History of First Presbyterian Church," available at http://www.pennyanpresbyterian.org/PYPC_history.shtml. *Penn Yan Democrat*, August 12, 1927, 3; "First Presbyterian Church, Newburgh, Orange County, New York," available at http://www.newyorkgenealogy.org/orange/newburgh-first-presbyterian-church.htm. Program for Installation

Service, October 2, 1947, Montauk Community Church. Minutes of Session, June 1, 1949, Montauk Community Church. Minutes of Session, October 19, 1949, Montauk Community Church.

37. Charles K. Imbrie, "How Would You Like to Become Pastor of Montauk Community Church," June 30, 1949, Montauk Community Church.

38. *New York Times*, June 27, 1958, 25.

39. Arthur J. LeVeer, Statement of Military Career, Archives, Diocese of Burlington.

40. *St. Albans Messenger*, September 2, 1964, 1–2; Clergy Biographical Data, Archives, Diocese of Burlington.

41. Service Record, Form No. 84d-1, A.G.O., New York State Archives. *New York Times*, October 29, 1955, 19; *Catholic News*, vol. 70, no. 14 (November 5, 1955), Archives, Archdiocese of New York.

42. Diocesan Appointments, Archives, Archdiocese of Omaha. Newspaper Article, Tucson, April 24, 1950, Archives, Archdiocese of Omaha.

43. Newspaper Article, Tucson, April 24, 1950, Archives, Archdiocese of Omaha.

44. George J. Jonaitis to Joseph F. Rummel, September 18, 1934, Archives, Archdiocese of Omaha.

45. Joseph F. Rummel to Jonaitis, September 20, 1934, Archives, Archdiocese of Omaha.

46. Jonaitis to James H. Ryan, May 2, 1936, Archives, Archdiocese of Omaha.

47. Harry E. Thompson to James H. Ryan, December 23, 1936; Jonaitis to James H. Ryan, December 29, 1936, Archives, Archdiocese of Omaha.

48. L. D. McGuire to James H. Ryan, October 1, 1937, Archives, Archdiocese of Omaha.

49. Diocesan Appointments, Archives, Archdiocese of Omaha. Newspaper Article, Tucson, April 24, 1950, Archives, Archdiocese of Omaha.

50. *Omaha World Herald, Morning Edition*, December 27, 1963, 36; *Omaha World Herald, Morning Edition*, December 28, 1963, 36.

51. Service Record, Form No. 84d-1, A.G.O., Pennsylvania State Archives. *Alumni Directory of Yale University* (New Haven: Yale University Press, 1920), 163; "Rectors of St. Peters," available at http://stpetershistory.org/stpetershistoryrectorsc.html. Eddy, "According to This Beginning," 48. "Epiphany Rector Resigns to Accept Long Island Parish," April 8, 1927, Scrapbook, Parish of the Epiphany.

52. Allen Evans, Jr., "Rector Evans' Plea for Christian Unity," April 1, 1927, Scrapbook, Parish of the Epiphany.

53. "Epiphany Rector Resigns to Accept Long Island Parish," April 8, 1927, Scrapbook, Parish of the Epiphany. *New York Times*, December 18, 1960. "Rectors of St. Peters," available at http://stpetershistory.org/stpetershistoryrectorsc.html.

54. *New York Times*, December 18, 1960.

55. *Hartford Courant*, April 8, 1919. Service Record, Form No. 84d-1, A.G.O., MANG. Assignment Record, Archdiocese of Boston, ADB.

56. *Daily Mining Gazette*, June 10, 1950, 10; Service Record, Form 84d-1, A.G.O., Wisconsin Office of Veterans Affairs.

57. Service Record, Form No. 84d-1, A.G.O., MANG. *New York Times*, May 11, 1919. *New York Times*, June 9, 1923; USTA Yearbook, Adult & Senior Cups (Church/Sears Cup). "The Church Cup was donated by George Meyers Church for competition between men's teams representing Boston, New York and Philadelphia." Available at http://www.usta.com/About-USTA/Organization/Yearbook/23088_

2008_USTA_Yearbook. 1920 U.S. Census, Massachusetts, Suffolk, Boston (Series T625, Roll 742, Page 172); *Inquirer and Mirror*, September 19, 1963.

58. *Inquirer and Mirror*, November 26, 1948. *Inquirer and Mirror*, November 20, 1948. *New York Times*, September 16, 1963, 35; *New York Times*, September 17, 1963, 35; *Inquirer and Mirror*, September 19, 1963.

59. Frederick Spring Osborne, *Princeton Herald*, reprinted with permission in the *Inquirer and Mirror*, September 26, 1963.

60. 1920 U.S. Census, Virginia, Roanoke County, City of Roanoke (Series T625, Roll 1912, Page 102). *Mobile Register*, January 19, 1933; *Mobile Register*, January 20, 1933.

61. 1920 U.S. Census, District of Columbia, City of Washington (Series T625, Roll 213, Page 182).

62. *Washington Star*, December 24, 1961; *Washington Post*, December 24, 1961.

63. Service Record, *Vermont Roster 1917-1919*, Vermont Office of Veterans Affairs. *New York Times*, August 20, 1921.

64. Laura Schiavo, "1923 Tree, The Elipse," available at http://www.nps.gov/whho/historyculture/1923-national-christmas-tree.htm.

65. *New York Times*, July 18, 1927, 20.

66. *New York Times*, August 20, 1947, 21; *Obituary Record of Graduates of Yale University Deceased during the Year 1947-1949*, Bulletin of Yale University 1, series 45 (January 1, 1949): 63-64.

67. 1920 U.S. Census, West Virginia, Kanawha County, City of Charleston (Series T625, Roll 1958, Page 112).

68. *New York Times*, June 29, 1956, 2.

69. *New York Times*, June 25, 1957, 25.

70. *New York Times*, August 6, 1957, 27; "Biographical Sketch," *A Finding Aid to the Israel Bettan Papers*, American Jewish Archives, Hebrew Union College, available at http://americanjewisharchives.org/aja/FindingAids/Bettan.htm.

71. Paul Sullivan, "Judaism Loses Master of Preaching," *Cincinnati Times-Star*, n.d., IBP 6.4.

72. Service Record, Form No. 84d-1, A.G.O., MANG. *Harvard College Class of 1896, Thirty-fifth Anniversary Report, June, 1931* (Norwood, MA: Plimpton Press, 1931), 92.

73. Markham W. Stackpole, *World War Memories of Milton Academy, 1914-1919, with Service Records of Masters and Former Students* (Cambridge, MA: Riverside, 1940).

74. Stackpole, "The War Memoirs of Milton Academy," *Milton Bulletin* 3, no. 2 (May, 1940): 19-21.

75. *Alumni Award Winners: Classes of 1884-1925*, available at http://www.colgateconnect.org.

76. Cyril H. Jones, "Mr. Stackpole," *Milton Bulletin* 8, no. 2 (May, 1945): 10-11.

77. *Milton Record*, March 19, 1948, 6.

78. Service Record, Form No. 84d-1, A.G.O., New York State Archives; Albert G. Butzer, Biographical Sketch, AGB. 1920 U.S. Census, New York State, New York County, Borough of Manhattan (Series T625, Roll 1208, Page 25). *New York Times*, September 7, 1920, 13.

79. Emily P. Aumiller and Abigail Gary, *A History of the West Side Presbyterian Church, Ridgewood, New Jersey: In Celebration of the 90th Anniversary, 1912-2002* (Ridgewood, NJ: The West Side Presbyterian Church, 2002), 18-22. Available at www.westside.org.

80. Butzer, Biographical Sketch, AGB.

81. *New York Times*, August 24, 1942, 13. *New York Times*, June 26, 1944, 22.

82. *Buffalo Courier-Express*, November 29, 1967, 8; Butzer, Biographical Sketch, AGB. *New York Times*, January 19, 1959, 22.

83. *Buffalo Evening News*, January 6, 1962.

84. Albert G. Butzer, Farewell Sermon, September 30, 1962, AGB.

85. *Buffalo Courier-Express*, November 29, 1962.

86. Ford, *The Fighting Yankees*, 187. The Archdiocese of New York established Most Holy Trinity Catholic Chapel on the grounds of the United States Military Academy in 1900. The chapel is wholly owned by the Archdiocese, and it is considered a parish church. Since its establishment, until the appointment of the first Catholic military chaplain at West Point in the 1970s, the Archdiocese appointed a pastor or administrator of the parish to serve the needs of Catholic cadets. Rev. Michael P. Morris, Archdiocesan Archivist, to the author, February 10, 2012, and February 13, 2012. Avela, "John J. Mitty," 49; "Reverend John J. Mitty, D. D.," *Yankee Doings* 7, no. 7 (July–August 1926): 24; John J. Mitty to Patrick Cardinal Hayes, October 20, 1925, ADNY.

87. Avela, "John J. Mitty," 49–55.

88. Military Record, Kansas Historical Society; Sibley, *With the Yankee Division*, 346. *The First Presbyterian Church of Wichita, Kansas, Founded March 13, 1870* (n.p., n.d.), 14–15, Archives, Fourth Presbyterian Church, Chicago, IL.

89. Scroggs, *A Light in the City*, 118.

90. *Korematsu v. United States*, 323 U.S. 214 (1944).

91. Scroggs, *A Light in the City*, 120–21; *New York Times*, May 25, 1951, 23. *New York Times*, July 5, 1952, 8.

92. Scroggs, *A Light in the City*, 121–22.

93. Harrison Ray Anderson, Compilation of Notes and Writings, HRA.

94. Peabody, Chapter 8, Autobiography, MPP 15.1.

95. Service Record, Form No. 84d-1, A.G.O., MANG. 1920 U.S. Census, Massachusetts, Essex County, City of Lawrence (Series T625, Roll 692, Page 166). *New York Times*, June 21, 1974, 40; "Biography," Mary Peabody Papers, Schlesinger Library, Radcliffe Institute, Harvard University, Cambridge, MA.

96. Naulty, "Very Reverend J. Francis Tucker," Archives, Oblates of St. Francis de Sales.

97. *Evening Bulletin*, November 4, 1972.

98. Thomas Guthrie Speers, III, to author, January 23, 2013.

99. Speers, Chaplain's Notes, June 5, 1919, TGS.

100. Ibid., May 20, 1919, TGS.

101. Ibid., June 4, 1919, May 31, 1919, May 23, 1919, and May 20, 1919, TGS.

102. Ibid., May 26, 1919, TGS.

103. Ibid.

104. Ibid.

105. Ibid.

106. Ibid.

107. Ibid., June 1, 1919, TGS.

108. Ibid., May 30, 1919, TGS.

109. Ibid., May 28, 1919, TGS.

110. Ibid., June 3, 1919, TGS.

111. *New York Times*, February 28, 1920; Ibid., April 19, 1920, 14. "The First Presbyterian Church in the City of New York, History," available at http://www.fpnyc.org/about-us/history.html.

112. Speers, Interview, October 6, 1978, TGS. *New York Times*, November 29, 1926, 21. Ibid., December 27, 1926, 18.
113. *New York Times*, September 29, 1928, 22. Ibid., October 1, 1928, 26.
114. Speers, Interview, October 6, 1978, TGS. *New York Times*, May 28, 1928, 20.
115. *New York Times*, February 7, 1931, 13.
116. Ibid., April 26, 1936, 28.
117. Ibid., June 17, 1940, 34.
118. Brown Memorial Park Avenue Presbyterian Church, "A Brief History," available at http://www.browndowntown.org/index.php?s=history. *New York Times*, March 15, 1954, 19.
119. *Baltimore Evening Sun*, May 11, 1984, C4.
120. Charles L. Wagandt to the Editor, "A Hero Departs," *Baltimore Sun*, 1984, Archives, Brown Memorial Park Avenue Presbyterian Church.
121. David W. Malone, "In Remembrance: T Guthrie Speers, Pastor 1928–1957," Archives, Brown Memorial Park Avenue Presbyterian Church. Mrs. F. R. Leiss to Thomas Guthrie Speers, February 9, 1919, TGS.

Afterword

1. Budd, *Serving Two Masters*, 88 and 102. Coffman, *The Regulars*, 231; Budd, *Serving Two Masters*, 131 and 134–36.
2. Library of Congress, Biographical Note, Charles Henry Brent Papers, available at http://www.loc.gov/rr/mss/text/brent.html; James Kiefer, "Charles Henry Brent, Missionary Bishop, 27 March 1929," *Biographical Sketches of Memorable Christians of the Past*, available at http://justus.anglican.org/resources/bio/116.html; "Memorial Sermons for Charles Henry Brent, Bishop and Doctor (1929)," available at http://anglicanhistory.org/asia/brent/memorial_sermons1929.html.
3. Budd, *Serving Two Masters*, 84–86 and 133–36. Biographical Information, A. A. Pruden Papers, 1898–1931 (#04997-z), University of North Carolina, available at http://www.lib.unc.edu/mss/inv/p/Pruden,A.A.html.
4. Daniel 3:13–26.

Appendix

1. I have attempted to compile the most comprehensive list of designated Chaplains and other men who served with or regularly conducted religious services for the 26th ("Yankee") Division at some time during the First World War. Except where indicated, all of the foregoing have been mentioned by at least one source as having done so. Any omission on my part is accidental. In the absence of a designated chaplain, or in conjunction with one, many men in nongovernmental organizations like the YMCA, Red Cross, Jewish Welfare Board, and Knights of Columbus served the spiritual needs of the YD men on an ad hoc basis, as a part of their other duties. I have referred to these men throughout the text.

2. Although he was never formally appointed as an Army chaplain, Charles "Doc" Hesselgrave voluntarily looked after both the spiritual and temporal needs of the men of the 101st Machine Gun Battalion from early 1918 up until the assignment of Earl Taggart as chaplain in October. Accordingly, I have listed him with the other YD chaplains.

References

PRIMARY SOURCES

Books and Pamphlets

Adjutant General, State of Connecticut. *Service Records, Connecticut Men and Women in the Armed Forces of the United States during World War 1917–1919.* Hartford: Office of the Adjutant General, 1920.

Albertine, Connell. *The Yankee Doughboy.* Boston: Branden Press, 1968.

American Battle Monuments Commission. *26th Division: Summary of Operations in the World War.* Washington, D.C.: GPO, 1944.

Archdiocese for the Military Services, U.S.A. *Priest's Manual, Appendix.* Washington, D.C.: Archdiocese for the Military Services, U.S.A., 2009.

Avela, Steven M. "John J. Mitty, Archbishop of San Francisco, 1935–1961," in *Catholic San Francisco: Sesquicentennial Essays*, edited by Jeffrey M. Burns. Menlo Park, CA: Archives of the Archdiocese of San Francisco, 2005.

Benwell, Harry A. *History of the Yankee Division.* Boston: Cornhill, 1919.

Cabot, Charles R., Regimental Historian. *History of the 103rd U.S. Infantry, 1917–1919.* N.p.: 103rd U.S. Infantry, 1919.

Carter, Russell Gordon: *The 101st Field Artillery A.E.F., 1917–1919.* Boston: Houghton, Mifflin, 1940.

Cushing, Harvey. *From a Surgeon's Journal.* Boston: Little, Brown, 1936.

Duane, James T. *Dear Old "K."* Boston: Thomas Todd Co., 1922.

Eddy, Bradford Updike. "According to This Beginning: A Brief Account of the Development of the Parish of the Epiphany at Winchester, Massachusetts 1882–1954," *An Anthology of Epiphany History 1888–1988.* Winchester, MA: N.p., 1954.

Egan, Maurice Francis, and John James Bright Kennedy. *The Knights of Columbus in Peace and War.* Vol. I. New Haven: Knights of Columbus, 1920.

Fifield, James H. *The Regiment: A History of the 104th U.S. Infantry, A.E.F. 1917–1919.* Springfield, MA: Springfield Union, 1946.

Ford, Bert. *The Fighting Yankees Overseas.* Boston: McPhail, 1919.

George, Albert E., and Edwin H. Cooper. *Pictorial History of the Twen-*

ty-sixth Division, United States Army, with Official Government Pictures Made by United States Signal Corps Unit Under Command of Captain Edwin H. Cooper. Boston: Ball, 1920.

Havlin, Arthur C. *The History of Company A, 102nd Machine Gun Battalion, Twenty-Sixth Division, A.E.F.* Boston: Harry C. Rodd, 1928.

Herzog, Stanley J. *The Fightn' Yanks.* Stamford, CT: Cunningham, 1922.

History of Battery B, One Hundred Third Field Artillery, Twenty-Sixth Division, April, 1917 to April, 1919. Providence, RI: E. L. Freeman, 1922.

History of the 101st United States Engineers American Expeditionary Forces, 1917-1918-1919. Cambridge, MA: Harvard University Press, 1926.

History of the One Hundred Second Field Artillery, July 1917-April 1919. Boston: N.p., 1927.

Holy Cross Service Record. Worcester, MA: Holy Cross College, 1920.

Honeywell, Roy J. *Chaplains of the United States Army.* Washington, D.C.: Office of the Chief of Chaplains, 1958.

Johnson, Douglas V., II, and Rolf L. Hillman, Jr. *Soissons 1918.* College Station: Texas A & M University Press, 1999.

Kernan, W. F., and Henry T. Samson, eds. *History of the 103rd Field Artillery (Twenty-Sixth Division, A.E.F.) World War, 1917-1919.* Providence, RI: Remington Printing, n.d.

Lawson, Kenneth E. *A Historical Overview of the Militia Chaplaincy in Massachusetts from the Puritan Period to the Massachusetts Army National Guard (1620-1996).* N.p., 1997.

Levinger, Lee J. *A Jewish Chaplain in France.* New York: Macmillan, 1921.

Liggett, Hunter. *A.E.F.: Ten Years Ago in France.* Cranbury, N.J.: Scholars Bookshelf, 2005.

Marshall, George, C. *Memoirs of My Services in the World War, 1917-1918.* Boston: Houghton Mifflin, 1976.

McCarthy, Robert John, ed. *A History of Troop A Cavalry, Connecticut National Guard and Its Service in the Great War as Co. D, 102nd Machine Gun Battalion.* Westville, CT: Tuttle, Morehouse, 1919.

McGovern, Lane, ed. *An Anthology of Epiphany History: 1888-1988.* Winchester, MA: Parish of the Epiphany, 1991.

Mead, Frederick Sumner, ed. *Harvard's Military Record in the World War.* Cambridge, MA: Harvard University Press, 1921.

Miles, Dorothy F. *Church of Our Fathers: A Brief History of the Anglican Tradition at St. Michael's Church.* Marblehead, MA: St. Michaels Church, 1984.

Pershing, John J. *My Experiences in the First World War.* New York: Da Capo, 1995.

Putnam, Eben. *Report of the Commission on Massachusetts' Part in the*

World War, Vol. I, History. Boston: Commonwealth of Massachusetts, 1931.

———. *Report of the Commission on Massachusetts' Part in the World War, Vol. II, The Gold Star Record of Massachusetts*. Boston: Commonwealth of Massachusetts, 1929.

Rogers, Horatio. *World War I through My Sights*. San Rafael, CA: Presidio, 1976.

Samson, Henry T., and George C. Hull. *The War Story of Battery C, One Hundred and Third U.S. Field Artillery, France, 1917–1919*. Norwood, MA: Plimpton, 1920.

Sanborn, Robert. *The Immortal Yankee Division, 1917-1919*. Boston: Young Men's Christian Association, 1919.

Shay, Michael E. *A Grateful Heart: The History of a World War I Field Hospital*. Westport, CT: Greenwood, 2001.

———. *Revered Commander, Maligned General: The Life of Clarence Ransom Edwards, 1859–1931*. Columbia: University of Missouri Press, 2011.

———. *The Yankee Division in the First World War: In the Highest Tradition*. College Station: Texas A & M University Press, 2008.

Sibley, Frank P. *With the Yankee Division in France*. Boston: Little, Brown, 1919.

Sirois, Edward D., William McGinnis, and John Hogan, eds. *Smashing through "The World War" with the Fighting Battery C, 102nd F. A. "Yankee Division," 1917–1918–1919*. Salem, MA: Meek Press, 1919.

Stackpole, Everett S. *History and Genealogy of the Stackpole Family*. Lewiston, ME: Press of Journal Company, 1899.

Stover, Earl F. *Up from Handymen: The United States Army Chaplaincy, 1865–1920*. Honolulu: University Press of the Pacific, 2004.

Strickland, Daniel W. *Connecticut Fights: The Story of the 102nd Regiment*. New Haven, CT: Quinnipiack Press, 1930.

Swan, Carroll J. *My Company*. Boston: Houghton Mifflin, 1918.

Taylor, Emerson G. *New England in France, 1917–1919: A History of the Twenty-Sixth Division U.S.A.* Boston: Houghton Mifflin, 1920.

Thompson, Joseph J. *A History of the Knights of Columbus in Illinois*. Chicago: Universal Press, 1921.

United States Army in the World War, 1917–1919. 17 volumes. Washington, D.C.: GPO, 1968.

U.S. Army Center of Military History. *Order of Battle of the United States Land Forces in the World War: American Expeditionary Forces, Divisions*. Washington, D.C.: GPO, 1988.

Wainwright, Philip S., ed. *History of the 101st Machine Gun Battalion*. Hartford, CT: The 101st Machine Gun Battalion Association, 1922.

Welcome Home: In Commemoration of the Foreign Service and Home-Coming of the 26th Division. Boston: Committee of Welcome, 1919.

Westbrook, Stillman F. *Those Eighteen Months, October 9, 1917–April 8, 1919.* Hartford, CT: Case, Lockwood, 1934.

Zack, Charles S. *Holyoke in the Great War.* Holyoke, MA: Transcript Publishing, 1919.

Newspapers

Baltimore Evening Sun
Boston Globe
Brattleboro Daily Reformer
Bridgeport Standard Telegram
Buffalo Courier-Express
Buffalo Evening News
Burlington Free Press
Cadiz Republican
Catholic Transcript (Hartford)
Clifton (Illinois) *Advocate*
Concord Daily Monitor/New Hampshire Patriot
Daily Hampshire Gazette
Daily Mining Gazette
Danbury Evening News
Evening Sun
Framingham News, Framingham Evening News
Hartford Courant
Hartford Times
Holyoke Daily Transcript-Telegram
Huntington Herald-Dispatch
Inquirer and Mirror
Lowell Courier-Citizen
Meriden Morning Record
Mobile Register
Natick Bulletin
New Bedford Standard
New London Day
Newton Graphic
New York Sun
New York Times
Omaha World Herald
Pen Yan Democrat

The Pilot
Pittsburgh Press
Rogers (Arkansas) *Democrat*
Shoreline Times
St. Albans Messenger
Washington Post
Washington Star
Waterbury (Vermont) *Record*
Windham County (Connecticut) *Observer*
Worcester Telegram

Manuscripts and Special Collections

Anderson, Harrison Ray, Jr., Bellingham, WA
    Letters and Papers of Harrison Ray Anderson, Sr.
Archdiocese of Boston, Archives, Boston, MA.
Archdiocese of Hartford, Archives, Hartford, CT
Archdiocese of New York, Archives, Yonkers, NY
Archdiocese of Omaha, Archives, Omaha, NE
Archdiocese of San Francisco, Archives, San Francisco, CA
Butzer, Albert G., III, Virginia Beach, VA
    Letters and Papers of Albert G. Butzer, Sr.
Connecticut Historical Society, Hartford, CT
    Charles E. Hesselgrave, Typescript
Connecticut State Library and Archives, Hartford, CT.
Dewart, Murray, Brookline, MA
    Letters of Murray Wilder Dewart
Diocese of Burlington, Archives, Burlington, VT
Diocese of Fall River, Archives, Fall River, MA
Diocese of La Crosse, Archives, La Crosse, WI
Diocese of Peoria, Archives, Peoria, IL
Diocese of Springfield, Archives, Springfield, MA
Fourth Presbyterian Church, Archives, Chicago, IL
Georgetown University Library, Special Collections Division, Washington, D.C.
The Jacob Rader Marcus Center of American Jewish Archives, Hebrew
    Union College, Cincinnati, OH
    Israel Bettan Papers
Library of Congress, Washington, D.C.
    Charles H. Brent Papers
George C. Marshall Library, Lexington, Virginia.
    Pierpont L. Stackpole, Diary

Massachusetts Historical Society, Boston, Massachusetts.
    Clarence Ransom Edwards Papers.
    Potter, Frederick Wells, Letters
Massachusetts National Guard Military Museum and Archives, Concord, Massachusetts.
Twenty-sixth Division ("Yankee"): Miscellaneous Papers/Orders:
    Austin, John F., Letters
    Brent, C. H., *Final Report of Senior Chaplain, GHQ, AEF*
    Burnham, Kenneth N., Letters
    Buswell, Elmer N., Diary
    Chase, Porter B., Diary
    Connolly, John Leo, Letters
    Dankert, James Harrison, Letters
    Harding, Carl O., Diary
    Lamb, Henry L., Letters
    Leahy, Thomas A., Letters
    O'Connor, Fred L., Diary
    Packard, A. L., Letters
    Porter, R.S., *History, 101st Sanitary Train, 26th Division, A.E.F.*
    Priest, Karlton K., Letters
    Streeter, Charles M., Letters

Miscellaneous Service Records

Military History Institute, Carlisle, Pennsylvania.
    Chase, Donald S., Questionnaire
    Dinsmore, Donald, Letters
    Heilman, Albert M., Jr., Letters
    Horace P. Hobbs Papers
    Hugh A. Drum Papers
    Taylor, Everett, Letters
    Wright, Harry G., Typescript
National Archives and Records Administration, College Park, Maryland.
    Twenty-sixth Division ("Yankee"), Official Papers/Orders, Record Group 120
National Library of Medicine, Bethesda, MD
    Stanhope Bayne-Jones Papers
New York State Archives, Albany, NY
    Miscellaneous Service Records
Oblates of St. Francis de Sales, Archives, Childs, MD

Schlesinger Library, Radcliff Institute, Harvard University Library, Cambridge, MA
   Mary Peabody Papers
Stewart-Smith Research Center, Henry Sheldon Museum, Middlebury, VT
   Ruth Hesselgrave Papers
United States Army Chaplains' Museum, Ft. Jackson, SC.
United States Military Academy Library, Special Collections and Archives, West Point, NY

Secondary Sources

Books and Pamphlets

Allen, Hervey. *Toward the Flame*. Lincoln: University of Nebraska Press, 2003.
Asprey, Robert. *At Belleau Wood*. Denton: University of North Texas Press, 1996.
Braime, Paul F. *The Test of Battle: The American Expeditionary Forces in the Meuse-Argonne*. Shippensburg, PA: White Mane, 1998.
Browne, George. *An American Soldier in World War I*. Edited by David L. Snead. Lincoln: University of Nebraska Press, 2006.
Budd, Richard M. *Serving Two Masters: The Development of American Military Chaplaincy, 1860–1920*. Lincoln: University of Nebraska Press, 2002.
Coffman, Edward M. *The Regulars: The American Army 1898–1941*. Boston: Harvard University Press, 2007.
———. *The War to End All Wars: The American Military Experience in World War I*. Madison: University of Wisconsin Press, 1986.
Cooke, James J. *Pershing and His Generals: Command and Staff in the AEF*. Westport, CT: Praeger, 1997.
Corby, William, and Lawrence Frederick Kohl, eds. *Memoirs of Chaplain Life: Three Years with the Irish Brigade in the Army of the Potomac*. New York: Fordham University Press, 1992.
Cowdrey, Albert E. *War and Healing: Stanhope Bayne-Jones and the Maturing of American Medicine*. Baton Rouge: Louisiana State University Press, 1992.
Donovan, Charles F. *Boston College's Boston Priests*. Chestnut Hill, MA: Boston College, 1993. Available at http://escholarship.bc.edu/donovan/18.
Duggan, Thomas Stephen. *The Catholic Church in Connecticut*. New York: States History, 1930.

Ellis, Edward Robb. *Echoes of Distant Thunder: Life in the United States, 1914–1918.* New York: Kodansha, 1996.

Ellis, John. *Eye Deep in Hell.* Baltimore: Johns Hopkins University Press, 1989.

Emmanuel Church in the City of Boston, 1860–1960: The First One Hundred Years. Boston: Vestry of Emmanuel Church, 1960.

Ferrell, Robert H., *America's Deadliest Battle: Meuse Argonne, 1918.* Lawrence: University Press of Kansas, 2007.

———, ed. *In the Company of Generals: The World War I Diary of Pierpont L. Stackpole.* Columbia: University of Missouri Press, 2009.

Gilbert, Martin. *The First World War.* New York: Henry Holt, 1994.

Goldstein, David, and Martha Moore Avery. *Campaigning for Christ.* Boston: Pilot Publishing, 1924.

Graves, Robert. *Good-bye to All That.* New York: Anchor, 1985.

Grotelueschen, Mark E. *The AEF Way of War: The American Army and Combat in World War I.* Cambridge: Cambridge University Press, 2007.

———. *Doctrine under Fire: American Artillery Employment in World War I.* Westport, CT: Greenwood, 2001.

Hansen, Arlen J. *Gentlemen Volunteers: The Story of American Ambulance Drivers in the Great War, August 1914—September 1918.* New York: Arcade, 1994.

Harbord, James G. *Leaves from a War Diary.* New York: Dodd and Mead, 1925.

Harries, Meirion, and Susie Harries. *The Last Days of Innocence: America at War, 1917–1918.* New York: Random House, 1997.

Harris, Stephen L. *Duffy's War: Fr. Francis Duffy, Wild Bill Donovan, and the Irish Fighting 69th in World War I.* Washington, D.C.: Potomac Books, 2006.

Hill, Everett G. *A Modern History of New Haven and Eastern New Haven County.* Vol. 1. New York: Clarke, 1918.

Hoehling, A. A. *The Great Epidemic.* Boston: Little, Brown, 1961.

Horne, Alistair. *The Price of Glory: Verdun, 1916.* London: Penguin, 1993.

Keegan, John. *The First World War.* New York: Knopf, 1999.

Kennedy, David M. *Over Here: The First World War and American Society.* New York: Oxford University Press, 1982.

Ketchum, Richard M. *Decisive Day: The Battle for Bunker Hill.* New York: Henry Holt, 1999.

Lengel, Edward G. *To Conquer Hell: The Meuse-Argonne, 1918.* New York: Henry Holt, 2008.

Lockhart, Paul. *The Whites of Their Eyes: Bunker Hill, the First American Army, and the Emergence of George Washington.* New York: HarperCollins, 2011.

McCallum, Jack. *Leonard Wood: Rough Rider, Surgeon, Architect of American Imperialism.* New York: New York University Press, 2006.
Mead, Gary. *The Doughboys: America and the First World War.* Woodstock, NY: Overlook, 2000.
Meinig, D. W. *The Shaping of America: A Geographical Perspective on 500 Years of History, Volume 3, Transcontinental America, 1850–1915.* New Haven: Yale University Press, 1998.
Palmer, Frederick. *Newton D. Baker: America at War.* 2 vols. New York: Dodd Mead, 1931.
Pottle, Frederick A. *Stretchers: The Story of a Hospital Unit on the Western Front.* New Haven: Yale University Press, 1929.
Saint Bridget's Church, 75th Anniversary, 1878–1953. Framingham Center, MA: n.p., 1953.
Schaffer, Ronald. *America in the Great War: The Rise of the War Welfare State.* New York: Oxford University Press, 1991.
Scroggs, Marilee Munger. *A Light in the City: The Fourth Presbyterian Church of Chicago.* Chicago: Fourth Presbyterian Church, 1990.
Smythe, Donald. *Pershing: General of the Armies.* Bloomington: University of Indiana Press, 2007.
Stallings, Laurence. *The Doughboys: The Story of the AEF, 1917–1918.* New York: Harper Row, 1963.
Trask, David. *The AEF and Coalition Warmaking, 1917–1918.* Lawrence: University Press of Kansas, 1993.
Wilson, Dale E. *Treat 'em Rough!: The Birth of American Armor, 1917–1920.* Novato, CA: Presidio, 1989.
Winter, Denis. *Death's Men.* London: Penguin, 1979.
Wright, William M. Robert H. Ferrell, ed., *Meuse-Argonne Diary: A Division Commander in World War I.* Columbia: University of Missouri Press, 2004.
Young, Hugh. *A Surgeon's Autobiography.* New York: Harcourt, Brace, 1940.

Articles

Denis, Leon F., "The Cruise of the Montpelier." *Yankee Doings* 8, no. 7 (July/August 1927): 9–10.
Greely, John Nesmith, and Dwight E. Aultman, eds. *The Field Artillery Journal* 6 (1916): 101.
"The Knights of Columbus War Service." *Catholic Educational Review* 17 (January–May 1919): 113–17.

Moody, Paul D. "Practical Work for the Soldiers." *The Missionary Review of the World* 40, no. 7 (July 1917): 529–30.

Nickols, James P. "Religious Pluralism: A Challenge to the Chaplain Corps." *Military Chaplains' Review* 15, no. 4 (Fall 1986): 85–100.

Index

Acting rabbi, 7, 115, 176
Adams, Chauncey Allen, 27, 138, **139**, 171
Ahearn, George T., 14
Aisne-Marne, 51, 67, 74–76, 78, 82, 107
Albertine, Connell, 18, 99, 109, 192n11
Alexander, George, 85
American Battle Monuments Commission, 120
American Expeditionary Forces (AEF):
—Armies: First, 74, 87; Third, 116, 117
—Corps: Third, 107
—Divisions: 1st, 52, 89, 107; 2nd, 61, 67, 68, 70, 74, 79, 88, 107, 113; 3rd ("Rock of the Marne"), 72, 85; 26th (*see* "Yankee Division"); 32nd, 107; 34th, 101; 42nd ("Rainbow"), 52, 76; 77th, 195n14; 79th, 97, 107, 108
—Regiments: 23rd Engineers (512th Bn.), 28; 12th Field Artillery, 61, 68, 79, 88, 113; 127th Field Artillery, 101; 49th Infantry, 104; 313th Infantry ("Baltimore's Own"), 107
American Field Service ("AFS"), 26–27, 71
Anderson, Harrison Ray, xvii, 27–28, **69**, 70, 75, 78, 79, 81–82, 89, 91–92, 99, 103, 108, 109, 110, 111, 112, 117–18, 123, 157–58, 171, 179n2
Anderson, P. A., 163
Andrew, Abram Piatt. *See* American Field Service
Apremont (*Bois Brûlé*), 54, 55, 56, 131
Archdiocese for Military Services, U. S. A. *See* Military Ordinariate
Armistice, 7, 107, 108, 111, 113, 121, 124, 129, 168
Army Chaplain Corps, 167
Army Chaplain School. *See* Camp Zachary Taylor
Arnold, P. A., 112, 157
Axton, John T., 167

Barry, Jack, 193n12
Bayne-Jones, Stanhope, 73, 192n4

Bearss, Hiram, 88, 89, 93–94
Bettan, Israel, 7, **21**, 22, 23, 114–16, 151, 171
Bittings, Arthur, 162
Board of Chaplains (AEF), 5, 6, 69, 85
Boston College, 20, 58
Boucher, Osias, 39, 41–42, 47, 58, 66, 73, 81, 136–37, 169, 171–72, 186n29
Brent, Charles Henry (Bishop), **3**, 4–5, 6, 24, 28, 29–30, 38, 42, 80, 81, 85, 105–6, 117, 122, 167
Brest, 13, 28, 113, 125, 130
Brodney, Edward, 132
Bundy, Omar, 71
Bunnell, George W., 112, 122
Burke, Mary, 160
Burnham, Kenneth N., 59
Buswell, Elmer, 72, 189n11
Butzer, Albert George, **82**, 109, 123, 125, 153–55, 172

Cabot, Charles Ray, 153
Camp Bartlett (Westfield, MA), 9, 10, **11**
Camp Devens (MA), 9, 129, 132, 152, 155, 159
Camp Pontanezan (Brest), 125
Campbell, Robert, Jr., 19, 42, 80–81, 87, 89, 97, 99, 102, 109, 110, 117, **119**, 122, 123, 125, 126–27, 139, 172
Champagne-Marne, 67
Chaplains:
—Chaplaincy: Board of Chaplains, 5, 6, 69, 85; Chaplain Corps, formation of, xiii, 167–68; denominations, xiv, 2, 6, 28, 34, 44, 73, 117–18, 135, 138, 146, 157, 158, 165, 167; formation of, xiii, 167–68; history, 1; insignia, 8; non-governmental organizations, role of, 4–5, 42, 202; rank, 8, 167–70
—Duties: athletics, 32, 80, 123, 125; burial detail, 57, 58, 70, 72, 75, 80, 81, 95, 103, 118, **119**, 120, 195n26; education, 2, 28, 34, 123; in general, 2, 32, 80; morals, 5, 29–30, 122; recreation, 28, 34

Chaplain Schools (AEF):
—American Expeditionary Forces: Château d'Aux (Louplande), 96; Neuilly-sur-Suise, 6, 26, 46, 82, 96
—United States: Fort Monroe (VA), 6; Camp Zachary Taylor (KY), 6, 7, 12, 21, 63, 71, 78, 84, 85, 96, 107, 146, 188n32
Chase, Donald S., 67
Chase, Porter B., 184n61, 196n31
Château-Thierry, 51, 67, 71, 72, 81
Châtillon-sur-Seine, 87
Chaumont, 3, 5, 6, 46, 55, 63, 69, 77, 80, 85, 96
Chemin des Dames, 5, 19, 35, 39, 47, **48**, 49, 52, 64, 82, 131
Chevalier, John, v, xiii
Christianson, Henry, 95
Cochrane, James E., **11**, 178
Coëtquidan, 31
Coffin, Henry Sloan, 85
Cole, Charles H., 79, 124
Collins, Edward Day, 150
Collins, James H., 162
Committee on Public Information, 22
Congdon, Harry W., 166
Conlon, Christopher Michael, 193n12
Connor, George S. L., 10, **17**, 34, 107, 140, 172
Corcoran, John E., 196n40
Cormerais, Harry D., 66
Creighton, John Harvey, 19, **103**, 148–49, 172
Cushing, Harvey, 24, 25

Danker, Walter Stoutenburgh, **11**, 15, 43, 46, 54, 55, 57, 64, **65**, 66, 117, 129, 172–73, 194n3
Danker, William, 66
Dankert, James Harrison, 43
Dawes, Ralph M., 56
Degoutte, Jean (Gen.), 74
Dell, Burnham North, 77–78, 127, 147–48, 173
De Valles, John Baptist, 18, 47, 48–49, 54, 55, **56**, 57, 66, 71, 90, 99, 100–101, 108, 109, 117, **126**, 130–31, 169, 173, 197n8
Dewart, Murray Wilder, 15, **16**, 17, 30, 31, 32–33, 34, 35, 38–39, 47–48, 52, 53–54, 75, 76–77, 80, 112, 125, 132–35, 146, 173, 181n31, 184n5
Dickinson, Myron D., 59

Dinsmore, Donald, 64
Doherty, Francis B., 5, 80
Donahue, P. J. (Bishop), 23
Donifan, Patrick R., 116
Duane, James T., 63, 73, 187n7
Dunn, Joseph H., 95

Ecumenism, 38, 113, 117, 141, 155
Edwards, Clarence Ransom (Maj. Gen.), 8, 9–10, 30, 71, 74, 85–86, 96, 98, 105, 118, 130, 131
Edwards, Henry Boyd, 29, 34, 39, 46, 72, 77, 95, 98, 112, 116, **126**, 137–38, 173
Englander, Henry, 114, 115
Evans, Allen, Jr., 70, 87, 108, **126**, 146–47, 173, 194n35
Evers, Johnny, 101

Farrell, William J., 34, 58, **59**, 60, 62, 73, 100, 108, 112, 117, 131–32, 174, 192n11
Feehan, D. F. (Bishop), 18
Flu (See Influenza)
Fosdick, Harry Emerson, 160

Gibbons, James (Cardinal), 20
Goldberg, Martin, 155
Graves Registration Service, 118, 120
Graves, Robert, xiv, 71
Groves, Leslie, xiv

Hale, Harry C., 122
Hamilton, Reuben G., 95
Hanson, Roy, 93, 94
Harbord, James Guthrie (Brig. Gen.), 28, 79
Hardwick, Sydney C., 56
Harvard University, 1, 4, 24, 148; Divinity School, 12, 15, 19, 146; Medical School Unit, 24, 25
Hayes, Patrick (Cardinal), 155, 156
Hebrew Union College, 114, 151
Hedum, Arthur, 162
Heights of the Meuse, 88, 89, 91, 93, 98, 101
Hesselgrave, Charles Everett, 18–19, 36, 44, 67, 92, 96, 135–36, 174, 202
Hobbs, Horace P., 74, 91, 106, 111
Holy Cross College, 13, **14**, **17**, 34, 140
Houghton, Roy M., 19
Houlihan, Frank L., 118, 195n22
Hume, Frank M., 79

Influenza ("Flu"), 33, 98, 105, 106, 110, 113
Imbrie, Charles K., 82–83, **84**, **126**, 140–41, 174

Jewish Chaplains Association, 115
Jewish Welfare Board, 4, 7, 18, 42, 114–15, 195n14
Jonaitis, George Fediles, 20–21, 107, 142–46, **143**, 174

Kernan, Walter N., 34
Knights of Columbus, 4, 7, 18, 34, 39, 42, 44, 77, 82, 101, 104, 115, 117, 130, 140, 142, 172, 173, 174, 175, 197n9, 202n1

La Voi-du-Châtel, 70, 73
Lamb, Henry L. ("Harry"), 64, 188n34, 194n33
Langres, 17, 77, 80, 125, 133
Lawrence, William (Bishop), 10, **11**, 16, 138
Leahy, Thomas A., 42
Lejeune, John A., 74
Lerry, Ben, 192n12
LeVeer, Arthur Joseph, 95, **96**, 97, 106, 112–13, 123, 125, 142, 174
Libert, Lucien Gaspard, 77, 112, 132, 174–75
Liggett, Hunter (Lt. Gen.), 74
Lipsie, Leo J., 41
Loew, Ralph W., 155
Logan, John, 35, 66, 129

MacArthur, Douglas (Gen.), 155
Marchéville-Riaville, 92–95, 160, 161–62
Marshall, George C., 186n33
Maurer, Oscar E., 19
Mayotte, Anselm Joseph, 44, **45**, 46, 60–61, 68, 79, 88, 113–14, 129, 175, 186n38
Meuse-Argonne, 92–93, 98, 104, 107, 156
Middlebury College, 18, 134, 138, 149, **150**
Miel, Charles ("Duke"), 26
Miel, Ernest DeFremery, 26, 127
Military Ordinariate, 140, 179n5
Miller, Gale, 120, 161
Mitty, John Joseph (Archbishop), 104, 127, 155, **156**, 175
Montiéramey, 126
Montigny-le-Roi, 111–12, 125

Moody, Paul Dwight, 5–6, **11**, 36, 69, 77, 80, 112, 125, 133–34, 138, 139, 149, **150**, 175
Murray, John Gardner (Bishop), 134

Neptune Sector. *See* Verdun
Neufchâteau, 31, 34, **36**
Nilan, John J. (Bishop), 44, 46
Nivard, Michael, 82, **83**, 147, 175

O'Connor, Michael J., xiii, xv, 13, **14**, 30, 33, 34–35, **48**, 54, 58, 66, **68**, 105, 106, 112, 117, 118–19, 121, **126**, 127, 129, 136, 169, 175–76, 198n24

Packard, A. L., 186n32
Packer, William S., 135
Page, Herman Riddle, 11, 178
Parker, John Henry, 57, 61
Peabody, Malcolm Endicott (Bishop), **24**, 25, 85, 100, 104–105, 110, 113, 117, 121–22, 124, 125, 127, 158–59, 176
Pershing, John Joseph (Gen.), 2, 3, 4, 6, 8, 9, 29, 51, 74, 98, 106, 112, 121–22, 124, 167, 169
Petty, Orville Anderson, 12, 35, 60, **61**, 85, 127, 137, 169, 176
Pierce, Charles C., 120
Plattsburg (NY) Officer Training, 23, 71
Potter, Frederick Wells ("Fritz"), 44, 74, 75, 122, 125
Princeton University, 26, 77–78, 82, 85, 148
Pruden, Aldred Adino, 2, 3, 6, **7**, 8, 167, **168**

Red Cross, 4, **24**, 25, 26, 42, 44, 81, 104, 113, 127, 202n1
Riseman, Benjamin, 7, 176
Robinson, Harold B., 155
Rodger, James Y., 44
Rollins, Lyman, xv, 9, 14, 33, 34, **36**, **37**, 38, **48**, 54–55, 58, 62, **63**, 85, 86, 101, 112, 117, 121, 127, 129, 176, 188n32
Roosevelt, Theodore, 6, 76, 116, 190n24
Root, Elihu, 1, 7, 9
Rummel, Joseph F. (Bishop), 144

Salvation Army, 4, 18, 42
Scott, J. E., 23
Seicheprey, 54, 57–58, 59, 60, 108
Sewell, Wilbur S., 65
Shelton, George, 64, 91, 106, 130